MIRACULOUS IMAGES OF OUR LADY

THIS BOOK

BELONGS TO BOB BARR

Our Lady of Confidence
A seventeenth-century Italian portrait by Carlo Maratta.

MIRACULOUS IMAGES OF OUR LADY

100 FAMOUS CATHOLIC STATUES AND PORTRAITS

By

Joan Carroll Cruz

"I am the mother of fair love, and of fear, and of knowledge, and of holy hope. In me is all grace of the way and of the truth, in me is all hope of life and of virtue. Come over to me, all ye that desire me, and be filled with my fruits. For my spirit is sweet above honey, and my inheritance above honey and the honeycomb. My memory is unto everlasting generations."
—Ecclesiasticus 24:24-28

TAN BOOKS AND PUBLISHERS, INC.
Rockford, Illinois 61105

OTHER BOOKS BY THE AUTHOR

Secular Saints
Prayers and Heavenly Promises
The Incorruptibles
Eucharistic Miracles
Relics
The Desires of Thy Heart

Nihil Obstat: Father Terence J. Tekippe
Censor Librorum

Imprimatur: ✠ Most Rev. Francis B. Schulte
Archbishop of New Orleans
May 22, 1992

The Nihil Obstat and Imprimatur are the Church's declarations that a work is free from error in matters of faith and morals. It in no way implies that the Church endorses the contents of the work.

Cover Picture: *Mater Admirabilis,* or "Mother Most Admirable," a miraculous fresco that has been of spiritual benefit to many. (See Chapter 59.)

Library of Congress Catalog Card No.: 92-62149

ISBN: 0-89555-484-4

Printed and bound in the United States of America.

TAN BOOKS AND PUBLISHERS, INC.
P.O. Box 424
Rockford, Illinois 61105

1993

"There is not a church without an altar in her honor, not a country nor a canton where there are not some miraculous images where all sorts of evils are cured and all sorts of good gifts obtained."

—St. Louis Marie De Montfort
True Devotion to Mary

CONTENTS

FRANCE

GERMANY

HUNGARY

IRELAND

ITALY

THE NETHERLANDS

THE PHILIPPINES

POLAND

PORTUGAL

SPAIN

SWITZERLAND

UNITED STATES OF AMERICA

INTRODUCTION

Catholics do not adore statues or other representations of Our Lord, His Mother or the Saints, nor do we pray to these images. In early childhood we are taught from our Catechism that "We do not pray to the crucifix or to the images of Christ and of the Saints, but to the persons of whom they remind us." Because they represent holy persons, images are treated with becoming reverence, even as the picture of one's mother would be.

This subject was clarified by the Council of Trent during its twenty-fifth session in December, 1563:

> Moreover, [the faithful must be instructed] that the images of Christ, of the Virgin Mother of God, and of the other Saints are to be placed and retained especially in the churches, and that due honor and veneration is to be given them. . . because the honor which is shown them is referred to the prototypes which they represent, so that by means of the images which we kiss and before which we uncover the head and prostrate ourselves, we adore Christ and venerate the Saints whose likeness they bear. That is what was defined by the decrees of the Councils, especially of the Second Council of Nicaea (787 A.D.) against the opponents of images.

From the earliest days of the Church, images were painted on the walls of the catacombs as religious expressions of the faithful, as acts of veneration and as aids in visualizing Our Lord, His miracles and His holy Mother. We are told by St. John of the Cross in Book III, Chapter 35 of *The Ascent of Mount Carmel:*

> The Church established the use of statues (and images) for two principal reasons: the reverence given to the Saints through them and the motivation of the will and the awakening of devotion to the Saints by their means. Insofar as they serve this purpose their use is profitable and necessary. . .

The Saint also tells us that "Since images serve as a motivating means toward invisible things, we should strive that the motivation, affection, and joy of will derived from them be directed toward the living object they represent."

Without question, the most popular image of a saint found in churches throughout the world is that of the Queen of Saints, the Blessed Virgin Mary. One would be hard pressed to find a church, chapel or oratory that does not contain an image of the Mother of God.

Of these images of our Holy Mother, some have been identified as being miraculous. It is not that the statue or painting is miraculous of itself, but it does seem that Our Lady favors certain of her replicas and often honors the requests of those persons who visit them to express their needs and their love of her.

The purpose of this work is to identify 100 of these favored images and to chart their histories and the reasons for their designation as miraculous objects. It must be understood that the Blessed Virgin does not perform the miracles by herself. It is ultimately our Heavenly Father who performs the miracles according to His holy Will at the request of Our Lady. For this reason the Virgin Mary is known as the Mediatrix of All Graces who pleads our cause before God's holy throne.

For an image to be included in this collection, the painting or statue must fit into one or more of the following categories:

- It must have had a miraculous origin, such as the image of Our Lady of Guadalupe;
- It must be composed of an unusual substance, such as the portrait of Absam, Austria;
- It must have bled, wept, exuded manna or changed location, such as the portrait of Our Lady of Good Counsel;
- Something unusual must have happened to it, such as that which affected the statue of Our Lady of the Thunderbolt;
- And finally, it must have a reputation for miraculous cures and favors.

Many of the 100 images included in this volume fall into two or more of these categories.

It must be noted that all the images mentioned in this volume were thoroughly studied by Church authorities before ecclesiastical permission was granted for the images to be enshrined and honored in their respective churches or shrines.

The sanctuaries which house these miraculous images were especially selected by Our Lady. In keeping with her humble life at Nazareth, Our Lady chose places which were beautiful in their quiet simplicity. In almost every instance, the corner chosen was retiring and withdrawn from the world. A few of these shrines have maintained their reverent isolation, but in many instances a chapel located outside a village eventually became embraced by the houses and businesses of an expanding population. For this reason some shrines are now surrounded by great cities. To accommodate the growing numbers of Our Lady's devotees, many of the simple chapels that were first erected to house her images developed into churches, and finally into magnificent basilicas.

As Henry Martin Gillett noted in his *Famous Shrines of Our Lady:*

> Once Our Lady has been given a shrine, it may be said that the site belongs to her for all time. For one reason or another her subjects may forget their allegiance and even blot out every trace of the original sanctuary; but the site remains hers. And sooner or later she comes back to her own. Sometimes people are moved to restore the old. At other times her more faithful children, quite ignorant of past history, are inspired to establish a "new shrine" quite near the old foundations.

The reader will find that such has happened repeatedly, due to marvelous and unusual promptings.

Although many of the miraculous images of Our Lady are exquisitely beautiful, the reader will discover that some of them are regarded as being miraculous even though they are of poor workmanship. Many have been damaged by time, while some are downright unflattering representations of our beautiful Madonna. St. John of the Cross, in Book III, Chapter 36 of his *Ascent of Mount Carmel,* explains:

> Experience even teaches that if God grants some favors and works miracles, He does so through some statues

> that are not very well carved or carefully painted, or that are poor representations, so that the faithful will not attribute any of these wonders to the statue or painting.

St. John of the Cross has dedicated Chapters 35, 36 and 37 of his *Ascent of Mount Carmel* to the subject of miraculous images, the benefits to be derived through their veneration, and valuable precautions to be observed. The reader is encouraged to study these chapters, written by a Doctor of the Church who is also acknowledged as a master of the spiritual life.

The author feels bound to address the claim made by many writers that certain portraits of Our Lady were painted, and that some statues were sculpted, by St. Luke the Evangelist. This claim is made in spite of the fact that the styles and techniques of these paintings and statues are vastly different. Moreover, the churches which enshrine these images have on record either the approximate dates, or the actual dates of their origins—dates which do not correspond to the lifetime of St. Luke. One writer recorded that the claim originated somewhere around the sixth century, another that it was from the ninth century. It has also been noted that there are no works of art supposedly executed by St. Luke that sustain historical scrutiny in his favor.

Mrs. Anna Murphy Jameson, in her *Legends of the Madonna,* records that:

> The legend which represents St. Luke the Evangelist as a painter appears to be of Eastern origin and quite unknown in Western Europe before the first Crusade. It crept in then, and was accepted with many other oriental superstitions and traditions. It may have originated in the real existence of a Greek painter named Luca—a saint also, for the Greeks have a whole calendar of canonized artists. . .and this Greek San Luca may have been a painter of those Madonnas imported from the ateliers of Mount Athos into the West by merchants and pilgrims; and the West, which knew but one St. Luke, may have easily confounded the painter and the evangelist.

Finally, Alfred Plummer tells us:

> It is certain St. Luke was an artist, at least to the extent that his graphic descriptions of the Annunciation, Visitation, Nativity, shepherds, Presentation, the Shepherd and lost sheep, etc., have become the inspiration and favorite themes of Christian painters.

The only portraits discovered by this author that *might* have been painted by St. Luke—if indeed he was artistic—are the images of Our Lady of Mellieha on the island of Malta and that which is revered in St. Mary Major Basilica in Rome.

According to St. Alphonsus de Liguori,

> The divine Mother has shown by prodigies how pleasing to her are the visits paid to her images. But if we are unable to visit her miraculous images which are far from home, we should visit her shrines which are readily available.

The Saint continues:

> If we also desire the happiness of receiving the visits of this Queen of Heaven, we should often visit her by going before her image, or praying to her in churches dedicated to her honor.

This is a lovely suggestion which we might well take to heart and put into practice. Until we are able to make such visits in person, may this book serve to take us in spirit and in our hearts to Our Lady's shrines around the world.

DECLARATION OF OBEDIENCE

In obedience to the decrees of several Roman Pontiffs, in particular those of Pope Urban VIII, I declare that I in no way intend to prejudge Holy Mother the Church in the matter of miracles. Final authority in such matters rests with the Church, to whose judgment I willingly submit.

—Joan Carroll Cruz

MIRACULOUS IMAGES OF OUR LADY

— 1 —

OUR LADY OF LUJAN

(Our Lady of Consolation)
Lujan, Buenos Aires, Argentina
1630

Following the discoveries of Magellan, Cortez and others, South America in the sixteenth century provided a vast new land where the Faith could take root and devotion to Our Lady could thrive. The land was soon graced with many shrines, but that of Our Lady of Lujan is perhaps the most famous and the most historic in all of South America. It is said to bear every mark of a true, chosen sanctuary of Our Lady.

The history of the shrine begins in 1630, with a farmer who emigrated to Argentina from Portugal. Coming from a place where the Faith flourished, he was saddened at the lack of religious influence in his adopted district, and in particular his village of Sumampa. He decided to help the situation by building a chapel on his land. Writing to a friend in Brazil, he asked the friend to send him a small statue of Our Lady for the chapel. The friend, unsure of how the farmer wanted Our Lady to be depicted, sent two statues—one of the Madonna with Child, the other a representation of the Immaculate Conception.

Having at first been transported by sea, the images were then placed on a cart for the journey inland. Because of hostile natives in the region, a number of carts and pack horses banded together in a caravan. When darkness overtook the travelers after leaving Buenos Aires, they camped at the isolated ranch of Don Rosendo de Oramus. Early the next morning, the wagons and animals were readied for the rest of their journey. One by one the carts began to move, all except the one that carried the images of Our Lady. Progress was stalled when the driver was unable to coax the animals forward. The other drivers in the caravan came to help—but all efforts were unsuccessful. Finally, it was decided that the animals might somehow be influenced supernaturally. And so it seemed, since the animals willingly moved when the statue of the Immaculate Conception was removed from the cart.

The statue of the Madonna and Child continued its journey and arrived safely in Sumampa, where it is still venerated under the title of Our Lady of Consolation.

As for the statue of the Immaculate Conception that was taken off the cart, it was solemnly carried to the ranch and enthroned in a room of its own. This room soon became a popular shrine and remained so for the next 40 years.

A small, eight-year-old black slave from Angola in Africa now appears in the history of Our Lady of Lujan. Manuel had been traveling with the caravan and became intrigued by the incident of the stubborn animals. When the statue of Our Lady was removed from the cart, he begged to remain as a little servant of the Mother of God. Don Rosendo made arrangements with the boy's owner and brought Manuel to the ranch, where he worked as a sacristan and edified everyone by his charity and piety. As he grew, he devoted himself to the care of the sick and afflicted. Many of the villagers gave him alms, which he saved for Our Lady's "purse."

When Don Rosendo de Oramus died in 1670, a pious lady, Dona Ana de Mattos, obtained permission to move the shrine to a chapel on her own property some 15 miles away on the other side of the River Lujan. The ranch of Don Rosendo, it was decided, was too remote, and it was in constant danger from Indian attack. Even so, Manuel was left behind to care for the property.

When the statue of the Immaculate Conception arrived on the property of Dona Ana it was taken to the chapel and reverently enshrined. Following prayers of welcome to the Mother of God, the shrine was securely locked for the night. The next morning it was discovered that the image had disappeared. Looking about, the men finally found the statue at the ranch, on its former pedestal. Once more it was carried to the chapel of Dona Ana.

This time, in addition to the locked doors, a guard was placed to keep watch. But again, the statue vanished and was found at its former location.

Manuel was at first suspected of having removed his beloved statue, but the charge was dismissed when it was proved that it was impossible for him to have been involved. Dona Ana then turned for advice to the Bishop and the Governor of the Province, both of whom made an official inquiry. Afterwards it was decided that the shrine should be removed to the property of Dona Ana, since the ranch posed a real danger to pilgrims because of savage Indians who roamed the area.

To ensure that the statue would remain in Dona Ana's chapel, the Bishop and the Governor carried the statue to the chapel in solemn procession. Taking part was Manuel, who would thereafter remain with his beloved statue as its caretaker. Now that the Blessed Mother had her favored sacristan with her, the statue of the Immaculate Conception seemed content to remain at its new location.

The popularity of the shrine soon required larger accommodations. The foundation stone for the new church was laid in 1677 by Fra Gabriel, a Carmelite Friar. It was during that year that the first recorded miracle occurred. The miracle was in favor of Fr. Pedro de Montalbo. Other miracles are known to have occurred before this date, but unfortunately, these were not carefully recorded.

In 1710 another recorded miracle took place. This was the cure of a malignant throat tumor suffered by Fr. Bernabe de Gutierrez. Oil from the lamp of Our Lady's shrine helped to effect the miraculous results.

We are told that Our Lady revealed to the humble Manuel the date of his death and assured him of his eternal salvation. Manuel died a holy death on the date Heaven had revealed. The faithful sacristan who had attended Our Lady during almost all of his life, was not to be separated from her in death. He was buried in a tomb at the foot of the altar whereon his beloved statue was enshrined.

A still larger church was required for the ever-increasing number of pilgrims. A church started in 1730 was soon abandoned in favor of one built in 1763, the year Our Lady of Lujan was declared patroness of Buenos Aires. For the next 100 years, several orders of priests labored at the shrine and succeeded in gaining a worldwide reputation for the shrine of Our Lady in Lujan.

One of the strange occurrences that helped to spread the miraculous aspects of Our Lady of Lujan took place on August 28, 1780. On that date news arrived at the shrine that a large group of Indians were slaughtering all the people in their path as they advanced ever closer to Lujan. The news threw the people into a panic, and they fled to the shrine to pray for the protection of Our Lady. While they prayed, a mysteriously dense fog gathered quickly throughout the town, thoroughly hiding it from the advancing enemy so that they lost their way and traveled elsewhere. All the faithful agreed that they had been saved by virtue of the miraculous Lady of Lujan.

When parts of Argentina were afflicted with the much-dreaded cholera epidemic, Archbishop Aueiros vowed to make a pilgrimage to Lujan if his archdiocese were spared. While many cities suffered grievously, Buenos Aires—both city and province, including Lujan—was singularly and blessedly spared, as all acknowledged.

Because of the reputation of the shrine, Pope Leo XIII decided in 1886 to honor the miraculous statue with a papal coronation. On September 30 of that year he blessed the crown, which was made of pure gold set with 365 diamonds, rubies, emeralds and sapphires, 132 pearls and a number of enamels depicting the emblems of the Archbishop and the Argentine Republic. The papal coronation of Our Lady of Lujan took place on May 8, 1887. The celebrant chosen by the Pope for this event was Archbishop Aueiros, who made a pilgrimage at that time in thanksgiving to Our Lady for sparing his archdiocese from the scourge of cholera.

Other Popes who have honored the shrine are Clement XI, Clement XIV, Pius VI, Pius IX and Leo XIII. Fr. John Mastai Ferretti visited the shrine in 1824. He later became Pope Pius IX. It is interesting to note that it was this Pope who, on December 8, 1854, defined the dogma of the Immaculate Conception.

The Lazarist Fathers who had custody of the shrine at this time envisioned a grand basilica for Our Lady, a building that would merit the distinction of being a national monument. In 1904, when the monument was almost completed, the miraculous image of Our Lady of Lujan was triumphantly transferred to the basilica, where she was enshrined in the center of a camarin behind the high altar.

The Blessed Virgin stands atop a jewelled crescent moon in an attitude of prayer, with her hands joined at her breast. A mere 23 inches high, the statue has a pleasant, oval face. Her eyes are clear blue. A halo of 12 stars encircles her head, but behind this extend 15 large rays made of solid gold. The Virgin's robe and mantle are delicately embroidered with golden thread and enriched with sprays of gems. Made of baked clay, it is surprising that a statue of such delicate material could have survived so many transfers during its more than 350 years of existence. We can only credit Manuel's loving care of the statue and the cautious handling of it by those who followed him.

The shrine at Lujan is literally covered with votive offerings in the form of silver hearts, as well as miniature renditions of arms, legs and body parts, all attesting to the miracles of healing granted by Our Lady.

Many are the pilgrims from throughout Argentina who visit the shrine of their Madonna. Many, too, are the pilgrims from throughout the world who, while visiting Buenos Aires, journey 40 miles to the west to visit this world-renowned, miraculous image of Our Lady of Lujan.

— 2 —

GREAT MOTHER OF AUSTRIA

Mariazell, Styria, Austria
1157

The little town of Mariazell is situated on a gentle slope at the eastern end of the Austrian Alps, some 80 miles south of Vienna. Regarded as the most frequented pilgrimage site in central Europe, its documented history begins in the year 1025. A century later the Benedictines erected a monastery there, which they dedicated to St. Lambrecht. It is this place of prayer that gave rise to the now famous basilica-shrine of Mariazell.

According to the history of the shrine, a monk named Magnus, feeling called to live a more solitary existence, left the Benedictine monastery in the year 1157. One of the few possessions he took with him was a wooden statue of the Blessed Virgin, which would later become known as the Great Mother of Austria. A popular legend relates that Magnus progressed deep into the forest, only to find his way blocked by dense growth and boulders. After he prayed fervently before his beloved statue, a path through the thicket was miraculously opened; but instead of traveling along this path, Magnus decided to stay at the site. He placed the statue on a linden tree and there, with the help of shepherds and hunters to whom he ministered and instructed in the Faith, he built a little chapel in which he enshrined his statue. Regarded by the early visitors as a monastic cell of the Virgin Mary, it was for this reason that it became known as Mariazell.

Fifty years later, in 1200, a Romanesque church was built on the site, a project that can be linked with a legendary pilgrimage to Mariazell by Moravian Margrave Henrich and his wife. In 1370 the structure was enlarged. This was financed by King Louis I of Hungary, who also donated the "Treasury Picture" which is sometimes termed Mariazell's second miraculous image of the Blessed Virgin. First built in the Romanesque style, the church was later enlarged and embellished in the Gothic manner. Still later, in 1644, work was started on the church's conversion to Baroque. Crowned with two baroque spires and one gothic spire, the interior is regarded as Christendom's most beautiful specimen of Baroque art.

The town and the church were severely damaged by fire in 1827, but contributions for the work of reconstruction came swiftly from all parts of Austria and Hungary.

The year 1907 is notable in the history of this shrine for two reasons: the designation of the church as a papal basilica, and the official coronation of the ancient statue of Our Lady of Mariazell. Measuring a mere 47 centimeters high, the seated figure of the Virgin Mary supports the Infant Jesus with her right hand as He sits upon her lap. The Infant holds an apple and a fig, which are regarded as symbols of Christ's Redemption of mankind. Customarily dressed in ornate, heavily embroidered garments, both Mother and Child wear their gold- and jewel-encrusted crowns and hold court in a splendid gold and silver shrine. Above the miraculous statue is a silver canopy supported by 12 pillars. The altar beneath the statue was made in 1727 by an Augsburg goldsmith; the shrine's enclosing grille of silver, a gift of Maria Theresa, was crafted in 1756.

The Lady Chapel, which is also known as the Miracle Chapel, is located over the exact spot where the monk Magnus first established his cell in the year 1157. During the last reconstruction of the basilica, the remains of the original linden tree were discovered. Evidence reveals that this is the tree on which Magnus first placed the miraculous statue in his woodland hermitage.

Known as the most popular shrine of Our Lady in central Europe, Mariazell has been visited throughout the centuries by countless pilgrims from Hungary, Germany, Yugoslavia, Czechoslovakia, Poland and Russia and by the devout from throughout Austria. Many of these pilgrims have been recipients of miraculous cures which have been documented. Ex-votos of the fifteenth to twentieth centuries, located in one of the two Treasuries, attest to the gratitude of many who have been graced with a miracle. Also found in the Treasury are a number of elaborate garments worn at different times by the miraculous statue.

Benedictine monks from the nearby monastery have always been in charge of the shrine, and it was they who celebrated two milestones in the history of Mariazell: the Eighth Centennial celebration of the shrine in 1957 and the historical visit of Pope John

Paul II on September 13, 1983.

The most solemn ceremonies at Mariazell are observed on August 15, the Assumption of the Blessed Mother, and on September 8, the Nativity of the Blessed Virgin. During the summer months large crowds assemble on Saturday evenings, when a great torch-light procession takes place.

GREAT MOTHER OF AUSTRIA: The Romanesque statue of Our Lady located in the famous basilica-shrine in Mariazell, Austria. Pilgrims from all walks of life have prayed to Our Lady at the shrine, including King Louis of Hungary (1326-1382), asking for intercession and protection from evil.

ANCIENT STATUE: The famous statue of Mariazell, minus the ornate garb in which it is customarily clad. The Infant Jesus holds an apple and a fig (disguised here as a pear), symbols of Christ's redemption of mankind. Measuring only 47 centimeters high, the linden-wood statue is kept in the "Lady Chapel" located where the miraculous shrine's history began in 1157.

CHRIST'S INFINITE MERCY is symbolized by the light that bathes the statue of Our Lady nestled on the altar in the Mariazell shrine. Above the statue, a silver canopy is supported by twelve columns. Mariazell is the most popular shrine of Our Lady in central Europe.

— 3 —

OUR LADY OF THE BOWED HEAD

(Mother of Grace)
Vienna, Austria
1610

One evening in the year 1610, Venerable Dominic of Jesus and Mary was inspecting an old, dilapidated house that had been purchased with the intention of converting it into a monastery for the Discalced Carmelite friars. While walking around the outside of the building he passed a heap of rubbish, but paid no attention to it. But when he was examining the rooms of the building, he had an interior impulse that attracted him to the heap of rubbish and made him return to it. He lit his lantern and carefully examined the trash until something in the shadows attracted his attention. What he saw was an oil painting depicting Our Lady.

Being a devout child of Mary, Dominic was grieved to see a picture of her in such poor condition. After begging Our Lady's pardon for the ill treatment her portrait had endured, he carried it off, cleaned it, repainted the damaged parts and placed it in his cell. There he venerated it with great confidence.

One evening, after having swept his cell, Dominic noticed that dust had settled upon his treasured picture. Regretting what had happened, he begged Our Lady's pardon, and taking his woolen handkerchief he dusted the picture, saying with childlike simplicity: "O purest and holiest of Virgins, nothing in the whole world is worthy of touching your holy face, but since I have nothing but this coarse handkerchief, deign to accept my good will."

While he continued dusting the picture with great care and humility, the face of Our Lady suddenly became animated. She smiled at Dominic and nodded her head in token of her gratitude. Because Dominic was deeply confused and feared that he might be experiencing a diabolical illusion, the Queen of Heaven dispelled his concern with the words: "Fear not, my son, for your request is granted." (Dominic had earlier requested a favor of her.) "It will be accomplished, and will be part of the recompense that you are to receive for the love that you bear my Divine Son and myself." Our Lady then told Dominic to express to her with all confidence any favor he might desire. Dominic fell on his knees and offered himself entirely to the service of Jesus and Mary, and knowing by revelation that the soul of a benefactor was suffering in Purgatory, he asked its deliverance. The most Holy Virgin promised the soul's release if sacrifices and several Masses were offered for the soul. The apparition then ended.

Dominic hastened to do as Our Lady had requested, and a short time later, as he was kneeling before his miraculous picture, Our Lady appeared to him with the soul of the benefactor, which had been delivered from Purgatory. The benefactor thanked Dominic for his prayers and sacrifices. Then the Mother of God encouraged Dominic to ask for yet more favors. The holy religious asked Our Lady if she would listen mercifully to the prayers of all those who honored the picture and invoked her aid. Our Lady offered this assurance:

> All those who implore my protection, devoutly honoring this picture, will obtain their petitions, and will receive many graces. Moreover, I shall hearken in a special manner to the prayers that shall be addressed to me for the relief of the souls in Purgatory.

Since the promise was intended for all Our Lady's devotees, Dominic felt that he could no longer retain the picture for his own personal use. For this reason he had the portrait placed in the Oratory of St. Charles, connected to the Church of Santa Maria della Scala. It remained there until his death, becoming the object of fervent veneration, which was rewarded with many singular favors. Reproductions were made of the portrait, and soon it was venerated in several places.

A close friend of Dominic and the Carmelite Order was Maximilian, Duke of Bavaria. As a personal favor, he asked the Reverend Father Nicholas of the Immaculate Conception, who was the Vicar-General of the Order, if he might borrow the portrait. His request was granted.

The picture was brought to Munich by a pious lay brother, Brother Anastasius of St. Francis, who had been Dominic's traveling companion for more than 15 years. Brother Anastasius of St. Francis wrote and signed under solemn oath a document attesting to all that he had heard from Dominic concerning the picture and the miraculous events relating to it. The document is dated August 7, 1631.

Maximilian kept the portrait for a time and then gave it to the Carmelite Fathers of Munich. Shortly thereafter, the Superiors of the Province loaned it as a token of gratitude to the Emperor Ferdinand II, a great benefactor of the Order, having founded the convents of Vienna and Prague. By virtue of this loan the miraculous portrait arrived at the Imperial Court of Vienna in 1631. It was received with great joy by the Emperor and his wife, Eleanor, who placed it in the private chapel of the palace. There they richly decorated it. Ferdinand had perfect confidence in the portrait, and in all his difficulties he never ceased to invoke Our Lady's intercession. It is said that he even took the picture with him on all his travels.

Upon the death of Ferdinand, Eleanor retired to the convent of the Discalced Carmelite nuns which she had founded in Vienna. She had the holy picture transferred to the same convent and placed over the high altar. Upon her death on June 27, 1655, the picture was returned to the Carmelite friars.

Having been restored to the veneration of the public, Our Lady did not cease to draw multitudes and to bestow on them singular favors and graces in accordance with her promise to those who honor her image. The miraculous portrait was transferred on December 14, 1901 to the new church and monastery that the Discalced Carmelites had built on Silbergasse, Silver Street. The first altar erected in this church, by the generosity of benefactors, was dedicated to "Our Lady of the Bowed Head," and here the treasure of the Viennese Carmel is kept and venerated.

The Reverend Dominic of Jesus and Mary, who was favored with the animation of the portrait and the promise of Our Lady, became the fifth General of the Discalced Carmelite Order. He died in Vienna on February 16, 1630. His cause for beatification was introduced 46 years later, on January 29, 1676. Following a study and examination of his heroic virtues, Dominic of Jesus and Mary was declared Venerable in 1907 by Pope St. Pius X.

RESCUED FROM RUBBISH: The oil painting which depicts Our Lady of the Bowed Head was retrieved in 1610 by Venerable Dominic of Jesus from a rubbish heap. He was led to it by an interior impulse as he looked over a dilapidated house that was to be converted into a monastery. The holy religious was rewarded for his care of the miraculous portrait when the face of Our Lady became animated and spoke to him. The most Holy Virgin, Mother of Grace, assured Dominic that "Those who implore my protection, devoutly honoring this picture, will obtain their petitions."

— 4 —

OUR LADY OF THE WINDOW PANE

Absam, Austria
1797

Located near Innsbruck, the village of Absam is nestled among the majestic mountains of the Alps. During the winter months the beauty of the place is rarely appreciated since the weather is harsh and dreary. It was in the middle of winter, January 17, 1797, a day that was dark and snowy, that the miracle of Absam occurred.

It was between three and four in the afternoon when Rosina Buecher, a girl of 18, began to sew in the dim light provided by an overcast sky. After a few moments an interior prompting encouraged her to look at the window, where strange markings appeared on one of the window panes. She looked closely and then called excitedly to her mother. Together they looked upon the face of a woman, whom they quickly identified as the Blessed Virgin. Little time was lost in calling neighbors and the parish priest to see the wonder that had mysteriously appeared.

As an insulation against the harsh winters of the Alps, the windows of many cottages are doubled, creating an inside and an outside window. The image of the Blessed Virgin was in an upper pane of the inside window, one that could be opened only from inside the cottage.

After examining the image, the parish priest asked that the pane of glass be removed so that it could be more closely examined by experts in painting and glasswork. During this examination it was discovered that the image disappeared when the glass was submerged in water, but that the likeness of the Virgin *reappeared* as soon as the pane was dried. The image was also analyzed chemically, but the process by which the image was applied to the glass was never discovered. Eventually the experts declared that it was created in a miraculous fashion.

The reason for the appearance has been a matter of speculation. It is thought that Rosina's mother suspected it to be a warning of future troubles. Another theory is that Rosina believed it to be a heavenly sign that her father and brother would safely return home, which they did, after having narrowly escaped injury in an accident. Whatever the reason for the appearance, after the glass was examined by countless experts both the parish priest and the Bishop of the diocese declared it to be a miraculous favor.

The glass was eventually returned to the Buecher family. Because it was so highly regarded by the villagers, who thought it should be more easily available for their veneration, the Buechers gave the image to the parish church. Here it was visited not only by the villagers, but also by countless pilgrims who journeyed to Absam after hearing of the miracle and the placement of the image in the church.

Miracles of healing soon began to occur. Proof of these heavenly favors is given by a number of the ex-votos kept in the church. During the early 1800's many of the ex-votos were in the form of small paintings. Some of these depict the sick lying in their beds or the petitioner kneeling in prayer. Sometimes both the sick and a praying figure are shown. The word "ex-voto" and the date are usually given, and in all cases a miniature reproduction of the miraculous image is added.

Measuring a mere seven inches long and five inches wide, the glass on which the image of the Virgin Mary miraculously appeared is kept today on a side altar in the beautiful church of Absam. On its altar of gold it is surmounted by a golden crown and surrounded by golden rays that are embellished with golden flowers and precious jewels. The miraculous image appears somewhat dark and humble in appearance, but it is regarded as a precious treasure and as an indication of the Heavenly Mother's love for the people of Austria, and the people of Absam in particular.

AUSTRIA'S TREASURE. In 1797, an image of the Blessed Virgin Mary appeared on a window pane. Credited with miracles of healing, the glass is kept today in a church in Absam, Austria.

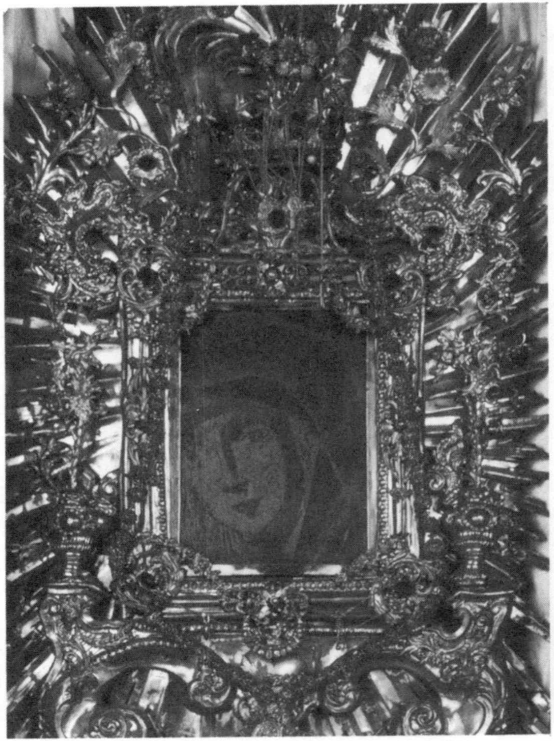

— 5 —

OUR LADY OF WALCOURT

Walcourt, Namur, Belgium
c. 347

No less than six fires either scorched or destroyed the buildings in which the wooden statue of Our Lady of Walcourt was enshrined, but in each instance, the statue escaped injury. These miraculous escapes on their own would cast an aura of virtue upon the statue, but a still more wonderful spectacle occurred (which will be noted later).

Tradition relates that while the fierce tyrant Arbeus was terrorizing merchants and travelers in the Heure Valley, St. Maternus, an apostle of the region, came upon him, instructed him in the Faith and converted him. As though to confirm or reinforce the religious conversion, or perhaps to place it under the protection of the Mother of God, St. Maternus thought to build an oratory to the Virgin Mary. The place chosen for the chapel was a spot in the very shadow of Arbeus' stronghold. In this oratory St. Maternus is said to have placed a figure of Our Lady which he carved himself. Since St. Maternus died in 347, Walcourt can be regarded as one of the oldest shrines of Our Lady in the world.

The oratory, which was no doubt kept in repair from the time of St. Maternus, was burned by Norman pirates about the year 992. During the same year Seigneur Wilderic began the rebuilding of another chapel, which was completed by Odwin, his successor. Consecrated by Reginald, Bishop of Liege in 1026, the chapel became a popular place of pilgrimage.

During the thirteenth century the deliberate setting of the second fire reduced the chapel to ashes. It was during this fire that an astounding spectacle took place.

The record tells us that:

> All the townsfolk witnessed the prodigy; they saw the holy image rise from the midst of the flames, lifted

> by a supernatural force and borne to a nearby place called "Jardinet," where it was set on a tree. In spite of all their efforts, the people were unable to remove it and the miraculous statue dwelt on the tree until the day when they besought the intervention of Count Thierry de Rochefort, the Seigneur of Walcourt. The Count rode out to the tree, followed by his squire, but his horse recoiled before the statue of the Virgin Mary, which was surrounded by a host of angels.
>
> Thrice did the Count try to advance. Then, dismounting, he knelt at the foot of the tree and vowed to found a monastery in that valley and to rebuild the burnt chapel. Then, to the amazement of the people, they saw the miraculous statue leave the tree and descend into the arms of the Count, who hastened to carry it back to Walcourt.

Faithful to his vow, Count Thierry founded the Cistercian Abbey of Jardinet, which existed until the eighteenth century. Ruins of the buildings can still be seen.

In memory of the miraculous escape from the fire and its transport to Jardinet, every year on Trinity Sunday a memorial procession is observed which travels the route taken by the statue to and from Jardinet.

The chapel erected by Count Thierry has suffered a number of fires. When enemy soldiers set fire to it in June of 1477, the statue and other articles were saved, but the archives were lost. In 1615 a fire devoured some 200 houses of the village. The bell tower collapsed, and serious damage was suffered by the church. During the Napoleonic War the church served as a barracks for some of the soldiers, who amused themselves by bayoneting the statues carved on the rood-screen that had been given by Emperor Charles V. After the villagers hid a bell that the enemy had intended to melt down for bullets and cannonballs, the enemy retaliated by setting fire to the church. Fortunately, the fire was extinguished before serious damage was done.

Yet another war posed a threat to the church when in August, 1914 German occupiers deliberately set fire to the church, claiming that the French used the tower as an observation post. With some thousand or more soldiers watching the flames, Abbe

Guillaume broke through the ranks and entered the church in search of the miraculous statue. The Lady Chapel was almost completely engulfed in flames when he reached it, but fortunately the statue had been placed above the high altar for the Feast of the Assumption. If this transfer had not taken place, the statue might have been destroyed. The church was later repaired, but traces of the numerous fires are still evident.

In addition to the recovery of the miraculous statue, many valuable articles were likewise saved from destruction, including a medieval Sacrament House in the sanctuary. Also saved were the rood-screen, which had been given by Emperor Charles V in 1531, a great crucifix and the ornately carved choir stalls.

The miraculous statue of St. Maternus that escaped so many threatening fires is found on the Lady Altar amid countless ex-votos and seventeenth-century paintings depicting the more important miracles attributed to Our Lady of Walcourt. A record of other miracles is kept in the archives of Walcourt and Namur.

The miraculous statue depicts Our Lady in a sitting position with the Christ Child resting against her chest. The Virgin wears a very solemn expression, while looking downward in a pensive attitude. The statue is covered with plates of silver that are regarded as being ancient. These were undoubtedly attached as a means of protecting it from future harm. It is known that some restoration was made to the statue in the thirteenth century. In 1626 the feautres of Mother and Child were redefined before a silversmith did some minor restoration.

Because of the many miracles attributed to Our Lady of Walcourt, Msgr. Jean de Wachtendonck, the Bishop of Namur, erected a Confraternity in her honor in the year 1663. Numerous indulgences were accorded its members by Pope Alexander VII in 1665.

A crown of gem-encrusted gold was placed upon the brow of Our Lady of Walcourt when Pope Pius XI ordered a papal coronation in 1875.

Still observed is the Trinity Sunday procession, which commemorates the translation of the statue in the thirteenth century to Jardinet. The villagers, wearing costumes of the period, first attend Holy Mass before processing along a six-mile route around the town. Along the way are fifteen chapels. At each chapel the procession pauses for the recitation of prayers and the singing of special antiphons. When the group approaches a designated tree which represents the tree at Jardinet, one of the villagers slowly approaches the small fourteenth-century silver replica of the miraculous figure which earlier had been hung from one of the limbs. A traditional prayer is recited before the image is placed in the arms of the villager who represents Count Thierry. The tree is then practically torn to bits by the participants who take pieces for mementos.

It is said that not even the terrors of the French Revolution interrupted this annual procession.

The image of Our Lady of Walcourt is truly miraculous, having survived so many fires in which its existence was threatened. Additionally, there have been countless miracles attributed to Our Lady's intercession. But what seems to be the greatest miracle of all is that Our Lady of Walcourt has been honored without interference where St. Maternus first established her shrine over 1,600 years ago.

ANCIENT IMAGE SURVIVES FIRES. After having resisted six fires 1,600 years ago, the wooden image of Our Lady of Walcourt (above) rose supernaturally from the blaze that razed the chapel where it had been kept.

— 6 —

OUR LADY OF HAL

Hal, W. Vlaan Deren, Belgium
1267

The original owner of the statue known as Our Lady of Hal was St. Elizabeth of Hungary, and it was this saint who gave the statue to her daughter, Sophie. She in turn gave the statue to her neice Alice, the Princess of Holland and Zeeland. Finally, it was Alice who donated the Black Madonna to the church in Hal in the year 1267.

Our Lady began almost immediately to disperse her favors to the countless pilgrims who flocked to her. So numerous were these spiritual graces, and so many were the healings of afflicted bodies, that pilgrims from throughout the country made their way to the church containing the miraculous image of the Queen of Heaven. A few years later an important confraternity was established which received recognition and favors from Popes Martin V and Eugene IV.

With the donations of pilgrims and the gifts from many nobles, a new church was started in 1341 which rose to become one of the most splendid of all the Gothic churches of Belgium. Although it is not the largest church in Belgium, its artwork is said to equal, or in some cases to excel, that of the country's other sanctuaries. Hal's carvings and ornaments are so intricate and artistically appealing that they delight the eye and prompt appreciation for the skill of the craftsmen, while the soul soars heavenward with admiration for the Heavenly Father, who inspired the work and bestowed talent to the hands that beautified the sanctuary of the Mother of God.

Because of the many persons of nobility and influence who were visiting Our Lady, a Registry of Visitors was initiated in 1344. Signing this book were kings, emperors, queens, princesses and princes. Also signing was King Edward III of England and William II, Duke of Brabant.

In time it became the practice for towns throughout Belgium to reserve a day for a yearly pilgrimage. At one time there were

45 such reservations. We report with admiration that almost entire towns participated in these pilgrimages.

Our Lady of Hal became so famous that even King Henry VIII of England knew of her. His majesty had apparently appealed to her for help, since in 1513, as a symbol of the King's gratitude for his victory over Louis XII of France, he presented the shrine with a splendid monstrance which is still viewed in the treasury of the church. This presentation occurred, of course, before the King initiated his dispute with the teachings of the Catholic Church.

The wooden figure of Our Lady, which gives every indication of its antiquity, was at some ancient time encircled with plaster-stiffened bandages which were then covered with silver. These wrappings, which cover only the trunk of the statue, are hidden under regal vestments which were donated by ladies of the nobility. In some cases these ladies embroidered the garments with elaborate designs. The statue is therefore robed in queenly fashion as she holds the Infant King of Heaven.

Our Lady's queenship is also affirmed, as is the kingship of her Child, by the crowns which were placed on their heads in 1874 in the name of Pope Pius IX. Crafted 400 years earlier, the crowns were made of silver overlaid with gold and encrusted with precious stones of great beauty and value.

Of interest at the shrine of Our Lady are 32 cannonballs which are kept in a niche of the tower. A nearby commemorative plaque bears the date "9 and 10 July, 1580." These cannonballs recall the time when Hal was besieged by the army of William the Silent. While the defenders of Hal courageously confronted the enemy, the women flocked to Our Lady of Hal to pray for deliverance. Although vastly outnumbered, Hal was, of course, victorious. The cannonballs are those which fell harmlessly around the shrine.

In commemoration of this great and unexpected victory against a formidable enemy, medals were struck with the image of Our Lady of Hal standing atop a number of cannonballs.

Hal was once more delivered from danger by way of Our Lady's protection when a group of Protestant extremists marched through Belgium, destroying everything that hinted of Catholicism. When Hal was spared desecration, Philip de Croy, the Catholic leader of the resistance, visited the shrine and attached a medal of Our Lady to his hat. His example was imitated by countless others, who in this way exhibited their devotion and loyalty to Our Lady of Hal.

When the Eucharistic Congress was held in London in 1908, Our Lady of Hal once again came to prominence when the monstrance given to the shrine by King Henry VIII was borrowed for the festivities. The Blessed Sacrament within this monstrance was carried by Cardinal Bourne in the procession in which all the participants in the Congress took part.

For 650 years Our Lady of Hal held court in her own chapel, but in 1910, to mark the fifth centenary of the consecration of the church, a new high altar was erected—and it was here that the miraculous statue was transferred. After removal to this place of honor, the statue of Our Lady became more accessible to the huge crowds that visited her. From her throne Our Lady is said to have favored the afflicted with more than a hundred miracles which have been recognized as authentic.

On the day of liberation from the Germans in 1945, British soldiers who were in the area could find no better way to celebrate the victory and show their appreciation than to form a procession through the streets of Hal, carrying on their shoulders the miraculous statue of Our Lady.

Finally, Our Lady was honored by the saintly Pope Pius XII on August 15, 1946, when His Holiness raised the sanctuary to the rank of minor basilica. By virtue of this distinction, the Pope recognized the church as a privileged house for its renowned and revered resident, the 700-year-old miraculous statue of Our Lady of Hal.

— 7 —

OUR LADY OF THE POTTERY

Bruges, Belgium
Thirteenth Century

Amid the Old World charm of steeply roofed gables and turrets, on the site where members of the Potters' Guild had their sheds and their wheels during the thirteenth century, now stands a church with a miraculous statue known as Our Lady of the Pottery.

Unlike other miraculous statues which were presented under unusual circumstances or were the result of a vision or other event, Our Lady of the Pottery was a large statue, erected under ordinary circumstances that gave no hint of its future renown or miraculous tendency—a tendency that would prevail for more than seven centuries.

When the potters of the early thirteenth century were practicing their trade, they built a chapel nearby which they dedicated to St. Catherine. This seemed appropriate, since St. Catherine was tortured on what came to be known as a "Catherine Wheel." The Saint's wheel was likewise depicted on the badges of Potters' Guild members.

Adjacent to the Potters' Chapel a hospice was founded on December 22, 1276 for the care of the destitute sick and infirm. Well-preserved documents in the hospice archives reveal that the community of five sisters observed the Rule of St. Augustine. The superior of the group was Mother Sara. Also assisting in the care of the patients was a master, a chaplain and a bursar.

A chapel in honor of Our Lady was started by the nuns in 1290 and was completed two years later. When a larger chapel was required, the sisters incorporated the Potters' Chapel of St. Catherine next door into the plan. The statue, which was later revered as miraculous, was made of stone and was placed outdoors, with only an iron grille and a penthouse roof to protect it from the weather.

Persons of importance then figured into the history of Our Lady of the Pottery. Alard Lam in 1302 arranged for a daily Mass to be offered in honor of Our Lady (this occurred about the same time that the Battle of the Spurs took place). A charter was granted by Philip "The Fair" of France, and in 1304, prior to the Battle of Mons-en-Pevele, the men of Bruges made a vow known as the Brugeois Promise. This required them to present to Our Lady, on a yearly basis, a wax candle of not less than 36 pounds. From that time on, devotion to Our Lady of the Pottery steadily increased.

In the mid-fourteenth century a larger church was needed. Dedicated to the Holy Spirit, it was consecrated on Passion Sunday, 1359.

By the year 1529 the wonder-working statue of Our Lady had been moved from the outside shrine to a new shrine within the church. During the year 1622 more space was needed for its visitors. It was then decided to build a chapel adjacent to the south side of the nave. A fine altar of carved oak and a triptych of the Assumption by the artist Vleys was donated by Jean Lucas, a native of Bruges who was then the Apostolic Vicar of Peru. When the chapel was completed, a ceremony of translation took place on the octave of the Assumption, 1625.

An elaborate and lofty altarpiece was positioned in the chapel in 1691. Surrounded by marble pillars, figures of the four Evangelists, and with the Holy Dove and angels hovering overhead, the miraculous statue was enthroned with great ceremony. For the benefit of the stranger who might not have heard of the wonder-working statue, a long marble scroll is near the image of Our Lady. Inscribed thereon are the words, *"Door Miraakelen Vermaert,"* or "Famous for Miracles."

Here on this elaborate altar the miraculous statue remained until 1917. During that year a restoration of the statue was decided upon. The task was entrusted to the artist Alphonse De Wispelaere, who first removed the paint. It was then realized that the statue had been separated into two pieces sometime in the remote past. It was theorized that this had been done so that the heavily embroidered mantles might hang to better advantage. It was detached at the waist, and a layer of cement had been wedged between the two pieces to give the statue a more upright posture. But the statue, now without its mantles, was seen to be disjointed and unnatural. As another insult, the Christ Child's right arm had been completely detached. When the wedge was removed, the two sections fitted perfectly together and gave the figure a pleasing form, with the

Mother's body slightly arched to the side to accommodate the weight of the Child, who stands somewhat on her hip. The statue remains in its natural state, without paint.

Our Lady of the Pottery was sculptured with a crown, a wimple, dress, girdle and long sleeves. Her mantle is caught up beneath the left arm, although the arm is free to hold the Christ Child. With her two hands supporting the Child at His waist, the Mother looks lovingly and happily at Him. For His part, the Child holds an orb in one hand while dispensing a blessing with the other.

Among the ex-votos at the shrine is one that captures the attention. It reads, "A Hamburg ship, returning from San Sebastian in 1632, was saved during a violent tempest and brought into the port of Plymouth, England. George van der Kerkhove, citizen of Bruges, who was on board, made a vow to Our Lady of the Pottery—Hence this tablet here."

A valuable old book in the archives entitled *Book of Miracles of Our Lady of the Pottery* gives details concerning many of the favors granted. Some of these are depicted on three panels of tapestry which are dated 1550. Each year during the summer months these tapestries are hung beside the Lady Chapel.

To the left of the present church doorway is the outdoor shrine in which the statue of Our Lady of the Pottery was first placed centuries ago. In the course of time another statue of Our Lady was installed in the shrine behind the iron grille. As a symbol of the love and reverence which the people of Bruges maintain for Our Lady of the Pottery, and as a way of alerting the passersby to the blessed place where she once stood, a stone tablet at this outdoor shrine reads: "In memory of the statue of Our Lady of the Pottery, formerly venerated on this spot, which is now above the altar in the side chapel."

"FAMOUS FOR MIRACLES." The statue of Our Lady of the Pottery, erected in the potters' district of Bruges, Belgium in the thirteenth century, initially gave no hint of the marvelous reputation it was to gain.

— 8 —

OUR LADY OF LA SARTE

La Sarte, Huy (Liege) Belgium
Thirteenth Century

A well-worn path leads up the hill from the market town of Huy, Belgium, past seven chapels in honor of the Seven Sorrows of the Blessed Mother, to the summit and the shrine of Our Lady of La Sarte. Here at the top, in what is comparable to a broad terrace, is found the seventeenth-century shrine church, a House of Studies and a tall belfry which is surmounted by a golden figure of the Holy Virgin.

Experts agree that the statue dates from the thirteenth century. It is believed that the first chapel at La Sarte was built about the same time. We know that a chapel stood there in 1501, since documents preserved in the town archives speak about it. But, unfortunately, the chapel fell into ruins. A contemporary, Amborse de Warem, a Capuchin friar, wrote:

> The chapel in which the most Blessed Mary was venerated at La Sarte has become so old and ruined that scarcely one piece of wall remains intact. A stone jutting from a wall bore the image of the Blessed Virgin. As the roof had fallen, the statue had been exposed to the elements for years and was decayed, broken, and damaged to such an extent that children playing round about made fun of it.

What could have brought about a revival of devotion for a statue that had been abandoned and in such a sad state? It can be attributed to one Anne Hardy, who in the year 1621 paused by the ruins to rest after gathering wood in the nearby forest. When she stood up to resume her journey home, she saw the statue, and feeling sorry for its condition she tied it to her bundle of sticks, thinking to place it in a more sheltered location. But when she attempted to pick up the bundle of sticks she discovered that she was unable to do so, since the statue had become unaccountably heavy. A man and a woman passing by offered their help, but the three, in their joined effort, could not lift the sticks until the statue was removed.

This incident is like so many others in which the Blessed Mother indicated her preference for a particular place by a suddenly weighted statue. It is unlikely that these incidents, happening as they did in isolated and far-flung areas, could have been generally known in the seventeenth century so as to influence the people to imitate what had taken place elsewhere. Moreover, the people involved in these cases, for the most part, were humble and honest folk who respected all things relating to the Church. All of these unusual accounts have been fully investigated, as was this particular event.

Evidence was gathered; the three witnesses were questioned and their statements were taken under oath. In the end, the facts were accepted under the normal laws of evidence.

Yet another incident occurred which was to renew devotion to the weather-worn statue. There was in the village a woman named Anne Nandrin, who had suffered for 15 years from a chronic affliction, as well as from a hernia and periodic swoons due to cerebral anemia. Following a third severe attack she was given Extreme Unction. When her condition improved a little, she was urged by friends to visit Notre-Dame de Tilliesse, but the journey was entirely too long and difficult for one in her condition. Anne then remembered a story told by her mother about the ancient statue of La Sarte. Since it was still exposed in the ruins, Anne decided to visit the statue on six successive Saturdays.

While she was praying during her fourth visit, Anne fell violently ill and sat down. During the seizure she kept her eyes on the statue. When her pains diminished, it seemed to Anne that Our Lady's features had become animated and assumed a natural color. Then drops of liquid seemed to trickle down the face of the Madonna. Needless to say, the woman was astounded and did not know what to do. After a considerable time, Anne approached the statue, drew out her handkerchief and wiped the face of the image. The cloth became saturated. Falling to her knees, Anne prayed fervently. When she arose a few minutes later, she was completely cured. The townspeople rejoiced at the miracle, and we can be certain that many of them hastened to examine the statue.

Anne continued to visit the statue as she had promised, but

she did not spend all her time in prayer. Instead she spent part of the time in decorating the niche where the statue stood and in arranging the area in a more orderly fashion. This inspired the people to go still further toward the complete restoration of the sanctuary. But first, the unusual happenings had to be investigated.

It is from the writings of Fr. Ambrose de Warem that we learn of the official inquiry conducted in 1624. The investigating panel consisted of a Doctor of Theology, a number of assessors chosen from the Canons of the Collegiate church and various religious of Huy. The inquiry was conducted as though it were a court of law, and evidence was taken under oath and in writing, the documents being signed in the presence of witnesses. The investigation, which considered the cases of Anne Hardy and Anne Nandrin as well as other events, is said to have lasted six weeks.

When a favorable verdict was rendered, the governing magistrates were then approached concerning a land grant at La Sarte on which to build a spacious chapel. Since it was indicated that many benefits would be derived by the city from the pilgrims who would visit the shrine, the magistrates anticipated the profits to be gained and formally granted a piece of land on September 22, 1624.

Canon Precentor Servais Hoyoul was appointed the first administrator and was given the task of building the new sanctuary. Brother Noel, a hermit, helped in raising funds and later became the first guardian of the shrine. Another document still preserved is the expense book in which Canon Hoyoul kept meticulous accounts from 1645 until 1655.

When the church was completed in 1656 the miraculous statue, now somewhat restored, was borne in procession to the church in Huy at the bottom of the hill. After remaining there for nine days during a solemn novena, it was carried in a triumphal procession through the town of Huy and was then carried back to the top of the hill, where it was enthroned in a chapel of the new church.

During the novena, one of the intentions was for the end of a prolonged drought that had scorched the land and all its vegetation. It is reported that as soon as the statue was enshrined the heavens provided a downpour, whereas an hour earlier there had not been a cloud in the sky. One witness wrote,

> The Lord caused abundant rain to fall, and all the country round was refreshed. The sky gave rain on several successive nights; the earth brought forth its fruits, and the people, happy witnesses of such benefits, gave glory to God.

During various wars and the French Revolution, the figure of Our Lady of La Sarte was spared. Today, after a thorough restoration, it is beautiful and lovable. The throne on which the Virgin is seated with the Child on her knee was carved from one piece of oak and measures 33 inches in height. The Virgin holds a scepter in her right hand, while supporting the Holy Child with her left. The statue's original right hand had been removed and replaced by another. Also, the two hands of the Holy Child have been replaced. Mother and Child are finely sculptured, but are rarely exposed without their magnificent tunics and mantles. Heavy silver and gold crowns cover the wooden crowns originally carved on the heads of Mother and Child.

Located directly above and behind the high altar, Our Lady of La Sarte is considered to be one of the most popular shrines in Belgium, the figure being one of the finest and oldest in the Diocese of Liege.

— 9 —

OUR LADY OF MONTAIGU

Montaigu, Belgium
Fourteenth Century

Meaning "Sharp Hill" in French, Montaigu rises abruptly from the surrounding territory. At its summit grew a solitary oak tree that was known from the time of the Druids as the site of superstitious practices. During the fourteenth century the people decided to transform the pagan site to one of nobler purpose. To accomplish this, they placed a small figure of Our Lady in a natural cavity of the tree. Many of the distressed regarded the place as a favorite shrine where they could seek help and comfort from the Mother of God.

One day a simple shepherd grazing his sheep on the hill came upon the shrine and found that the wind had blown the statue to the ground. Picking it up, he thought to carry it home when suddenly he was unable to move except to return the statue to its niche. When the boy excitedly told people in the village about what had taken place, the shrine became more popular, even to attracting people of distinction including Alexander Farnese, the victor of the Battle of Lepanto.

It is believed that the statue was destroyed in 1579 by a band of heretics known as the Gueux, who attacked all things that hinted of Catholicism. But even though the statue was missing, visitors continued to flock to the empty shrine, and many favors are said to have been bestowed there by the Mother of God.

The theory that the statue was destroyed by the Gueux came to be doubted when, in 1586, a certain resident of Sichem who was devoted to Our Lady of Montaigu, visited a widow who lived in the nearby town of Diest. In this home, in a place of honor, was a statue remarkably similar to the statue that was missing from the shrine in the tree at Montaigu. The response of the widow as to the origin of the statue is unknown; but the statue was given to replace the one that had disappeared.

Once again the solitary oak tree was graced by a statue of Our Lady, but in 1602 it seemed necessary to provide a more fitting shrine for the image. That same year Abbe Van Thienwinckel built a small wooden chapel beside the oak tree. The statue of Our Lady was removed to a shrine inside the chapel, where she was visited with all love and devotion. The confidence placed in Our Lady of Montaigu was rewarded by the distribution of countless favors, so much so that the renown of these graces encouraged even larger numbers to climb the hill of Montaigu.

One year later, in January of 1603, the most wonderful of all events took place when three councilors of the parish, after leaving their meeting, stopped at the shrine for a visit. While praying before the statue of Our Lady, each saw—to their utter bewilderment—that drops of blood trickled from the lips of the statue. While the blood continued to drip, they advanced to the statue and carefully inspected it. There was no evidence that the statue had been recently painted, and there was no indication that the blood was perhaps moisture that had collected because of humidity or other atmospheric conditions.

The miraculous bleeding was duly reported by the three councillors to the Bishop and public officials, who subsequently held an official inquiry. The officials rendered a favorable verdict since the three men were known as upright, honest, respected and pious persons whose testimony agreed with the reports offered by other witnesses.

A commission was then organized to study the reports of the favors and miracles that were reported as a result of prayer before the miraculous statue. The respected historian Numan interrogated the recipients of these favors and questioned the older residents of the village about previously reported miracles. Numan recorded that after the placement of the statue in the oak, more than 200 cures had taken place.

The attention of Pope Pius V was directed to the shrine, and it was he who granted numerous indulgences for those who visited Our Lady of Montaigu. Archduke Albert and the Infanta Isabella likewise became interested in the shrine and placed it under their direct patronage.

The shrine that was built as a replacement for the original was soon destroyed by a band of heretics. Fortunately, the miraculous statue was rescued and hidden until peaceful times were restored.

After the destruction of this chapel, Albert and Isabella resolved to repair the sacrilege by building a larger and safer shrine. They envisioned something of a fortress, surrounded by bastions and battlements that would render it impregnable against future attacks. The area around the oak tree was made into a large park within a seven-sided enclosure of walls, with a bastion at each point. Since many pilgrims had killed the tree by hacking away pieces of the bark as souvenirs, the tree was removed. In its place was positioned the high altar.

No better disposition of the wood of the oak could have been devised than what next took place. The wood was cut up into small pieces, which were carved by local craftsmen into replicas of the miraculous statue of Our Lady of Montaigu. These statuettes were given to various persons as marks of high regard. It is said that wherever these figures were enshrined with honor, Our Lady seems to have sent her favors with them. The most celebrated of these daughter shrines is in a side chapel in the Church of Our Lady of Victories in Paris. Another is in the Carmel at Lanherne in Cornwall, where it is known under the title of Our Lady of the Oak of Sichem.

The royal governors devoted themselves to providing a most exquisite basilica for their revered statue. The foundation stone was laid in 1609, but it was not until 1627 that the work was completed. Adorned with gold from Mexico, silver from Columbia, gems donated by countless devotees and costly silks from the East, the shrine presented a royal atmosphere for the queenly enthronement of Our Lady above the high altar.

Exquisitely carved, Our Lady of Montaigu is beautiful and very small. The figure was polychromed in the eighteenth century and is usually clothed in heavy robes, beautifully embroidered and sprayed with gems. With her hair flowing over her shoulders, Our Lady of Montaigu holds a large scepter topped by a large star. The Christ Child, on her left, extends His right hand in blessing while holding a small orb in the other. As befits their royal station, both figures wear costly crowns.

Kept at Montaigu is the original register of membership in the Confraternity that was established at the shrine. The hand-illuminated volume bears coats of arms of illustrious signers. It is said that no single volume in the world contains such an array of eminent and historic signatures.

The treasury of the church is a veritable museum of art. Some articles date back to the first humble chapel. Others include golden crowns presented in 1603 by the city of Brussels, silver candlesticks, vestments embroidered by royal fingers, a monstrance presented by Empress Marie-Therese, a processional cross dating from the thirteenth century given by Pope Adrian VI, a vestment worn by St. Thomas of Canterbury, and other articles which provide a most interesting exhibit for visitors to the miraculous statue of Our Lady of Montaigu.

— 10 —

OUR LADY OF GOOD SUCCESS

Brussels, Belgium
1436

Formerly known as Our Lady of Aberdeen, this miracle-working statue was taken from Scotland during the Scottish Reformation and brought to the city of Brussels, where it became known as Our Lady of Good Success.

The origin of the statue is clouded in uncertainty. It is thought to have been enthroned in the Aberdeen Cathedral in 1436. When the Calvinists were intent on desecrating the cathedral, it escaped injury by being placed in hiding with a family of the city. After graces and blessings were showered on them, the family members returned to the practice of the Faith. They readily acknowledged that their conversion resulted from the presence of the statue in their home.

After a time the statue was given to the care of a Scottish Catholic, William Laing. Then, in 1623, it was given to the Archduchess Isabella of Belgium, whose devotion to Our Lady was well known. Having already contributed generously to the building of the shrine of Our Lady of Montaigu in Belgium (see Chapter 9 in this book), Isabella provided funds for the building of a fitting sanctuary for Our Lady of Aberdeen.

Judging from the royal reception accorded Our Lady on her arrival in Brussels, the statue apparently had, by this time, a reputation for dispensing favors and blessings.

The priest who bore the statue from Ostend to Brussels was Fr. de los Rois, an Augustinian, who brought the statue to the newly built Augustinian church on May 3, 1626. Present for this occasion were all the clergy, nobility and authorities of the city. Pope Urban VIII likewise expressed his devotion by granting a plenary indulgence to all who would assist at the ceremony.

The statue was greeted by a procession, the ringing of bells and the firing of canon. Properly dressed for the auspicious occasion,

Our Lady appeared in golden garments and wearing crown jewels. With Isabella walking behind the statue, they reached the Augustinian church, and there a Holy Mass was sung for the good success of her Royal Highness. Henceforth, the statue of Our Lady of Aberdeen was known as Our Lady of Good Success.

The festivities which followed the installation of the statue lasted ten days and included the founding of the Confraternity of Our Lady of Good Success. The first to be enrolled was the Archduchess Isabella. Mary de Medicis, wife of Henry IV, likewise inscribed her name while kneeling before the statue.

The arrival of the statue in Brussels was recorded by several chroniclers, especially Fr. Gilbert Blackall, Priest of the Scots Mission, who wrote his account in 1631, five years after the event. His record in Old English reads:

> And that same day that the shippe in which it did arrive at Ostend, the Princess Isabella did winne a battaile against the Hollanders, the people thinking that Our Ladye for the civil reception of her statu, did obteane that victorye to the Princesse, who did send for the statu to be brought to Bruselle, wher the princesse with a solemne procession, did receave it at the porte of the towne, and place it in this chapelle, where it is much honored, and the chapelle dedicated to our Ladye of bonne successe, which befor was pouer and desolat, now is riche and wel frequented.

From her shrine Our Lady reigned in peace for 150 years, until revolutionary troubles swept through France to Belgium. Once again Our Lady sought refuge. This time she was placed into British hands for safekeeping. An English Catholic named Morris kept the figure secure until 1805, when it was restored to its former shrine.

Nine years later, a Protestant sect obtained a decree giving them the use of the Augustinian church. So once again, but for the last time, Our Lady was moved to another home, to a niche in the parish church of Our Lady of Finistere.

Above the main altar in this church is found a small, smiling figure of Our Lady of Finistere. Our Lady of Good Success is found in a side chapel. Upon entering this chapel one is immediately aware of countless ex-votos and the subdued light and warmth of flickering votive candles.

The figure is of a standing Madonna holding her Child on her right arm, but the Child is not upright as one would expect; rather, He is reclining as a newborn in the arms of His Mother. The Madonna wears an exquisite robe and holds a large rosary and a still larger key, which represents Our Lady's freedom in the City of Brussels. The left hand of the Mother tenderly supports the right foot of her Infant Son.

From time to time a suggestion is made that the statue should be returned to Aberdeen, Scotland, but the people of Brussels have taken the Lady of Good Success to their hearts and have made her theirs by adoption. Moreover, since the figure of Our Lady has been in Belgium longer than she was in Scotland, the suggestions are promptly dismissed.

— 11 —

OUR LADY OF FOY

Foy, Belgium
1609

A woodsman was cutting down an old oak tree on July 6, 1609 when he discovered in the wood of the trunk what seemed to have been an old wayside shrine of Our Lady. Along with a tiny sandstone figure were some beads, a lock of human hair and three bars of iron that once must have been a protective grille. A farmer and a laborer who were nearby ran to the astonished woodsman. They examined the articles and agreed that the tree had once provided a natural niche for the statue, but that in time the bark had grown over it.

The statue was taken to the farmer's house, where it was cleaned and put on the kitchen mantle. It remained there for a month and a half until the Baron of Celles, who was the Lord of the Manor, ordered that a new shrine should be provided for it on a tree that was near the one in which it was found. The statue remained in its new shrine for four years, until someone attempted to steal it. The Baron then took it to his own private chapel with the intention of keeping it there until a more secure shrine could be provided for it.

The statue might have remained in the private chapel of the Baron had it not been for Martin Pieltemps, the father of the parish priest of Sorinne. In the year 1616 Martin became desperately ill due to a hernia. After praying to Our Lady of Foy, he was wonderfully cured and made a pilgrimage of thanksgiving to the little statue. Since he was well known and highly respected, his cure became widely reported. Others soon followed his example of praying to the Madonna of Foy for all sorts of graces and cures. When favors were dispensed by the benevolent Mother of God, visits of thanksgiving were made.

So many were the people who visited the small statue as the result of miraculous cures that the Baron petitioned the Bishop of Liege for permission to erect a chapel near the site where the original shrine had once been located. First a canonical inquiry was made, with the result that 20 miracles were formally approved. The bishop then gave permission for a new chapel which was soon built. The statue was enshrined there during splendid ceremonies on November 21, 1619, the Feast of Our Lady's Presentation.

This chapel, built by the Baron, was visited by so many pilgrimages within the next three years that an enlargement of the building was required. Since the number of pilgrimages and visitors grew more numerous, the chapel had to be replaced by a sizable church. Still kept are the records pertaining to the building of the church. From these we learn that lumber was provided when the Bishop donated 32 oak trees. Sixty-four were bought from Adrien of Sommiere and 137 from Louis of Malaise. One order of bricks numbered 150,000 from the brickyards of Fuma, and 11,628 pounds of iron were forged at Liege. After two years of construction, the building was consecrated in 1624.

With the Jesuit Fathers caring for the new church and the much revered statue of Our Lady, devotion to Our Lady of Foy became widespread. Replicas of the statue were dispersed throughout France, Germany and the Americas.

Our Lady of Foy reigned in peace in the Lady Chapel for only a few years before hostile enemies, on a number of occasions, forced its removal to places of protection. Finally in 1696 Dutch Protestants forced open the doors of the church and stole many valuables, including the precious statue of Our Lady.

The people of the little town of Foy were outraged! A week later the priest of St. Peter's Church in Huy, the Reverend Noel de Comblin, obtained from Captain Charles Linchet a statue identical to that of Our Lady of Foy. When this was examined and declared to be the statue stolen from Foy, the Count of Beaufort was notified; it was he who decided to keep it for his own.

It is said that a serious fight began in the sacristy of the church between the Count and Captain Linchet, who had rescued the statue. Evidently the Count prevailed, since the statue was kept at his chateau at Veves from that time until he was forced to surrender it under threat of excommunication.

After the French Revolution the shrine lost its popularity for a time, but it gained its former glory in the early 1900's due to the efforts of Abbe Felix Fries and Abbe Charles Petitjean, who restored the church and encouraged pilgrimages. Finally, in 1909

Pope Pius X ordered the coronation of Our Lady of Foy, with Bishop Heylen serving as the papal delegate.

Our Lady of Foy is a mere nine inches tall. Made of gray sandstone, the statue is kept in a bronze shrine which was a gift of Bishop Ferdinand of Bavaria. The features of the entire statue have been somewhat worn by the passage of time, but Our Lady maintains her regal stature as she holds the Christ Child on her left. Atop her short veil, the heavenly Mother wears a large crown that is part of the sculpture. The statue is a pleasing one, with Our Lady's garments flowing in graceful folds around her. Estimates of its age place it in the first half of the fifteenth century, and it is believed to have been crafted in Utrecht. A traveling merchant apparently brought it to Foy, where it was purchased for the niche in the oak tree that served as a wayside shrine.

This small statue is enthroned in a church that is regarded as one of the important artistic treasures of Belgium. Of special note are the ceiling panels painted before 1626. These depict the Mysteries of the Rosary and various saints. Most of the panels were donated as ex-votos for favors received from the miraculous Lady of Foy.

The site of the oak tree that was felled by the woodsman is marked by a calvary which dates from 1635.

— 12 —

OUR LADY OF CHEVREMONT

Liege, Belgium
Seventeenth Century

Long before the City of Liege came into being, the Romans claimed the area for the Roman Empire and established a stronghold on a nearby hill known as Chevremont. During the seventh century, Ansegise (Chancellor in the court of King Sigebert III) enters the stronghold's history. It was he who added ramparts, walls, and a Lady Chapel inside the enclosure. Ansegise's wife was St. Begga; his son was Pepin of Herstal, who founded at Chevremont a monastery and a hospice for travelers. While Chevremont was a center of devotion and prayer, it was also a citadel where the local people sought refuge during invasions. But this military and religious stronghold lasted only until the year 986, when Chevremont was besieged by Lothaire, the King of France. The fortress was destroyed and the Lady Chapel was severely damaged. Centuries later Our Lady arranged for the repairs.

After a few Jesuit priests came from England during the seventeenth century and built a college in Liege, they were soon inspired to build a small chapel for Our Lady on the summit of Chevremont. Although the first chapel suffered serious damage, there is evidence that devotion to Our Lady of Chevrement had remained constant. This is made evident in official papers of the Council of the Prince-Bishop Maximilian of Liege dated September 14, 1686 which state:

> The English Jesuit Fathers have shown that there was a small chapel of Our Lady of Chevremont, very restricted and decrepit, which was built of roughly dressed stones, without mortar. There, every Sunday and Feastday, is held a great gathering in devotion by the people from around, of a kind which they (the Fathers) hope may become larger. . .the Glory of God and devotion

> to the most Holy Virgin would be much increased. They humbly request us to grant them permission to build there another chapel less mediocre. We therefore permit and authorize the said Fathers to build there a moderate-sized chapel.

After obtaining permission, a simple chapel was erected, but in 1697 this "moderate-sized chapel" proved inadequate and had to be enlarged.

Although the chapel is not elaborate, it was handsomely crafted and is decorated with countless ex-votos which indicate the many miracles attributed to Our Lady of Chevremont. Situated at the top of the hill, the chapel affords a magnificent view of the countryside and is reached by a path marked with seven stations indicating the Sorrows of Our Lady.

During the French Revolution, many churches were closed or destroyed, but devotion at Chevremont continued. For centuries pilgrims have been wending their way up the hill to honor Our Lady and to present their needs.

When Pope Pius IX was in need of prayers during the year 1874, the Bishop of Liege, together with 20,000 people, made a grand pilgrimage to pray for him before Our Lady's image. The following day the Bishop was presented with hundreds of requests for a religious house to be established on the hill, since priests were needed to dispense the Sacraments and to offer Holy Mass for the pilgrims. The Discalced Carmelites were invited to fill this need. By 1878 a monastery had been completed and a community chapel established. Twenty-one years later a church of Gothic design was consecrated.

The chapel erected by the English Jesuits in 1688 was recognized by Pope Leo XIII in 1888, the Second Centenary of the chapel, with the granting of a plenary indulgence to all who should visit. The same indulgence was granted in 1913, for the 225th anniversary.

The greatest celebration witnessed at the shrine was the Papal Coronation which was granted by Pope Pius XI in 1923. Unlike other Papal Coronations in which two crowns were offered, one for the Mother and another for the Child Jesus, this time three crowns were used in the ceremony officiated by the Papal Nuncio. Due to the size of the statue, miniature crowns were given, one for Our Lady, the other for the Christ Child, and the third, a much larger one, was placed above the canopy of Our Lady's shrine. By this coronation, the Church recognized the people's long-standing love of the statue and the historic nature of the sanctuary.

Following the papal coronation, the number of pilgrimages increased and grew larger. Because of the popularity of the shrine, Pope Pius XI raised the new Carmelite church to the rank of Minor Basilica on August 24, 1928.

The church was admired and devotion to Our Lady flourished there until World War II. Unfortunately, the basilica was severely damaged by aerial bombardment. The roof of the basilica was blown off, stained glass windows were shattered and the high altar was badly damaged. A bomb that fell within a few feet of the chapel reduced a large tree to splinters. The chapel of Our Lady, however, remained intact. This alone was considered a miracle. What was also considered extraordinary was that, in spite of the immense vibrations caused by countless bombings, the statue of Our Lady remained standing peacefully in its place, perfectly undamaged.

The repairs to the basilica were costly, but expenses were in large measure defrayed by a surtax placed on Belgian stamps which depicted Our Lady's Shrine, the basilica and a portrait of St. Begga. The stamps were issued on April 8, 1948, when the restored high altar was consecrated.

The statue of Our Lady of Chevremont is one of the oldest of the miraculous images of Our Lady, and it is also one of the smallest, being only eight inches high.

Our Lady holds the Divine Child on her right arm; her left hand is positioned at her waist. The figures of Mother and Child are finely sculptured, with their robes nicely draped.

— 13 —

OUR LADY OF OOSTACKER

Oostacker, Ghent, Belgium
1872

An outdoor aquarium was the unlikely origin of a shrine in Belgium dedicated to Our Lady of Lourdes which has been the scene of numerous miracles and the destination of countless pilgrims.

The aquarium was to be located in a cave near the chateau of the Marquise de Courtbourne. The cave was known to her family as "the hermitage," because a brother of the Marquise had lived there for many years after illness forced him to leave the Trappists.

The plan envisioned by the Marquise was to build along the walls of the cave a number of tanks for her large collection of rare fish. When the aquarium was completed, the Marquise invited her friends and the parish priests to the festive opening. Since the famous apparitions at Lourdes had occurred 14 years earlier, one of the priests suggested that it might be possible to incorporate a figure of Our Lady as she had appeared to St. Bernadette.

The Marquise immediately arranged for a statue to be sculptured and set in place. For the ceremonial blessing of the statue she invited all the parishioners to attend. The grotto immediately became a place of great popularity with the people, and they asked permission to enter the property for Sunday visits. By 1873, the stream of visitors had increased to such proportions that arrangements were made to make the grotto permanently accessible to the public. The solemn inauguration of the place as a public shrine was witnessed by more than 2,000 persons.

Organized pilgrimages were soon arriving at the grotto. Within a year Oostacker had become famous throughout Europe, with visitors arriving at the shrine from Holland, northern France and throughout Belgium. Cures and favors were frequently reported to the local priests, with one of the most notable cures occurring on September 9, 1874 when a woman who had been ill and totally incapacitated for 12 years was suddenly cured after a few moments of prayer before the statue of Our Lady.

The most widely reported cure and the one which is perhaps the most sensational occurred one year later, in 1875, in favor of Peter de Rudder. Peter had been severely injured when a heavy tree fell across his body. Among his serious injuries was his mutilated leg, which was smashed a few inches below the knee. The bone is said to have been splintered and almost pulverized. For eight years Peter endured excruciating pain, especially when splinters of bone worked their way through a gaping wound near his ankle.

When Peter heard of the many cures that were taking place at Oostacker, he resolved to journey there despite the distance and the added pain he would be forced to endure. Journeying to the shrine on crutches, he arrived completely exhausted and fell on the grass before the statue. After a few moments he felt a curious inclination to throw aside his crutches and advance closer to the grotto. He submitted to the urge and walked—without a trace of pain—to the entrance of the cave before he realized that he had been completely cured. With cries of thanksgiving to Our Lady, he was taken to the chateau, where he was given a medical examination. Peter had been completely cured. A number of specialists, including the doctors who had treated Peter for his many injuries, could not explain the sudden and complete cure of the leg, although they soon deemed it to be the result of a miraculous intervention.

Before his death Peter bequeathed the bones of his legs to the shrine as proof of the cure. Accurate casts of these bones have been affixed to a plaque which is located beside the figure of Our Lady.

As a result of these and other cures, the grotto was recognized as a major shrine of Our Lady. A church, which was raised to the dignity of a basilica, was built beside the grotto, but the grotto has remained exactly as it was in the time of Peter de Rudder. The grounds have been landscaped, however, and there is a simulated Calvary, a Way of the Cross and a path denoting the beads of the Holy Rosary.

Known as the Belgian Lourdes, the grotto is not in competition with the French shrine. Rather, it is regarded as a simple shrine to Our Lady of Lourdes for those who are unable to journey further on to southern Francce and the hallowed place where Our Lady appeared to St. Bernadette. The basilica of Oostacker resembles a parish church, but inside is found a magnificent shrine and a statue of Our Lady of Lourdes which was crowned by order of the Holy See. Within the shrine are countless plaques, tablets and ex-votos which attest to the favors received by Our Lady's grateful children.

— 14 —

OUR LADY OF COPACABANA

Bolivia, South America
1583

The name Copacabana brings to mind a tourist retreat, a beach on the Atlantic coast southeast of Rio de Janeiro, Brazil. But the place we are considering is near the Pacific Ocean on Lake Titicaca, which spans the Peruvian-Bolivian border.

Two fishermen were one day fishing on Lake Titicaca when they were overtaken by a violent storm. When they seemed destined to drown, they appealed to Our Lady of Copacabana for her protection. They credited their survival to the devotion they had maintained for Our Lady at the nearby shrine containing her miraculous image. When the two fishermen moved from Bolivia to the Brazilian beach, they named the area Copacabana as a gesture of gratitude to Our Lady. This is supposedly how the retreat in Brazil received its name.

For the history of the Bolivian shrine and statue we must look back to pre-Christian days when there was a shrine to the Inca sun god high in the mountains of western Bolivia. The area still had a sinister history of idolatry and human sacrifice when it was evangelized during the sixteenth century. During a terrible famine which devastated the people in the year 1582, friars in the area regretted the absence of a statue of the Blessed Mother, for they sensed that such a figure would have been a comfort to the distressed. Prayers were offered and pious associations formed, but the famine continued.

Finally a young Indian named Francisco Tito Yupanqui decided to fashion a statue like those he had seen in La Paz. Although untrained in sculpture, he made a four-foot-high statue of maguey, wood, plaster and stucco. Even though he had done his best, the statue was not acceptable to the people. They complained that the face of the simulated Virgin was quite ugly. They ridiculed the crude work of sculpture, and no one was pleased with the idea that the statue, made by an unskilled artist, would be placed in their church. For this reason the young Indian placed his statue in the house of Fr. Francisco Navarrete, a Franciscan.

Sometime later the friars saw a mysterious light surrounding the statue. The whole image glowed—and by a miraculous transformation the face became quite beautiful. As a result of this phenomenon the statue was solemnly enshrined in the church on February 2, 1583. As soon as the statue was placed in the church the devotion of the people was awakened. Many favors were received and many cures obtained. Soon large crowds of suppliants filled the church, and it was not long before the old structure was too small to accommodate the enthusiastic crowds that hastened to the foot of Our Lady's altar. Eventually a new church was built for the miraculous image, and there the Indians have been untiring in their devotion.

The statue made by Yupanqui is situated in a lovely, jewel-sparkled shrine. It is reached by a double stairway, the steps of which are well worn by the feet of countless pilgrims who have visited the image for over 200 years. The power of Our Lady's intercession is demonstrated by the many ex-votos that are affixed to the walls of the shrine.

Our Lady of Copacabana evidently wished to endear herself to people of other countries, since an exact copy of the statue was placed in the Cathedral of Lima by St. Alphonsus Tiribio. Another copy was placed in the Church of St. Ildephonsus at Rome, while yet another copy was enshrined with great solemnity at Madrid.

The miraculous statue is never removed from the church; a duplicate is used for processions.

The miraculous statue is usually clothed in richly embroidered garments which have been donated by Our Lady's devotees. The Virgin Mother holds the Child Jesus on her left arm, and a jeweled scepter in her right hand. Dangling from the right arm is a golden basket containing two golden doves. A lacy veil and a tall golden crown adorn the head of the Virgin. The Child Jesus also wears a crown which is similar to that of His Mother. The statue is somewhat unusual in that the Child Jesus is at a curious angle, giving the impression that He is uncomfortable. Still, He raises His right hand in blessing, while holding a golden orb in the other.

During an Indian uprising in 1781, the church was desecrated and valuables were stolen, but the chapel of Our Lady remained untouched and intact.

The image was solemnly crowned in 1920. Twenty years later the church was elevated to the rank of Basilica.

The two main feasts of the miraculous statue are August 6 and February 2. These are celebrated with native dances which re-enact many events from the history of South America and Bolivia. The feasts are noted for the colorful costumes and the boisterous and enthusiastic dances of the participants.

A NEW FACE. (Above.) When the sculpture of Our Lady of Copacabana was first created in 1580 by Francisco Tito Yupanqui, people complained that the face was ugly and crude. They even refused the statue a place in the local church. They changed their minds, however, after a mysterious light surrounded the statue and the image was beautifully transformed. **(Right)** Our Lady of Copacabana, adorned with elegant garments donated by devotees.

— 15 —

OUR LADY OF THE HOLY ROSARY

Notre Dame du Cap
Cap-de-la-Madeleine, Quebec, Canada
c. 1845

When French Jesuit priests began to evangelize the eastern parts of Canada, their great devotion to Our Lady was manifested by the many shrines and chapels they erected in her honor. One of the settlements which benefitted from this devotion was the trading post named Three Rivers. Here, in 1634, a shrine was consecrated by the Jesuit missionaries to the Immaculate Conception.

In the mid-seventeenth century, a district adjacent to the Three Rivers trading post became a separate village and was promptly dedicated to the Blessed Mother. A fort and some houses were built there, as well as a church placed under the patronage of St. Mary Magdalene. Eventually the settlement became known as Cap-de-la-Madeleine, a name it has retained.

Constantly in peril from the Iroquois savages, the people put their confidence in Our Lady to protect them. They demonstrated their trust by erecting small shrines in their homes. There, every night, they would recite their family prayers and plead for heavenly protection.

Reinforced with stones gathered from the fields, the first chapel of 1662 became, 32 years later, the home of one of the earliest Confraternities of the Holy Rosary in Canada. Documents signed for the inauguration of this Confraternity are still kept in the archives of the sanctuary. Fr. Vachon, the founder of the Confraternity, is buried beneath the altar of the shrine. It is said that timbers used in the building of the primitive shrine bear Indian markings.

The eighteenth century is said to have been one of uneventful struggle in the settlement. Lacking a priest in residence who could celebrate the Holy Sacrifice each day and minister to the spiritual needs of the people, devotion waned. It was not until 1845 that the Bishop appointed Fr. Leandre Tourigny to be the settlement's resident priest. It was during his pastorate that a generous donor presented the Confraternity Altar with a large statue of Our Lady, in honor of the definition of the Dogma of the Immaculate Conception. This was also a reminder that the Jesuit priests had dedicated the region to the Immaculate Conception 200 years earlier. It is this figure of Our Lady which is the focus of Canada's most popular shrine of Our Lady.

The statue represents Our Lady standing in an attitude reminiscent of that on the Miraculous Medal. Her bare feet crush the serpent coiled on the top of a star-studded globe. Her head is covered with a white veil and adorned with a golden crown; her garments are gilded, ornamented and bordered with artistic figures. Perhaps the most outstanding feature of the statue is an oversized heart, encircled with roses and topped with a spray of flames. This is supported by a chain encircling the neck of the Madonna. The expression of Our Lady's face is pleasant; her eyes are modestly downcast.

Unfortunately, Fr. Tourigny was unable to rouse the people from their indifference. For this reason Bishop Cooke appointed Fr. Luke Desilets to help in revitalizing religious fervor. The method devised for this transformation was the building of a National Shrine of Our Lady.

This endeavor was to be proposed to the congregation, but on the eve of the Ascension, 1867, not one soul approached the confessional. Instead, Fr. Desilets discovered a pig in the church. Especially upsetting to the priest was the discovery that the pig was munching on a rosary. Overcome by the sight, Fr. Desilets fell to his knees to implore Our Lady's forgiveness and help. It was then that he was inspired to regain his lost flock through the promotion of the Holy Rosary.

The theme of his sermon the next day was, "The pig and the Rosary." There was an immediate awakening of fervor. Gradually the number of penitents and devotees increased, until the building of a new church became a necessity.

When the Bishop granted permission for this undertaking, the stones needed for the new church were cut and dressed at a quarry at S. Angele on the other side of the river. This task took two years, from 1877 to 1879. It was the intention of the builders to drag the stones across the frozen water of the St. Lawrence River during the winter, since thick ice customarily formed and provided a natural bridge. But the winter of 1879 proved to be an exceptionally mild one. During the month of March, the parishioners grew increasingly doubtful that they would be able to secure the needed stones from the opposite side of the river. Realizing that the plans for the new church would likely be abandoned, Fr. Desilets had recourse to urgent prayer and "bargained" with Our Lady. If the heavenly Queen would construct a bridge of ice sufficient to transport the stones, he would not supplement the supply of stones by taking the stones from her primitive church. He would instead preserve the old church and cause it to be dedicated for all time as a perpetual shrine of the Most Holy Rosary.

The holy prelate's prayers were answered almost immediately. On March 15, 1879, a violent gale began to pile up ice floes until a bridge of thick ice formed from one shore to the other. The next day, a Sunday, it was found that this bridge of ice could bear the weight of 30 or 40 men. The next day saw a steady stream of more than 150 horse-drawn sledges crossing and recrossing this bridge, carrying loads of stone. By the end of the week every stone needed was located on the church site. Then, when the ice bridge was no longer needed, a thaw set in. The next day, just as quickly as it had formed, the ice bridge was gone.

We are assured that the formation of the ice bridge is no imagined legend since newspapers of that time told of its mysterious and timely formation, as well as its sudden disappearance. The miraculous ice bridge is also recounted in a detailed letter written by Fr. Frederic, O.F.M. (d. 1916), whose cause for canonization was introduced in 1940. Moreover, the events relative to the ice bridge were regarded by everyone as extraordinary. A permanent marker was erected in the gardens of the sanctuary to memorialize the occasion of the marvelous bridge of ice.

The church that was built with the stones that had been transported across the ice bridge was opened on October 3, 1880. The primitive Lady Chapel was restored, but was not ready for use until June 22, 1888, when great ceremonies took place. It was during this observance that the small church was consecrated to the Virgin Mary as a pilgrimage site. Fr. Frederic, who had recently joined the pastoral team, delivered the sermon. He later became pilgrimage director and served in this capacity until 1902.

Of the many miraculous events that occurred at the shrine, one of the most notable took place on June 22, 1888, the same day that the small restored church was consecrated to the Virgin Mary. One of the pilgrims on that day was Pierre Lacroix, a sick man from Three Rivers. Because of his infirmity he was assisted into the chapel by Fr. Desilets and Fr. Frederic. While they were praying, all three independently observed that the eyes of the statue of the Blessed Mother, which had moments before been downcast, were then wide open and looking straight ahead. The men doubted what they were seeing until they questioned one another. Each man described the statue's eyes as "living eyes." Fr. Desilets recorded, "She raised her eyes and looked in front of her as if looking outwards, far into the distance. Her face was at times severe, and sometimes sad." Fr. Desilets died eight weeks after this miraculous event.

Detailed accounts of this occurrence are carefully preserved in the sanctuary archives, including the following declaration:

> I, Pierre Lacroix, engineman, resident of the City of Three Rivers, solemnly declare that in the month of June of the year in which, at the shrine of Our Lady of the Holy Rosary, at Cap-de-la-Madeleine, a great religious feast had been celebrated to mark the fact that on that day the statue of the Blessed Virgin which had formerly occupied the side chapel as altar of the Confraternity of the Most Holy Rosary, had been installed over the main altar.
>
> I went into the shrine about seven o'clock in the evening accompanied by Vicar-General Luc Desilets and the Reverend Fr. Frederic. I was walking between the two of them, being helped by them. We had taken our places before the altar rail in front of the main altar over which the statue had been placed, the Vicar-General and the Reverend Father on their knees, myself sitting between them on a chair placed there for the purpose, for I could not kneel because of my infirmity.
>
> After praying for a while, I looked up at the statue of the Blessed Virgin, which was facing directly towards me. As I did so, I most distinctly saw the statue with its eyes wide open in a completely natural manner. It was as if it had looked out over our heads, and it seemed to me to be looking at Three Rivers.

I examined this closely without saying anything. Then Vicar-General Desilets, leaving his place which was on my right, went over to Father Frederic and I heard him say, "Do you see it?" "Yes," said Father, "the statue has its eyes open, hasn't it?"

I then told them that I had seen the same thing for several moments, and I make this solemn declaration believing it in conscience to be true and knowing that it has the same force and the same effect as if made upon oath, under the jurisdiction of the act of proof in Canada, 1893, and I declare that I do not know how to write my name.

(Signed) Pierre Lacroix X (his mark.)

Taken before me at Three Rivers this fourteenth day of January in the year of Our Lord eighteen hundred and ninety-five.

(Signed) P. Desilets, N.P.

This declaration was certified as exact on all points by Fr. Frederic. In his historical report of 1897, Fr. Frederic wrote, "I continue to reaffirm my belief that I never had any doubts and the effect left by the long stare of the Virgin is still present to my eyes."

News of this miracle, as well as that regarding the ice bridge, prompted pilgrimages that have continued ever since and have increased in number until the shrine is regarded as the most frequented shrine of the Blessed Mother in Canada.

Between serene ponds and a lovely lake, a whole complex of buildings, gardens and devotional areas have developed around the shrine. Among the additions are a monastery of the Oblate Father of Mary Immaculate, a convent for Dominican nuns, a retreat house, a perpetual adoration chapel, restaurants, a building for lodging pilgrims and the basilica which was inaugurated in 1964. A Stations of the Cross is on the other side of the little Faverel River. Linking the shrine grounds to the Stations is the Rosary Bridge, named in memory of the historic episode of 1879. The bridge is decorated throughout with large chains resembling rosaries.

In 1904, Pope St. Pius X ordered the crowning of Notre Dame du Cap. Once again the statue was crowned when Pope Pius XII sent his delegate, Cardinal Valeri, to act in his stead. To this day, Notre Dame du Cap is the only Madonna to be crowned in Canada.

The shrine was also dignified by the visit of Pope John Paul II on September 10, 1984; 75,000 pilgrims joined in welcoming him.

The year 1988 was one of exceptional interest, since the centennial of the shrine was observed with special ceremonies. Also celebrated that year was the beatification of Fr. Frederic on September 25. Countless pilgrims who visit Notre Dame du Cap also journey to Three Rivers, where Bl. Frederic's tomb is found in the chapel of the Franciscan Order.

"THE PIG AND THE ROSARY" was the topic of a sermon in 1867 by Fr. Luke Desilets after he found a pig in his Quebec church munching on a rosary. Dismayed at the event and hoping to restore religious fervor to his parishioners, the priest implored Our Lady's forgiveness and help. His prayers were answered, and miraculous assistance spurred the construction of a new church. Pilgrimages to the shrine of Our Lady of the Holy Rosary have taken place for over a century.

— 16 —

THE VIRGIN OF CHARITY

Cobre, Cuba
1600

The origin of a statue venerated in Cobre, Cuba is lost amid legends and confusion. Some believe that the statue was hidden long ago in a cave on the island during a conflict between pagan natives and Spanish settlers. One theory holds that floodwaters dislodged it from its hiding place and washed it out to the Bay of Nipe.

What is accepted as certain is that two Indians and a black slave, all named John, were in a small skiff in the Bay of Nipe in the year 1600 when a raging storm threatened their lives. Far from shore, they were terrified and prayed fervently to Our Lady to help them. It is said that Our Lady appeared to them in a vision and promised them her maternal protection. Shortly thereafter, the winds grew quiet, furious clouds calmed, and the sun once again sparkled upon gentle waves. It was then that the slave saw in the distance a white object floating on the water. Since the object seemed to follow them, they decided to investigate and rowed their skiff toward it. As they drew near they saw that the object was a small statue of a Lady standing upright on a plank that floated easily on the water. They gently placed the statue in the boat and pulled the plank in. On the plank were carved the words: "I am the Virgin of Charity."

The three Johns decided to dock at the nearest port and leave the statue in the hands of a responsible person. They delivered it to a Spanish officer, to whom they told the details of their survival and the mysterious finding. Impressed with the story, the officer temporarily placed the statue in a small chapel.

The vision and the miracle of the Virgin floating on the waves stimulated the devotion of the people. Their enthusiasm reached such a pitch that a dispute arose over where the statue should be permanently enshrined. Since various signs indicated Our Lady's choice, the statue was delivered to Cobre.

The little statue, about 16 inches tall, has a round, pretty face that reflects the beauty of the Spanish people and their heritage. The Madonna holds the Christ Child in her left hand, while her right displays a small jeweled cross. The Virgin and Child wear exquisite garments of gold cloth, heavily embroidered with golden thread. Both figures wear regal crowns and are surrounded with a great golden halo. The statue is undoubtedly one of the most beautiful of the many miraculous images of Our Lady.

Appearing as she did to two Indians and a black slave, and favoring them with the finding of her statue, it has been noted that the Mother of God apparently wanted to express her love and concern for people who were then considered outcasts of the Spanish province in the New World. As the Virgin of Charity, she provided hope for her oppressed children. Even today, she is comforting Cuban exiles in this country as well as the oppressed people on the island who are struggling under the rigors of Communist domination.

When the evils of Communism forced more than a million people to flee Cuba, they settled in Miami and erected a church which honors the Virgin of Charity. On the facade above the main entrance a mosaic depicts the three Johns in their skiff amid heavy waves. A large mural behind the main altar displays the history of the island nation, various miracles of the Virgin and, in the middle, the Virgin of Charity and the three Johns in their skiff. Separated physically from their beloved statue, the Cuban people are consoled with another image of the Virgin of Charity which is enshrined in their church. This beautiful Madonna also holds the Child Jesus in her left hand and a crucifix in the right. Both figures also wear royal crowns and are surrounded with a magnificent halo.

MYSTERIOUS ORIGIN. The statue pictured at left was found in the year 1600, floating on a plank in the Bay of Nipe by men in a small skiff who had prayed for an end to a raging storm. The storm grew quiet, and then the mysterious statue made its appearance. The story of the Virgin of Charity, Patroness of Cuba, is represented above.

— 17 —

OUR LADY OF QUINCHE

Quinche, Ecuador
1586

During the year 1586 a wood-carver named Diego de Robles carved a statue of Our Lady from native cedar for the newly converted Carib Indians. Since they did not appreciate his work, he took the statue with him to Ecuador where another tribe of Indians lived who were also newly baptized converts. They immediately saw beauty in the statue and traded lumber for it. Since they did not have a chapel, they placed the little statue in a rocky niche near their place of work.

During the day the Indians noticed that little birds seemed to favor the statue by fluttering about it while chirping their praises. As if to continue the concert of the birds, the Indians began the practice of gathering in the evenings before the Madonna, singing and playing melodies for her on their crude musical instruments. In what seemed a sign of appreciation during these performances, the statue was often surrounded by a glowing light.

The women of the village wove a garment for their beloved statue, and it was the touching of this robe that effected numerous cures. There were so many, in fact, that news of the miracles alerted Indians of nearby tribes who began to pilgrimage to the wonder-working image.

In time a small chapel was built for the statue. Once again the wood-carver Robles steps into the statue's history. He was asked to exercise his skills by constructing a pedestal for the statue. The sculptor apparently took little interest in this new assignment and repeatedly made excuses for not beginning the work—that is, until one day when he was riding his horse to Quito. During this journey his mount stumbled on a jungle bridge spanning a swift river and threw him head first over the railing. It is said that Roble's spur caught in the rope of the bridge, saving his life but leaving him dangling by one foot. No doubt he made fervent promises to the Lady of Quinche because, immediately after being rescued, he set about designing and constructing the requested pedestal.

Many are the miracles attributed to Our Lady of Quinche, but one of the earliest and the one which attracted the most interest and drew countless pilgrims to the woodland shrine was that which took place when a young couple prayed fervently for the protection of their small baby. The couple had left the child sleeping in the shade of a tree while they helped in the construction of the chapel. On hearing the baby scream, they saw it being carried off by a large bear. They eventually found the child dead and badly mangled. While weeping and bewailing their loss, the parents carried the baby to the statue of Our Lady. There they were joined by all who had witnessed the attack. While they prayed fervently for resignation and consolation, the child opened its eyes and reached for the statue. All present acclaimed the recovery to be a miracle of Our Lady of Quinche.

Many are the miracles worked by Our Lady throughout the centuries for her beloved Indians and the people of Ecuador. Among them is the fact that it has never rained on a day when a procession was planned. Additionally, on many occasions Our Lady has also relieved Quinche of droughts and contagious diseases.

Affectionately known as "La Pequenita," "The Little Beloved One," the statue of Mother and Child is enshrined in the large, magnificent Church of Our Lady of Quinche which developed from the rudimentary woodland shrine erected by the Indians in the sixteenth century.

— 18 —

OUR LADY OF ALL GRACES

Chatillon-sur-Seine, France
Fourth or Fifth Century

The great St. Bernard of Clairvaux (d. 1153) figures prominently in the history of this miraculous statue. During the lifetime of the Saint the statue was venerated in the Church of St. Vorles and was even then considered to be extremely old. St. Bernard, who studied in a school under the jurisdiction of this church, was familiar with the holy image from childhood and it was he who much later changed the name of the statue from Our Lady of Chatillon to Our Lady of All Graces. The Saint, with the help of his cousin, Bishop Bruno de Langres, also constructed an abbey at Chatillon, which he dedicated to Our Lady of All Graces. Built in 1136, it was confirmed in a Bull of Pope Innocent II dated September 19, 1138.

The devotion expressed to Our Lady during the following centuries was marked with triumphant processions, particularly on the thirteenth of May—the anniversary of an apparition of Our Lady to St. Bernard, and on August 20, the feastday of the Saint.

Because of the wonders Our Lady performed and the many graces dispersed through her generosity, other towns asked for a visit of the miraculous statue. For these journeys the statue was placed on a platform with the reliquary of St. Vorles beside it and carried in procession to neighboring towns and villages. Of particular note were the processions to Clairvaux in 1583, Fontaine-les-Dijon in 1632 and the journey to Pontigny in 1639.

Pere Legrand, a Jesuit, wrote a history of the image that was edited in 1651. In this book he describes the image as being made of wood. He writes:

> The face is long and slender, the eyes are wide open. The nose is long with cheeks not too full nor is it harsh. The color is brown with age and by the art. She is

> sitting holding with her two hands the little Jesus on her lap. The statue was placed in a niche at the very center of an apse. It was the first Christian monument in that region in the fourth or fifth century.

During the Reign of Terror (1793-1794) the pilgrimages that had been held in honor of the Madonna were discontinued, but the love of the people continued. In fact, when the church was threatened, 24 men encircled the building and remained throughout the day and night to prevent it from being profaned. By their actions, the members of Our Lady's honor guard were ready to sacrifice their lives to protect the Madonna's shrine.

The statue of the Virgin was not in the church at this time, but had been safely hidden as a precaution against certain abuse. A doctor, M. Maurage, had carefully hidden it in the garden of a farm. Many years later, when the statue was taken from this hiding place, it was greeted with the immense joy of the people. Some, however, doubted that it was the miraculous statue. After it had been compared to the early records and matched in all respects to the statue that had been honored before the Revolution, the authorities testified that the statue was indeed the same one that had performed so many astounding miracles in the Church of St. Vorles. The age of the statue was noted, and the rudimentary throne on which the statue sat was recognized. After it was verified as the one known to St. Bernard, Our Lady of All Graces was clothed in garments made by the Visitadine nuns and was triumphantly restored to her devotees.

Since that time, the devout have continually surrounded Our Lady's altar, where she is credited with healings and the dispensing of extraordinary blessings and graces.

Our Lady
Of All Graces

— 19 —

THE VIRGIN OF THE SEA

(Notre Dame of Boulogne)
Boulogne-sur-Mer, Pas-De-Calais, France
636

An ancient chronicler relates how one day in the year 636, during the reign of King Dagobert and the episcopate of St. Omer, a mysterious boat—a boat without oars, sails or sailors—entered the mouth of the Liane River and docked where the port of Boulogne is now located. On board was found a statue of the Virgin Mary which had a strange radiance around it. The townsfolk flocked to the river bank, and taking hold of the statue they carried it to the upper town and placed it in a chapel that was later transformed into a church.

The statue stood approximately three and a half feet high. Sculptured wood, it depicted the Blessed Virgin holding the Christ Child on her left arm. The size of the statue is estimated from ancient seals and medallions that have been carefully kept. Unfortunately, the statue no longer exists, but because of its renown and the many miracles performed through the intercession of the Virgin of the Sea, we give here a brief history of the miraculous image, the abuses it endured, and its cruel destruction.

The city chosen by the Virgin of the Sea is located on the northwestern shore of France and is separated from England by the English Channel. Founded in the year 50 B.C. by Quintius Pedius, a Roman soldier, the city was introduced to Christianity in the year 170. It is claimed that St. Patrick resided there for many years.

After the statue's miraculous entrance into the city, it was placed in a chapel that had been built in 606 by Clothaire II, the eighth king of France. The veneration paid to the miraculous image by crowds of townspeople and pilgrims was such that a larger building was required. The chapel was finally enlarged in the year 1104 by Countess Ida de Bouillon, the mother of the Crusader Godfrey, who was proclaimed king of Jerusalem. This newer structure welcomed large pilgrimages from far and wide, especially in the year 1212, when pilgrimages flourished. From every corner of Europe and especially from France, England and Flanders, townspeople and lords, peasants and craftsmen, women and children, monks and beggars flocked to the feet of the Virgin of the Sea to beg her spiritual and temporal favors. Among these pilgrims were often found men and women who were compelled by the sentence of secular or ecclesiastical courts to take up the pilgrim's staff. As a souvenir of their visit, pilgrims purchased badges and small lead objects in the form of the Virgin in the boat. Gold and silver medals were also struck. The demand for these objects kept the smiths of the town occupied throughout the entire year.

On returning home the pilgrims told of numerous favors received, so that the Virgin of the Sea became well known. Because of these reports new places of worship were dedicated to the miraculous image.

From the thirteenth to the sixteenth century pilgrimages to Boulogne enjoyed extraordinary popularity. Chaucer, in writing his famous *Canterbury Tales*, names Boulogne as one of the most important shrines in Christendom. In the Prologue, Chaucer tells about the Wife of Bath in this manner:

> Now forth to foreign lands each year she fared, Since fate decreed she seek out every shrine... She'd seen Boulogne, and Rome, and Palestine, Spain and Cologne.

The popularity of the Virgin of the Sea flourished until the year 1544, when the soldiers of Henry VIII pillaged the church and took the miraculous statue to England. It remained there for many years before its return.

Later, in 1567, the Huguenots devastated the church. The ancient statue was stolen by one of them, the cruel Jehan de Frohart. At first he tried to burn the statue. When this was unsuccessful he took it to the yard of his manor at Honvault, a league outside the town, and buried the statue in a heap of manure. Three years later, when the statue was discovered unharmed, he threw it into the well located in his cellar. His wife, a good Catholic, retrieved it in secret and placed it in the safety of the rafters. Forty years after its abduction, in 1607, the aged Jehan de Frohart renounced Protestantism, repented of the abuse he had inflicted on the image, and restored it to the veneration of the people.

Pilgrimages once again wended their way to Boulogne; many a nobleman paid their respects to the miraculous image including 14 Kings of France. Also visiting the chapel of the Virgin of the Sea were St. Bernard, St. Jean Baptist de la Salle, St. Benedict Joseph Labre, Napoleon and the future Pope John XXIII.

The French Revolution proved fatal for the sanctuary and the statue of Notre-Dame de Boulogne. The sanctuary was seized by a gang of thieves while the miraculous statue of the Virgin and Child was claimed by Andre Dumont, who had the statue burnt with great ceremony in the middle of the present Godefroy de Bouillon square. He later wrote that the "celebrated and incomprehensible" Virgin had been "unmiraculously" reduced to ashes. Only a small part of the hand was salvaged. This can be seen through a small round crystal located at the top of its reliquary, which is in the shape of a hand. This is kept with great care in the Cathedral of Boulogne that was erected during the last century over the ruins of the chapel that had been enlarged centuries before by Countess Ida. Beneath the cathedral is found a Romanesque crypt and a great number of fragments from sculptures. Here are also found traces of a former building which must have been a Gallo-roman temple.

Two statues have replaced the miraculous image. One consists of a skiff in which the seated Virgin holds the Child Jesus. Entirely of white marble, except for the golden crowns and a golden heart held by the Virgin, the skiff and statue are placed on a rolling platform when it participates in processions. This statue has been lovingly called "Our Lady of the Great Return." The second statue is of carved wood. Standing elegantly with the Child Jesus on the left arm, the Virgin holds a golden scepter. Both Mother and Child are adorned with jeweled crowns.

The solemn crowning of the Virgin of the Sea took place in 1885. In 1938 a Marian congress in Boulogne attracted more than 200,000 people.

THE VIRGIN OF THE SEA is paid tribute by this marble sculpture. The original miraculous statue, which dated back to seventh-century France, was destroyed during the French Revolution.

ANCIENT CHRONICLES relate that in about the year 636 a mysterious boat without oars, sails or sailors entered the mouth of the Liane River near where Boulogne, France is now located. A statue of Our Lady was found on board, surrounded by a strange, glowing light. The stained glass window above, in Rigny-le-Ferron, recalls the extraordinary event.

A MOBILE SKIFF: Adorned with jeweled crowns, the sculpture of Our Lady, Virgin of the Sea and the Infant Jesus stands ready to participate in processions.

— 20 —

OUR LADY OF MIRACLES

St. Omer, Pas-de-Calais, France
636

On the ruins that had once been a temple of Minerva, the ancient pagan Roman goddess of wisdom and arts, St. Omer built a church in 636 which he dedicated to Our Lady. Located some 20 miles from the shore of the North Sea and the same distance from the border of Belgium, a township which adopted the name of the Saint eventually developed around the church. Here St. Omer was buried when he died in 670.

Because of the large number of miracles granted at his tomb, St. Omer became so famous that the original dedication of the church to Our Lady was practically ignored. For this reason, the people built another church for Our Lady in the marketplace. When this wooden structure was destroyed by fire they built another, which was similarly destroyed.

With the consent of the local Bishop, Count Robert II of Artois arranged for a stone church to be built in 1271. In 1280, nine years later, an historian wrote:

> In the town of St. Omer, in the great marketplace, there has been built in honour of the Virgin Mary and to the joy of the inhabitants a chapel called Our Lady of Miracles, on account of the number of wonderful cures granted there.

The title seems to have been justified, since a record of these favors published by Fr. Couvreur stated that numerous cases of drowning, paralysis, epilepsy, deformity, muteness and other infirmities were cured before the shrine of Our Lady.

In addition to the healing of bodily afflictions, other miracles occurred. For example, in 1638 the town of St. Omer was besieged by an army of 40,000. The fears and difficulties of the people prompted the Bishop to make certain promises before the miraculous statue and soon after this—on the Feast of Our Lady of Mount Carmel, July 16—the army quietly withdrew. Our Lady is also known to have saved the town from attack and destruction, not once, but on several occasions.

Although the Blessed Virgin saw to the protection of the city, she somehow permitted a catastrophe to befall her shrine. In spite of the people's prolonged and vehement protest, the aldermen of the city voted on January 23, 1769 to demolish the shrine because, as they alleged, the space was needed to extend the marketplace.

The miraculous statue was solemnly removed from the shrine and was settled in a new shrine in the original church of St. Omer, which had been designated a cathedral in 1559.

A miracle was declared by the people when they saw a bright star shining in broad daylight during the translation. Abbe Leroy noted this event in the record of the church.

During the French Revolution the statue was preserved through the efforts of the guardian of the cathedral, Francois Thomas. For a time it was hidden in the church of St. Denis. Finally, in 1803, Our Lady of Miracles was again restored to her place of honor in the cathedral. Although still referred to as a cathedral, the church of St. Omer was stripped of this distinction in 1801 when the See was removed to the City of Arras.

Although deprived of this privileged status, the church was nevertheless raised to the dignity of a basilica in 1879 by Pope Leo XIII. Four years earlier the miraculous statue had been crowned by Cardinal Regnier, Legate of Pope Pius IX.

Located in the south transept of the cathedral, the figure, four feet high, is found in a canopied shrine high above the altar. Here Our Lady sits with the Holy Child on her left knee. The most alluring attraction of this statue is the pleasant smile of both Mother and Child. Unlike many statues of Our Lady which are clothed in costly mantles and veils, the statue of Our Lady of Miracles and her Child wear only their sculptured clothing. The only exceptions are their two crowns and sometimes a white lace veil.

The sculptured clothing is simple. A long veil falls behind Our Lady's back. Her dress is fastened at the waist; her neckline is fastened with a large oval broach. A crown of fleur-de-lis, constructed of copper gilt, is on her brow. In her right hand the Blessed Virgin holds a long scepter topped with a fleur-de-lis which some consider to be symbolic of her virginity. Her left hand firmly supports her Son at His waist. The Holy Child holds a book in His left hand; the other is raised in regal Benediction. A crown, matching His Mother's, is also worn.

It is said that Our Lady of Miracles is never without her visitors. Yearly novenas are held, especially in July, when many parishes and societies take part. One of the most noteworthy of these took place on July 14, 1950 when, during the closing ceremonies, Our Lady of Miracles was visited by no less than 40 statues which were carried to St. Omer from shrines of Our Lady throughout the region.

In a monograph produced by Canon Coolen of St. Omer, he described every detail of the statue and wrote that:

> Our Lady's features are particularly delicate and of fine cut. They reflect her simplicity, purity and virginal frankness. Her lips are cut to suggest a smile infinitely spiritual. . .the interior light revealed by the expression of the face, all these denote an art highly developed and a hand skilled and sure.

One might also add that the sculptor's hand might have been supernaturally guided since this statue somehow stands apart from other statues, whether they be miraculous, more beautiful, or more elaborately adorned. It is without doubt the expression of dignified humor and love which make the devotee feel a genuine closeness to this Heavenly Mother of Miracles. It is no wonder that this smiling image of Our Lady is so highly revered and so frequently visited.

— 21 —

OUR LADY OF AVIOTH

Avioth, Meuse, France
Twelfth Century

When the Reverend Jean Delhotel became parish pastor in 1668, he interviewed the older members of his congregation to learn what he could about the history of the miraculous statue of Our Lady of Avioth. What he learned was recorded in *The Brief Account of Avioth*. The actual discovery of the statue, and construction of the chapel that was built to house it, had taken place in the twelfth century. Therefore, the history that was told to one generation after the other, and then finally to the Reverend Delhotel, can only be regarded as legendary; but then, some legends have a way of containing some elements of truth.

According to the legend, one day the citizens of Avioth discovered a statue of Our Lady in the shadow of a thornbush. They carried it to their church, believing all the while that it had been carved by angels. The next morning the statue was missing from the church. Somehow it had made its way back to the place where it had been discovered. Since everyone had appeared pleased to have the statue in the church, it seemed unreasonable that anyone would take it upon themselves to return it to the thornbush. It was then decided that the statue's mysterious relocation was Our Lady's way of indicating the site where she wished her statue to reside. The citizens then happily erected a modest chapel as a shrine for their statue of Our Lady.

When favors and miracles were granted to those who visited the statue, more and more pilgrims became attracted to the shrine. Soon the oratory gave way to a stone church that was built prior to the year 1131. Among the many pilgrims to the church was St. Bernard, a great devotee of the Blessed Mother who was later declared a Doctor of the Church. Pious tradition gives credit to St. Bernard for suggesting that the ancient hymn, the *Salve Regina* be sung "daily and reverently by a warden and scola, immediately after the Mass of the Day; and that the said warden be engaged for the purpose at the expense of the church." A "warden" in this case meant one who was the head of a college, guild or conventual church. Since the time of St. Bernard (d. 1153) the *Salve Regina* has been sung every day at the shrine and by members of the many pilgrimages who visit there.

Construction of the basilica that replaced the church was started in the fourteenth century and incorporated the remains of the twelfth-century church of St. Bernard's time. The basilica is a veritable museum of images representing Our Lady. Carvings, stained glass, the ornate pulpit, paintings and still more carvings depict scenes from her life. All of these representations attest to the love and devotion of the people of Avioth for their heavenly Mother.

The statue has been dated by more than one expert in such matters as being of the twelfth century. The Blessed Mother is seated on a throne which is situated above the fourteenth-century high altar. Blackened with time, but repainted this century, the statue is carved of oak and measures 35 inches in height. Unfortunately, the right hand of Our Lady and the figure of the Christ Child have been lost, but replacements were added later. According to the custom of dressing Our Lady in fabric, Our Lady of Avioth and the Child on her lap are clothed in regal garments. They wear golden crowns and hold scepter and orb. The figure of the Christ Child is unique in that on its chest is a heart surmounted by flames, a symbol usually reserved for depictions of Jesus as an adult.

The favors of Our Lady of Avioth have been sought especially by brides and mothers, but also by people who are thought to be possessed, as well as by the blind and the lame. These are perhaps especially attracted to Our Lady because of the favors she has bestowed upon others of similar concerns and situations.

When the Reverend Jean Delhotel was recording the history of Our Lady of Avioth in the seventeenth century, he also recorded that no less than 131 cures had taken place during his pastorate. The ex-votos that represented these and many other favors unfortunately were pillaged during one of the several wars of the seventeenth century.

The shrine of Our Lady of Avioth has a history of continuous activity despite the wars and unrest that have destroyed shrines or suppressed devotions at other places of prayer.

The principal feast of Our Lady of Avioth is observed on July 16, the feast of Our Lady of Mount Carmel.

— 22 —

OUR LADY OF ROCAMADOUR

Rocamadour, Lot, France
Middle Ages

During the Middle Ages the shrine at Rocamadour was ranked as one of the four most popular places of pilgrimage in Christendom, equal in merit with the Holy Places in Palestine, Rome, and St. James of Compostella in Spain. It is also one of the most unusual shrines in existence in that its location seems to defy gravity.

Rising 500 feet above the Alzou River and the lush green fields of a gorge, the buildings of Rocamadour seem to cling to the side of an almost vertical mountain. Three distinct levels are obvious. The lower tier has a long row of buildings, some of which have been converted into gift shops and hotels. The second tier is occupied by the basilica, many diverse chapels, the Lady Chapel and monastic buildings. The highest level is crowned with a modern bell tower, the bishop's residence and a castle with its ramparts.

At the time of medieval warfare, Rocamadour must have been impregnable. Fortified gateways and other fortifications protected the city and rendered it a veritable stronghold. One single path rises from the gorge and develops into a steep stairway of 216 steps which has been called *Via Sancta.* At the top of these steps is a sharp bend, then a second bend, and then, after a few more steps, one finds the small courtyard called the Place St. Amadour. From here seven churches are arranged at slightly different levels.

Adjacent to the basilica, but in a chapel of its own, is the shrine which legend says was hollowed out by St. Amadour for an oratory. Named the Chapelle Miraculeuse, it contains a miraculous statue of Our Lady that is reputed to be a thousand years old. Through a curious dimness, the image is found above the main altar.

The statue is perhaps one of the least pleasing portrayals of our beautiful Madonna. The wooden statue depicts Our Lady as being unnaturally thin, almost skeletal and elongated. A shoulder-length veil falls from beneath a short crown worn by the seated figure.

Unlike countless other images in which the Virgin holds her Child, or the Child Jesus embraces His Mother, the hands of Our Lady of Rocamadour touch the arms of her chair while her Son sits unsupported on her lap. The Child Jesus, also thin and elongated, holds a book in His left hand; His right hand rests on His knee. The gauntness of the statue is usually hidden beneath a simple robe, fastened at the neck and waist. The figure of the Child is customarily dressed in a matching garment.

At one time the statue was covered with silver, but the wood, which is thought to be cedar or walnut, is now dark with age. The bottom portion of the statue, from the knees of the Virgin to the base, is pitted and time-worn. The sad condition of this part of the statue substantiates the estimate that the statue is over a thousand years old.

The miraculous nature of the figure is manifested by the thousands of ex-votos that clutter the walls, the pillars, ceiling and every corner of the shrine. In addition to these little plaques, other symbols of gratitude take the form of lamps, banners, medals, crutches, braces, children's toys and countless hearts of both silver and gold. Among the most unusual of these tributes are chains and iron manacles given in gratitude by prisoners who were rescued or who escaped from the Saracens.

Although the shrine is far from the sea, many of the ex-votos were placed at the shrine by mariners in thanksgiving for favors received at sea. These, from French, Spanish and Basque sailors, testify to the popularity of Our Lady of Rocamadour.

Of great interest at the shrine is a wrought iron bell which is suspended from the ceiling within the chapel. Estimated to be 1,500 years old, the bell is said to "ring of its own accord" to announce the granting of a miracle in response to prayer offered to Our Lady of Rocamadour.

The ancient tradition of the shrine claims that the region was settled by Zaccheus, the Jericho publican with whom Our Lord conversed (*Luke* 19:1-10). Somehow the tradition weds Zaccheus to St. Veronica, who wiped the face of Our Lord during the carrying of the Cross. Driven from Palestine by persecution, Zaccheus and Veronica supposedly landed at Soulac (on the Bay of Biscay), where they founded an oratory to the Blessed Virgin which became known as Our Lady of Lands End.

When St. Veronica died, Zaccheus allegedly migrated to the heart of France. There he made a hermitage in a cave in the gorge of the Alzou River, taking the name of Amadour (Lover of God). When he died about the year 70, he was buried in a rock-hewn sepulcher beside his hermitage, hence the name, Roc-amadour. Human remains discovered in the year 1116 in a rocky sepulcher at Rocamadour were accepted as those of Zaccheus.

The legend of Zaccheus and Veronica is accepted by many as being trustworthy, since it coincides accurately with the ancient traditions of the shrine at Soulac approximately 150 miles away. But this legend has been questioned and criticized throughout the years by many of both the critical and traditional schools. Most of these scholars, as well as recent authors, have suggested that Amadour was not Zaccheus, but simply a hermit who lived in the region.

Even though the origin of the shrine is lost in antiquity and the miraculous statue itself is deprived of its early history, the place has not been harmed. On the contrary, the place seems to be especially favored by the Mother of God.

From its earliest years, Our Lady and her shrine have been held in the highest veneration and have been visited by the most distinguished and royal personages, including Charlemagne (d. 814); Henry II, King of England (d. 1189); St. Louis and his mother Blanche, who visited in 1245; King Charles IV, the Fair, who came in 1324 and King Louis XI, who visited in 1463. Other visitors include St. Dominic; St. Bernard; John, King of Bohemia and Philip VI.

The wayward have also found their way to the shrine. Heretics who repented, and hardened sinners who converted, were often sent on a pilgrimage to Rocamadour as a penance. Dressed in clothes covered with crosses, a big hat and a staff, the penitent traveled on foot. Upon reaching his destination he was bound with chains before he climbed the 216 steps on his knees. Standing before the Blessed Virgin, he first pronounced his *amende honorable*. This was followed by a priest's recitation of purification. The chains were then removed and the penitent, now forgiven, received a certificate and a medal depicting the miraculous statue, as proof that the penance had been performed.

Rocamadour reached its height of popularity in the thirteenth century; but later, despite its many fortifications, it was sacked several times. Thankfully, the miraculous statue of the Blessed Virgin has never been harmed. For a time the abbey remained idle, until it was finally extinguished by the Revolution. In the nineteenth century, however, the bishops of Cahors revived the pilgrimage, and devotion to Our Lady of Rocamadour once again flourished.

The annual retreat and novena at Rocamadour extend from September 8 to the 15th. Arriving at dawn, many of the people climb the *Via Sancta,* the 216 holy stairs, on their knees while singing hymns and reciting ejaculations. So great is the influx of visitors that additional confessors are brought in. Holy Communion is given at all hours of the morning, and preaching and devotions fill the rest of the day. The interests of all are directed to the shrine of Our Lady, as she is presented with countless prayers of petition and sentiments of gratitude for favors received.

THOUSAND-YEAR-OLD PORTRAYAL. The statue of Our Lady of Rocamadour, France attracts the prayers of pilgrims each year who climb—on their knees—the *Via Sancta*, or 216 holy stairs, which long ago were carved into a deep gorge.

— 23 —

OUR LADY OF LIESSE

Liesse, Picardy, France
Twelfth Century

Long before pilgrims directed their steps to Lourdes, the shrine of Our Lady of Liesse was regarded as the most popular pilgrimage site in France.

Dating back to the twelfth century, the story of the statue's origin has been preserved not only in France but also in the Holy Land, where it mysteriously appeared during the time of the Crusades. The traditional account of its history is as follows.

When the King of Jerusalem, Foulques of Anjou, rebuilt the fortress of Bersabee to protect his kingdom against the incursions of the Moslems, he placed it in the care of the Knights of St. John. One day some of the knights were caught in an ambush, and in spite of their valiant efforts at defending themselves they were captured and secured with chains. After they had been taken to Egypt, it was discovered that three of the knights, who were brothers, were members of the prestigious house of Eppes in Picardy, France.

Seeing their proud bearing and learning of their willingness to die rather than deny their faith, the Sultan was determined to have them renounce their belief in Jesus Christ and turn instead to Mohammed. After learning that the three remained staunch in their faith despite the cruel conditions of their imprisonment, the Sultan tried a different approach. This time he offered them gold, their freedom, and a position of honor. But instead of relenting, the pious knights seemed inspired by the Holy Spirit to defend their Christian faith by preaching to their guards and to all who would listen.

As a final effort to achieve his evil desire, the Sultan sent his daughter, who was a virtuous maiden, to warn the knights about the frightful punishments reserved for them. The knights listened respectfully to the princess, thanked her for her concern, and spoke to her of their beliefs. They spoke in such a persuasive manner that the princess began to reflect seriously on all that had been told to her. That night she dreamed of Christ and His Blessed Mother.

During that same night a resplendent statue of the Blessed Mother was brought to the prisoners by angels. Realizing that the statue could not have entered the prison except in a supernatural fashion, the young princess was converted.

One night she released the prisoners after bribing the guards with gold, and fled with the knights from her father's palace. After crossing the Nile the fugitives set their course for Alexandria, hoping to conceal themselves for a time in the Coptic monasteries of St. Macarius. After walking for some hours, the princess was exhausted and wanted to rest. Despite the danger, the knights decided to keep guard over her and seated themselves at a respectful distance. The princess soon fell asleep. The knights, although struggling against drowsiness, nevertheless succumbed to a profound slumber. It is not known how long they slept. The eldest of the brothers was the first to awaken to the singing of birds and a soft glow of sunlight. Then, looking at the landscape with great surprise, he realized he was no longer under palm trees by the Nile, but under an oak beside a gentle brook. The members of the little party were bewildered, but a passing shepherd who was driving his sheep to pasture relieved their confusion by stating that the castle in the distance belonged to the knights' father and that they were indeed in France.

The knights and the princess had fallen asleep in Egypt—only to awaken in France. Much to their relief, the little oriental statue of the Blessed Virgin had traveled with them, and it was for her that they built a handsome church to enshrine the statue. The Moslem princess, we are told, received Baptism in the Cathedral of Laon.

Historical accounts assure us that the statue was indeed brought to France from the Holy Land by three lords of Eppes, Knights of St. John of Jerusalem, although there is mention that it could also have arrived through natural means.

Since this account is so unusual and is sometimes met with skepticism, we might mention here two instances recorded in Holy Scripture where a similar transport occurred. The first was experienced by Habacuc; he was told by an angel to carry food to Daniel, who was then in the lions' den at Babylon. "And Habacuc said: Lord, I never saw Babylon, nor do I know the den. And the angel of the Lord took him by the top of his head, and carried him by the hair of his head, and set him in Babylon over the den. . . And Daniel arose and ate. And the angel of the Lord presently set Habacuc again in his own place." (*Daniel* 14:33-39).

The other instance of unusual flight takes place in the *Acts of the Apostles* (Chapter 8:26-40) when the Apostle Philip was instructing an Ethiopian eunuch. As they went along the way, the eunuch saw a body of water and asked to be baptized. Then, "When they were come up out of the water, the Spirit of the Lord took away Philip; and the eunuch saw him no more. . . But Philip was found in Azotus; and passing through, he preached the gospel to all the cities, till he came to Caesarea."

Whether the unusual transfer of the knights is true or not, it is certain that the miracles performed by Our Lady at Liesse were so many that the shrine attracted the attention of countless royal personalities who visited and signed the registry of pilgrims. These notables include the Duke of Burgundy, the Duke of Bourbon, Prince Henry, Louis the Duke of Orleans, King Charles VII, King Rene, Louis XI, Francis I, Henry II, Charles IX, Queen Mary of Medicis, Louis XIII, Anne of Austria, Louis XIV and many others.

Unfortunately, the costly gifts offered to Our Lady by these nobles and other wealthy visitors also attracted the attention of the greedy, who pillaged the shrine. The Huguenots and the Revolutionaries also visited the shrine for unlawful purposes.

The shrine of Our Lady of Liesse is still very popular, despite the many French shrines to Our Lady which also vie for the attention of the devout.

— 24 —

OUR LADY OF VIRTUES

Ligny-en-Barrois, France
Twelfth Century

There are 13 Madonnas in France which carry the name of Our Lady of Virtues, but the portrait enshrined in the parish church of Ligny is the original for which the others are named. According to the experts who have examined the portrait, it is believed to have originated in the twelfth century.

The miraculous properties of the painting were experienced almost from its beginning and were so extraordinary and so well known that the cousin of Pope Urban IV visited the portrait in 1264 to appeal for the cure of his crippled and afflicted condition. His cure was attributed without doubt to the influence of the holy image. As a result of this miracle, the portrait found its way to Pope Urban IV, who entrusted the precious portrait to Charles d'Anjou in 1265.

The portrait eventually was given by the religious of Capri in 1435 to Antoine de la Salle, who saw to its enshrinement in the parish church of Ligny in 1459.

The image rested in peace and honor atop its altar until 1544. Its reputation then aroused the evil inclinations of an imperial representative who visited the church with a band of terrorists. Approaching the altar with an air of audacity, he removed the portrait and maliciously carried it off. This sacrilege distressed the people, particularly Margaret of Savoy, the Countess of Ligny, who was Our Lady of Virtues' most ardent devotee. For 37 years the location of the portrait was unknown, but in 1581 it was discovered at Bouchon and was triumphantly returned in procession to Ligny.

In the presence of two archbishops, four bishops, nine priests and countless members of the parish, Our Lady of Virtues was given a papal coronation in 1894.

A church historian once described the oil painting as being mediocre. The frame, which has a series of painted roses, pansies and poppys, is also regarded as being of inferior workmanship. Yet the painting displays a simple charm and an appealing quality. Our Lady is dressed in red with a blue veil covering her head. Her hair is black, parted in the center and twisted into two plaits. The Madonna inclines her head toward the Child she holds in her hands. The Child for His part is naked, but smiles lovingly at His Mother, while offering her a rose with His left hand. Two angels are also featured in the portrait. The angel on the Madonna's right plays a primitive mandolin; the angel on her left plays a flute.

The people of Ligny celebrate the solemnity of the portrait on the Friday preceding the fifth Sunday after Easter.

Our Lady's miraculous portrait is still kept in the parish church, where it is much loved and where it is regarded as valuable and miraculous.

LIGNY'S MIRACULOUS LADY: The miraculous properties of the portrait above were evident as early as 1264. The oil painting is credited with the cure of Pope Urban IV's cousin, who was crippled. Today the portrait is kept in the parish church at Ligny, France.

— 25 —

OUR LADY OF MYANS

Myans, Savoie, France
Twelfth Century

A favorite of St. Francis de Sales, the shrine of the Black Virgin of Myans is located on a little hill between Chambery and Modane, approximately 50 miles from Italy's border. The shrine is easily located against the huge mountains of the Chartreuse Massif since an imposing statue of the Virgin Mary is situated atop the shrine's belfry. The shrine is said to be the most interesting and important of Our Lady's shrines in the Alpine regions.

The early history of the Black Virgin and the origin of the shrine are lost to us. However, reference to the shrine is made in the twelfth century Chartulary of St. Hugh, who belonged to the Charterhouse which is located a few miles away. Likewise St. Anthelme, Prior of the Charterhouse in the twelfth century, also had a strong affection for Myans.

The shrine came into prominence in 1248 as the result of a catastrophe. On the evening of November 24 of that year, a tremendous earthquake shook the region. The gigantic force caused Mont Granier, the tallest mountain of the Chartreuse Massif, to disintegrate into huge boulders which came crashing down into the valley. The boulders, some as big as a house, crushed 16 villages and some 5,000 people.

The church of Myans on its rocky hill was spared, miraculously it would seem, since gigantic boulders were hurtled to its very door. These are still located on the church grounds.

For 200 years the ancient chapel stood alone atop its hill as the center of a strong local devotion. Then, like many an ancient shrine that was incorporated into a larger structure, the original shrine of Our Lady of Myans became the crypt of an outer church. The expense of this undertaking, as well as the building of a convent, was met in 1458 by Jacques de Montmayeur, and Rene, son of Philip, the Duke of Savoy. The coat of arms of both benefactors may be seen in several places in the church.

The popularity of Our Lady of Myans was such that processions representing 60 to 70 parishes from throughout Savoy were known to have arrived at the shrine at the same time. Many villages made it a yearly event to journey there in procession. One of the largest processions consisted of 6,000 people from the little town of Bugey. This was led by a close friend of St. Francis de Sales, Bishop Camus of Belley.

A marvelous answer to prayer occurred in 1534 in favor of Jean Grandis of Savoy, who was on a vessel bound from Genoa to Leghorn. When the ship was threatened during a tempest and seemed likely to sink, Jean Grandis called upon Our Lady of Myans, Queen of Savoy. Battered by the waves, the ship foundered and sank. Jean Grandis was the only survivor. As a gesture of thanksgiving, he traveled barefoot to the shrine and there placed his ex-voto. It is said to be one of the oldest to survive.

Another miracle attributed to Our Lady of Myans was in favor of the brother of St. Francis de Sales, Count Louis de Sales, who in 1603 was traveling to the Chateau of Cusy to marry Claudine-Philiberte de Pingon. Since there was no bridge in sight, the Count attempted to cross the River Cheran at a place that he thought was shallow and safe. However, the Count was swept away by floodwater. Invoking the name of Our Lady of Myans and promising to make a pilgrimage, he was suddenly thrust onto an obstruction that saved his life. The wedding ceremony was conducted on April 2. The next day St. Francis de Sales offered a Mass of thanksgiving in the little crypt chapel before the miraculous image of Our Lady of Myans.

When France was in chaos during the French Revolution, the people of Savoy suffered religious persecution. The shrine was closed, but only after the miraculous figure of Our Lady had been hidden and smuggled away. Even so, despite the efforts of the revolutionaries to suppress devotion to Our Lady, the traditional pilgrimages were observed. It is estimated that on one day alone, between 15,000 and 20,000 pilgrims gathered to pray outside the church. The people's love for Our Lady of Myans was so strong and constant that there was no need to revive the devotion following the Revolution, since it had never ceased.

When religious freedom was restored in France, the ruined church was repaired and the clock tower was rebuilt. In 1855 the figure of Our Lady, 15 feet tall, was placed above the belfry.

The miraculous statue of Our Lady of Myans calls to mind the passage in Solomon's *Canticle of Canticles,* "I am black but beautiful." (*Cant. of Cant.* 1:4). The features of the Madonna are indeed beautiful, even though her complexion is black with age. Made of cedar wood, the 28-inch statue sits regally on her throne, while her left arm supports the Christ Child on her knee.

The robes of the Mother and Child are made of cloth of gold and are embellished with 500 precious stones. Grateful clients have contributed these, as well as crosses, rings and chains, which the figure also wears. The veil of the Blessed Virgin is of lace made with golden thread. The garments beneath the jeweled mantles are of a silver cloth. The crown of the Christ Child, composed of silver overlaid with gold, has more than 800 jewels; 100 gems sparkle on the crown of His Mother.

Pope Pius X honored Our Lady of Myans with a Papal Coronation in 1905. The ceremony was conducted by his legate, Cardinal Couille, Archbishop of Lyons and Primate of Gaul.

When the dogma of Our Lady's Assumption was declared on November 1, 1950, a great procession of pilgrims from Chambery arrived in Rome for the occasion. At the head of the procession was their archbishop and the miraculous statue of Our Lady of Myans. After the ceremony, Pope Pius XII granted an audience to the group. Also attending the audience was Our Lady of Myans.

— 26 —

OUR LADY OF THE GUARD

Marseille, Bourches-du-Rhone, France
Late Twelfth Century

Located in southern France on the shore of the Mediterranean Sea, Marseille is a port city with a shrine that claims seven centuries of history.

It is told that during the last years of the twelfth century a lone fisherman of the city was overtaken at sea by a great tempest. While struggling against the elements, his boat sprang a leak while the agitated sea claimed the rudder. Realizing that nothing less than a miracle could save him, he thought of his children and his dear wife, who would be forced to struggle without him. His thoughts then turned to Our Lady and the hymn known to almost all the mariners, *Ave Maris Stella,* Hail Star of the Sea. With his voice competing against the roar of the wind, his attention was directed toward shore and the mountain that overlooked the sea. On the summit of the rock he saw a strange apparition, a transparent form which seemed to hold out its hand to him in an encouraging manner. At that moment he knew that the Blessed Virgin, the Star of the Sea and the ever-ready helper of poor mariners, had come to save him. While he was still singing the *Ave Maris Stella,* the boat began to move toward the shore as if guided by a powerful hand. Upon reaching land, the fisherman jumped ashore and clambered up the mountain, but when he reached the top, the apparition vanished. On his return home he happily related his miraculous rescue and all that had taken place.

Everyone who heard of the fisherman's safe return realized it had been a miraculous rescue, and no one doubted that he owed his life to the intervention of the Blessed Virgin. Other seamen also related how they had several times seen the same figure, which appeared at the summit of the mountain during storms at sea. Shortly after its appearance their safety was assured when the wind and the sea became calm. It was apparent to all that the Blessed Virgin had chosen the mountain as the place from which she loved to guard and protect helpless mariners. For this reason a chapel was built on the summit in 1214 by a young priest, Master Peter.

In 1477 the chapel was rebuilt, and in 1833 a silver statue was fashioned by Chanuel. In 1853 the foundation stone of the basilica was laid and in 1864 the completed structure was consecrated by the saintly Bishop de Mazenod (who was beatified in 1975). The beautiful silver statue of Our Lady was situated above the main altar of the basilica during the year of its consecration.

Atop the main tower of the basilica a huge pillar was erected in 1870. This was built to support a monumental statue of Our Lady de la Garde. The Virgin Mother wears a crown atop the tresses that fall around her shoulders. She stands majestically while holding the Child Jesus on her left arm. The Child Jesus seems to look toward the port while He raises both hands as though signalling to the mariners. Facing the sea, the Blessed Mother seems ever ready to help the distressed seaman, while below, at the foot of the mountain, she overlooks the welfare of her children in the city of Marseille.

It is not only the sailors who experience the marvelous help of Our Lady de la Garde, but countless others as well. When cholera visited the city in 1833, every household had at least one sick member. In desperation, the people assembled in the public squares and pleaded with the priests to carry the statue of Our Lady in procession. Vested in penitential robes, the clergy, together with the soldiers of the garrison, all the seamen in the port and all those who were still healthy, went to the shrine and carried the statue of Our Lady in procession to the city and through the streets. The sick saluted Our Lady from windows or beds while children scattered flowers and sang hymns. Whereas the pestilence had raged the day before, on the day of the procession it was dismissed by Our Lady.

The numerous ex-votos which adorn the walls of the chapel of Our Lady give evidence of the many benefits received through her powerful intercession. Likewise the whole complex of connecting buildings which covers the mountain is a striking testimonial to the importance of the shrine and the faith placed in Our Lady's benevolence. The whole complex, with the basilica at its summit, reminds one of the great Mont-St.-Michel, the Benedictine Abbey in Normandy, France.

It is told that early in the twentieth century Our Lady again demonstrated her concern for seamen in distress when a violent storm overtook a ship in the Mediterranean Sea not far from Marseille. The steersman and the crew, realizing their inability to control the ship, fell to their knees and fervently implored the help of Our Lady. The passengers likewise knelt in prayer. Suddenly they all saw a dim figure at the wheel. Then, while they were still kneeling, they realized that the ship was being steered through the waves at a great speed. It was soon in calm waters and was gliding safely toward shore. When the ship docked, the 29 persons on board, although thoroughly wet, ascended the mountain to the chapel of Our Lady, and there they sang hymns of gratitude.

OUR LADY OF THE GUARD. The statue of Our Lady of the Guard, situated above the main tower of the basilica in Marseille. The Child Jesus waves to mariners at sea.

OUR LADY'S CONCERN for seamen has been demonstrated many times near the Mediterranean port city of Marseille, and the basilica/shrine pictured above bears testimony to the miraculous rescues reported following apparitions of the Blessed Virgin.

THE SILVER STATUE of Our Lady holding her Son, pictured above, was fashioned in 1833. For seven centuries, the faithful have called upon Our Lady of the Guard for intercession.

— 27 —

OUR LADY OF THE THORN

(Notre Dame de l'Epine)
Chalons-sur-Marne, France
1400

During the years when the Church was undergoing the Western Schism which divided Christendom into two and then three papal obediences (1378-1417), France was enduring famines and epidemics brought on by wars and disturbances. It was during these troubled times, in the year 1400, that God granted relief by way of a miraculous appearance of the Blessed Virgin.

During the night of March 24, 1400, the eve of the Feast of the Annunciation, a group of shepherds were tending their flocks on a hillside a few miles from Chalons. To their amazement, they saw a bright light near the rustic chapel dedicated to St. John the Baptist. On approaching the light they saw a thornbush engulfed in flames, yet the thorns, branches and leaves seemed unaffected by the fire. In the midst of the flames stood a statue of the Blessed Virgin. Since the miracle continued all that night and the next day, it is not possible that the phenomenon was an illusion.

News of the miracle spread quickly. Many people rushed to see the burning bush which was reminiscent of the one witnessed by Moses on Mount Horeb. This burning bush was different, however, since above it stood the statue of Our Lady.

The Bishop of Chalons, Charles of Poitiers, also saw the burning bush and the miraculous statue, as did members of his chapter and the clergy. When the flames began to die down, the bishop reverently took the statue and carried it in his own hands to the Oratory of St. John.

On the very spot where the miracle had occurred, construction of a church was begun for the enshrinement of the miraculous statue. When completed, the Church of Our Lady of the Thorn proved to be so beautiful that the people considered it a worthy shrine for the Mother of God and a place of grandeur where their souls could expand in adoration of the Son of God, who inspired such marvels of design.

The people were so impressed with the beauty of the work and the relatively short time spent in its construction—a little over 24 years—that they started the charming legend which has it that angels took up the workmen's tools each night to continue the construction when the workmen left for home.

In this church the statue of the Blessed Virgin was enshrined, and here it received the homage of many generations until the time of the French Revolution. Many places of prayer were destroyed by the revolutionaries, but the Church of Our Lady of the Thorn was spared. On December 6, 1793, the pastor of the parish, M. Bertin, removed the miraculous statue to a place of greater security. It was replaced on its altar seven years later.

Clergy, laity and noblemen have venerated Our Lady of the Thorn. Their confidence in the Blessed Virgin has resulted in countless favors and miracles of healing, which have been properly documented and confirmed by attending physicians.

Among the noble visitors to the shrine can be counted Charles VI (who contributed to the construction of the church); Charles VII, who twice visited the Madonna; Margaret of Scotland, who made the pilgrimage from Châlons to l'Epine on foot; Louis XI, who came to fulfill the vow he had made in the prison of Peronne; Princess Palatine; Queen Marie Leczinska; Napoleon, in 1812; Charles X in 1828; and Louis Philippe in 1831. Also among these distinguished visitors can be counted St. Joan of Arc. The Saint reportedly visited the shrine on a number of occasions, both before and after her heavenly call to liberate France from the English.

The beautiful Church of Our Lady of the Thorn has been recognized by several popes, including Calixtus III, Pius II and Gregory XV. Pope Leo XIII, having heard the origin and history of the devotion and the marvelous benefits derived from the pilgrimages, said with emotion when the solemn coronation of the venerable statue was proposed, "Yes, Our Lady of the Thorn shall be crowned, and in my name. Prepare for her a diadem worthy of the Mother of God and of the people whom she protects. . ."

ATOP A BLAZING THORNBUSH, Our Lady appeared in the year 1400 to a group of shepherds tending their flocks. The flames did not affect the bush, and the statue of Our Lady that made its miraculous debut has been visited by pilgrims of all description over the years, including St. Joan of Arc.

— 28 —

OUR LADY OF THE WILLOW TREE

Plantees (Vinay), Isere, France
1649

The events relating to the origin of the shrines at Plantees would seem beyond belief were it not for the testimony of witnesses, the formal inquiry conducted by the bishop, and the documents which may still be seen in the Provincial Archives in Grenoble. Finally, the events were given Church approval when, on two occasions, Pope Pius IX ordered the solemn crowning of Our Lady of the Willow Tree (*Notre Dame de l'Osier*).

The main personage of this drama was Pierre Port-Combet, a farmer of the area who was a well-known follower of a heresy known as Calvinism. As such he harbored a great dislike for Catholics and all that represented the Faith. He had married a devout Catholic, Jeanne Pelion, but despite her protest, he disregarded his vow to permit her to raise their six children in the Catholic Faith and instead drew them into heresy.

On solemn holydays all work was suspended in the province so that the people might attend church services and spend the remainder of the day in private devotions. Pierre's great delight was to show public disregard for the Church, and in particular the holydays dedicated to the Blessed Mother. On that fateful day in 1649, on the Feast of the Annunciation, Pierre decided to show his utter disdain for the observances by performing work where all would see him. He chose to stand beside the road where the villagers would be passing on their way to Mass.

Drawing his knife, Pierre pretended to engage in manual labor by half-heartedly pruning a willow tree that grew beside the road. After his first stab at the tree he drew back in complete shock. The willow bled! Coming from the mark left by the knife were not just a few drops, but a large enough quantity to splash on Pierre's arms and hands. Pierre immediately thought he was injured, but he could find no wound on his arms or hands. After a moment of bewilderment, he stabbed at the tree once more—and again the tree bled.

At about that time Pierre's wife, who was on her way to church, drew near and saw the blood covering her husband's arms. Thinking he was seriously injured, she hurried to help him. While she searched for a possible injury, Pierre excitedly related what had taken place. Thinking to calm him, she took the knife and struck the tree, but nothing happened. More agitated than before, Pierre snatched the knife from his wife and cut off a small branch. The tree bled even more profusely than before.

A neighbor, Louis Caillet, was passing by at that time and was called over by the agitated Pierre, who by now was thoroughly frightened. Despite repeated efforts, Louis Caillet could not produce even a trace of blood. It was obvious that blood only appeared at the hand of the heretic.

Neighbors passing by and other villagers became aware of the marvel, and as though with one voice they agreed that the prodigy was a warning for Pierre to convert and, instead of giving public scandal, he should observe the laws of the Church.

There was also the law of the Province to contend with. Having gone contrary to the law by working on the feastday, Pierre was summoned to court. Testimony was heard from witnesses who had seen Pierre in the act of pruning the tree. The prodigy of the blood was likewise mentioned. As a result, Pierre received a fine for his disobedience of the law. The transcipt of this hearing is kept in the Provincial Archives in Grenoble.

When Church authorities heard of the case and the prodigy of the blood from the willow, they also took action. A tribunal of churchmen was gathered for a formal inquiry, as ordered by the Bishop. The testimony of Pierre was taken, as well as that of witnesses. In the end it was decided that Pierre had received a severe warning from Heaven.

Pierre took the decision to heart and was seen from time to time at the willow tree in profound prayer. Some of those who saw him were his friends of the Calvinist movement; they were unmoved, and even threatened bodily harm should he abandon Calvinism. For this reason, Pierre resisted his return to the Catholic Church for seven long years—until Our Lady herself intervened.

While Pierre was working in his fields on the Feast of the Annunciation, March 25 of the year 1656, he looked toward a small hillock called the Epinouse, or the Thornhill. There he saw a Lady clothed in white, wearing a blue mantle. Over her head was a black veil that partially hid her face. As the Lady advanced toward him, Pierre thought that she was lost and was coming to him for directions. Suddenly, displaying amazing speed, the Lady was standing next to him.

With a heavenly sweetness the lady addressed Pierre: *"A Dieu sois-tu, mon ami!"* ("God be with you, my friend!")

For a moment the sweet sound of the voice and the beauty of the woman caused Pierre to hesitate. The Lady again spoke, "What is being said about this devotion? Do many people come?"

"Yes, many people come," Pierre replied.

Seeming satisfied with Pierre's reply the Lady continued, "Where does that heretic live who cut the willow tree? Does he not want to be converted?"

When Pierre mumbled a vague answer, the Lady asked, "Do you think I do not know that you are the heretic?" Then, in a more serious tone, the vision warned, "Realize that your end is at hand. If you do not return to the True Faith you will be cast into Hell. But if you change your beliefs, I shall protect you before God. Tell people to pray to advantage, not to neglect the source of graces which God in His mercy has made available to them."

Pierre was overwhelmed with remorse and moved slightly away toward his oxen. Realizing his rudeness he turned back, but the Lady had moved away and was already near the Thornhill. Running after her, Pierre pleaded with her to stop and listen to his apology and his plea for help. The Lady stopped and turned. By the time Pierre caught up with her he noticed that she was suspended several feet in the air and was slowly fading from sight. Realizing that he had been granted a vision of the Blessed Virgin, he fell to his knees and while sobbing uncontrollably, he pledged a complete reform.

A few months later, on the eve of the Assumption, Pierre contracted a serious illness. The Augustinian Prior of Vinay heard his confession and accepted him back into the Church. Remembering that the prodigy had occurred on the Feast of the Annunciation, Pierre completed his conversion by receiving the Holy Eucharist on the Feast of the Assumption. Pierre's conversion influenced many others to return to the True Faith, including his son and five daughters, as well as many Protestants and Calvinists.

The Lady's words: "Realize that your end is at hand..." were realized five weeks later, when Pierre Port-Combet died. In accordance with his final wish, he was buried at the bottom of the willow tree.

With the approval of the directors of the Propagation of the Faith in Grenoble, the Reverend Fais, the parish priest of Vinay, helped Mme. de la Croix buy the field where Pierre had spoken to Our Lady. In due time, on the site of the apparition, a chapel was built which was dedicated to Our Lady of Good Meeting. Soon another even larger church was built at the site of the willow. This was dedicated to Our Lady of the Willow Tree. A statue sculptured according to Pierre's description was enshrined which soon attracted countless pilgrims.

Unfortunately, during the French Revolution terrorists from Grenoble pillaged and desecrated the sanctuary. The highly regarded statue of Our Lady was taken from its niche and hacked to pieces. These pieces were recovered by some valiant women who hid them until religious freedom was secured. Also saved was a portion of the willow tree that had been stored in a decorative box in the oratory.

Following the revolution, devotion to Our Lady of the Willow was revived. The Oblates of Mary Immaculate were given charge of the sanctuaries and in 1856, the second centenary of the apparition, Pope Pius IX decreed a solemn jubilee and a papal crowning for September 8. For this celebration more than 30,000 people and 400 priests attended. Another crowning was ordered by the same pontiff in 1873.

The meeting between Our Lady and Pierre is depicted on a large wall painting in the chapel of Our Lady of Good Meeting. Between this chapel and the Thornhill, where Our Lady left him, a specially marked path approximately 400 yards long indicates the route taken by Pierre when he ran after the apparition.

The church built where the willow once grew was raised to the dignity of a minor basilica by Pope Pius XI on March 17, 1924. Here is found the once-mutilated statue of Our Lady, and beneath her altar, the casket which contains the piece of the willow tree. Pierre's grave is at the foot of this altar. The casket containing a piece of the willow is located at about the same place where it formerly grew.

In the basilica, near the statue of Our Lady, are countless exvotos. Of all the miracles of healing worked as a result of prayer before this image, more than 100 are said to be undoubtedly genuine since they had been witnessed and sworn to by reliable people who testified under oath and affixed their names to written documents.

The shrines are located in the town of Plantees, five miles from Vinay. During the year, but especially on the feastdays of Our Lady of the Willow, March 25 and September 8 and 9, pilgrims wind their way from Vinay, up the terrain to Plantees to the shrine containing the image of Our Lady of the Willow Tree.

— 29 —

OUR LADY OF THE SMILE

Lisieux, France
1832

The statue which figured prominently in the life of St. Therese of Lisieux is not the only one of its kind. The statue was sculpted about the year 1832, and there are reports that others like it can still be found encased in the walls of a few old farmhouses in parts of Flanders. In addition, exact copies were made after St. Therese's death, as we will later relate.

The miraculous statue is made of plaster and is protected by an opaque varnish that gives it an ivory tint. Measuring 35 inches in height, it has been moved many times and, helped by several restorations, has endured the ravages of time. During one of these restorations a halo of stars was placed around the Virgin's head. A narrow band with a diamond serves Our Lady as a diadem.

The statue first enters into the life of Louis Martin, the father of St. Therese, after he completed his studies as an apprentice watchmaker in Paris. On his return to his native town of Alencon he was assisted financially in opening a jewelry and watch shop by a devout and charitable lady who also gave him the statue now known as Our Lady of the Smile. Louis Martin positioned the statue in a place of honor on his property amid flowers and shrubs. He spent his spare time before this statue, absorbed in prayer and spiritual reading.

After his marriage in July, 1858 to Zelie Guerin, the statue was enshrined indoors and was immediately established as the center of their spiritual life—and later became the center of their children's lives. The family's morning and evening prayers, as well as other devotions, were recited before the statue. The kisses of the children became so fervent at times that some of the statue's plaster fingers were broken off. They were, of course, lovingly restored. The children delighted in placing flowers and candles before the image of their Heavenly Mother, and especially in May their expressions of devotion could not be contained. Flowers, blossoms and all kinds of greenery are said to have been arranged around the statue.

The first unusual incident that took place regarding the statue involved the death of 5½-year-old Marie Helene. Zelie Martin was inconsolable because of what she considered her own negligence. A short time before the little girl's death, she had told her mother a small lie. Although the mother corrected her for it, Zelie Martin forgot to bring a priest to hear her confession and administer the Last Sacraments. The idea that the child was suffering in Purgatory because of her negligence grieved Zelie terribly. One day while praying before the statue and pleading for a sign that the child had escaped Purgatory, Zelie Martin distinctly heard a voice whispering in her ear: "She is beside me in Heaven." The voice brought relief and joy to Zelie Martin's tender heart and strength for her childlike faith.

After Zelie Martin's death from cancer of the breast, the grieving father moved his five daughters to Lisieux. The statue was likewise conveyed there since it was the mother's wish that the statue always remain with the family. At their new home, *Les Buissonnets* (the Shrubberies), the statue was placed in the room of the eldest girls, Marie and Pauline. The family's usual devotions before the statue were observed here at Lisieux as they had been at Alencon.

After the death of her mother, Therese became deeply attached to her sister Pauline, who became like a second mother to her. Then, when Therese was about nine years of age, Pauline entered the Discalced Carmelite convent at Lisieux. The sacrifice of parting brought to Therese's tender nature a prolonged grief. Later that year Therese became the victim of a strange illness from which she suffered intense headaches, nervous convulsions and morbid obsessions. Therese relates in her autobiography:

> Towards the end of the year, I began to have a constant headache. . .I believe the devil had received an external power over me but was not allowed to approach my soul nor my mind except to inspire me with very great fear of certain things. . .The sickness became so grave that, according to human calculations, I wasn't to recover from it. I can't describe this strange sickness,

> but I'm now convinced it was the work of the devil. . .I often appeared to be in a faint, not making the slightest movement and yet I heard everything that was said around me. . .I was absolutely terrified by everything: my bed seemed to be surrounded by frightful precipices; some nails in the wall of the room took on the appearance of big, black charred fingers, making me cry out in fear. One day, while Papa was looking at me in silence, the hat in his hand was suddenly transformed into some indescribably dreadful shape. . .Once it happened that for a long time I was without the power to open my eyes.

The affliction was so extreme at times that it was thought Therese would not survive. Everything revolved around her sickbed. Even though various remedies were administered, all were ineffective. Finally, Louis Martin arranged for a novena of Masses to be offered for Therese's recovery at the Sanctuary of Our Lady of Victories, a church he loved and frequented during his journeys to Paris.

It was Therese who acknowledged that Our Lady had performed a great miracle in healing her on Pentecost Sunday, May 13, 1883. Therese tells in her autobiography what took place when she looked upon the statue that had been moved into the sickroom:

> All of a sudden the Blessed Virgin appeared beautiful to me, so beautiful that never had I seen anything so attractive; her face was suffused with an ineffable benevolence and tenderness, but what penetrated to the very depths of my soul was the ravishing smile of the Blessed Virgin. At that instant all my pain disappeared and two large tears glistened on my eyelashes and flowed down my cheeks silently, but they were tears of unmixed joy. Ah! I thought, the Blessed Virgin smiled at me, how happy I am. . .

Sr. Marie of the Sacred Heart, St. Therese's sister, testified in the Process of Beatification:

> I saw Therese as in an ecstasy, and I understood that she was looking, not at the statue but at the Blessed Virgin. The vision seemed to last four or five

> minutes. . .and I knew she was cured. When I was alone with her I asked her why she shed tears. She hestitated to speak of the secret, but when she saw that I guessed it, she replied, "Because she had disappeared."

Following the vision Therese was completely cured.

At the age of fifteen, Therese joined her sisters Pauline and Marie in the convent of the Discalced Carmelites in Lisieux. After spending several years in religious life Therese contracted tuberculosis of the lungs. When the hemorrhages became quite serious and frequent, Therese was removed from her cell, which was on the second floor, to the infirmary on the ground floor. Her bed was placed in the middle of the room and at its foot, against the wall, was the miraculous statue of Les Buissonnets.

On September 30, 1897 (after having suffered from the disease for 18 months), Therese was at the point of death when suddenly, as if called by some mysterious voice, she raised her head and fixed her radiant gaze on a point above the head of the statue. Then after a few minutes of silent gazing, in an ecstasy of love, her head fell back, and with a last sigh her soul passed on to God.

Therese's sister, Marie of the Sacred Heart, who had witnessed Therese's first ecstasy and her miraculous cure at Les Buissonnets in 1883, also witnessed this final ecstasy. She wrote:

> Her gaze fixed a little above the statue vividly recalled the look which I had seen in her childhood, when the Blessed Virgin had appeared and cured her. It was impossible to describe—something heavenly. A sister passed a light before her eyes, but she did not seem to perceive it—for I am sure, she was already enjoying the light of God.

Following Therese's death, the house of the Martin family at Lisieux was restored. The room of the apparition was transformed into a small sanctuary, and an altar was placed where Therese's bed had been. When there was no further doubt about the favorable outcome of the Apostolic Process in Rome, a facsimile of the miraculous statue was also placed in the room. The copy of the miraculous statue was made by a Trappist sculptor, Pere Marie-Bernard. He made a cast of the statue in 1921. Several other copies were also made and were placed in appropriately selected places where Therese had lived and suffered. One copy is in the infirmary on the very spot it occupied when Therese had her last ecstasy. Another is in the antechamber of Therese's cell. Another was placed in the cell where Sister Marie of the Sacred Heart died in 1940.

The miraculous statue of Our Lady of the Smile is at the shrine of St. Therese at Lisieux. There it overlooks the reclining figure which contains the remains of the Saint.

PRAYER TO OUR LADY OF THE SMILE

O Mary, Mother of Jesus and our Mother too, who once by a visible smile didst graciously console and cure thy privileged child Saint Therese of the Child Jesus, we beseech thee, come to us also to console us in the troubles of this life.

Detach our hearts from earth, give to us health of soul and body, make us strong in hope, and obtain for us at last, that we may enjoy for ever in Heaven thy maternal and enrapturing smile. Amen.

OUR LADY OF THE SMILE, a statue which figured prominently in the life of St. Therese of Lisieux.

— 30 —

OUR LADY OF ALTÖTTING

Altötting, Bavaria, Germany
680

The highlands between the Alps and the Danube were controlled in the seventh century by the heathen Marcomannic tribe. A portion of this territory was placed under the control of Otto, one of their pagan chiefs, who was soon to come under the influence of St. Rupert (d. about 718). The Saint was successful in converting Otto in the year 680, together with many of his followers. A heathen temple with seven sides, which is thought to have been the place used by those who were devoted to the cultus of the Seven Planets, was converted into a Christian church for the baptismal ceremony. This chapel is today the seat of Our Lady's greatest sanctuary in Bavaria.

The chapel was a favorite of Karlmann, who was crowned in 875. One year after his coronation he founded a Benedictine monastery nearby which he richly endowed, together with the little chapel. The Benedictines controlled the religious affairs of Altötting for the next 400 years.

When the Hungarians invaded the area late in the ninth century, they destroyed a great deal, but they respected the Holy Chapel and the miraculous image of the Virgin Mary which tradition claims was a gift of St. Rupert himself. Still later, in 913, Duke Arnulf was successful in defeating another effort of the Hungarians during a fierce battle which took place within sight of the holy shrine.

Divine intervention is thought to have spared Altötting from further conflicts, as well as pestilence, famine, the Thirty Years' War and even the Black Death. When this last disease troubled the surrounding territory, thousands of pilgrims prayed at the chapel for relief and deliverance. The shrine was likewise spared during the Napoleonic era, as well as the First and Second World Wars. For this reason it is said that Altötting possesses a shrine of Our Lady which has never been destroyed or desecrated throughout the 13 centuries of its existence.

The number of pilgrims to the shrine had grown so large by 1490 that drastic alterations to the shrine became essential. This was accomplished by removing one of the shrine's seven sides so that the church could be attached. This alteration provided a large opening for better viewing of Our Lady's shrine by the large number of pilgrims who remained in the body of the church. The chapel of the miraculous statue remains, for the most part, as it was centuries ago.

One of the additions to the shrine was an outside arcade, which completely encircles the remaining six walls of Our Lady's shrine. This allows for an orderly passage for pilgrims. Here an ancient custom is perpetuated. A number of large wooden crosses are provided for the pilgrims who want to do penance by solemnly carrying one of these crosses around the arcade. Some pilgrims prefer to circumvent the church on their knees.

The shrine became so popular that it became necessary to build hospices, dispensaries, additional churches and other accommodations for the convenience of those who journeyed great distances. Many favors were received by the pilgrims, as indicated by the countless ex-votos which hang inside the arcade. Many of these ex-votos are in the form of pictures which indicate the favor received or the miracle obtained. These include pictures of the sick or crippled who were cured, the blind who received sight, children who were saved from harm, carriages at the brink of precipices, bombs that did not explode, ships that were saved from sinking and countless other infirmities and events. Of great interest are 59 pictures hanging in the nave which represent other important miracles which have been granted at the shrine.

The eastern alcove of the six-sided shrine is enriched from ceiling to floor with solid silver. Here stands the silver altar and the shrine which contains the Blessed Mother's miraculous image.

The statue, of wood, is 26 inches tall. The original statue given to the chapel by St. Rupert is believed to have been lost; the present statue is said to have originated in the thirteenth century. The Blessed Virgin carries the Christ Child on her left arm. Two features are of particular interest: the oversized hand of the Christ Child is said to symbolize the large number of graces He wishes to dispense; the other feature is the overly large head of the Virgin, which is disproportionate to the rest of the figure. She smiles gently at her Son, who holds a ball in His right hand.

The Virgin's garments fall in graceful folds and are a beautiful blue and rose trimmed by a border of gold. The colors are said to be the original which have survived the centuries. A golden scepter has been placed in the Virgin's hand, and her wooden crown has been gilded. But on festive occasions both figures are covered in exquisitely embroidered gowns which are embellished with costly jewels. On their heads are placed jewel-encrusted golden crowns which are said to be worth a king's ransom. These jewels and precious metals were given to Our Lady throughout the centuries as tokens of gratitude for answered prayers.

The Saint most closely linked to the shrine was St. Conrad of Parzham (d. 1894), a farmhand who became a Capuchin laybrother and porter at St. Anne's Friary a few yards from the shrine. Pilgrims frequently visit the Saint's tomb and his humble cell.

One unusual feature of the holy chapel is the great collection of human hearts. For generations it was the custom for the rulers of Bavaria, dukes and kings, to bequeath their hearts to Our Lady of Altötting as physical tokens of their love for her. Kept in the Holy Chapel are no less than 24 hearts, each in its own silver urn.

An important visitor to the shrine was Pope Pius VI, in 1782. Another visitor was Joseph II, the Emperor of Austria, who came in 1814 to thank Our Lady of Altötting for his victory against Napoleon. Other important visitors are the many pilgrims who visit the shrine each year to plead their needs before the miraculous statue of Our Lady of Altötting.

GRATITUDE FOR ANSWERED PRAYERS has been demonstrated by countless pilgrims to the shrine of Our Lady of Altötting in Bavaria, Germany over the past thirteen centuries (see pictures of the statue of Our Lady of Altötting shown in various states of dress on the next two pages). An unusual feature of the shrine is a collection of 24 human hearts kept there, bequeathed by rulers of Bavaria who wished to express their love for Our Lady of Altötting by specifying that their hearts be kept in silver urns in the Holy Chapel there.

— 31 —

OUR LADY OF THE VINEYARD

Dettelbach, Germany
1484

By the side of the road, about a mile from the old walled city of Dettelbach, a local vinegrower set up a small shrine which contained a statue depicting the Sorrowful Mother holding the lifeless form of the Crucified Christ on her lap. There was nothing original or ornate about the shrine, since wayside shrines were then common throughout Europe. The vinegrower's reason for erecting the shrine was the same as the intentions of the others who erected similar shrines: to provide the passerby and the vinedressers with a place to pause for a prayer and a moment of reflection. The year was 1484.

Twenty years later the shrine attracted special attention as the result of a fight which involved one Nicholas Lemmerer, a vinedresser, who lived outside the area. The confrontation occurred at a church fair when Nicholas was beaten so badly that he lay for almost a year in a semi-conscious condition. When all hope for his recovery seemed lost and he appeared to be at the point of death, Nicholas heard a gentle voice telling him that he could recapture his health if he would promise to visit the wayside shrine located where he formerly worked and there offer a blessed candle. Nicholas promised to do as the voice suggested. His recovery began at that moment.

A few months later, when his serious injuries were almost completely healed, Nicholas made the promised pilgrimage to the shrine. Upon his arrival there he offered the Sorrowful Mother the blessed candle she had requested.

Almost immediately the wayside shrine was visited by enormous groups of people who had heard the story of the hopelessly sick man who had recovered his health at the prompting of a heavenly voice. So many were the people who paused by the shrine to plead for help with their problems that one year later, in 1505, the town magistrate ordered the building of a small chapel to house the holy image.

This first chapel soon proved to be inadequate for the large groups of pilgrims. Another, larger chapel with three altars was erected in 1520. When peasant wars and religious disturbances of the sixteenth century nearly extinguished the enthusiasm of the people for the holy image, Bishop Julius of Wurzburg took the shrine under his personal protection. When improvements were made to the shrine and the whole church was redecorated and embellished by the most talented artisans of the region, the bishop appointed the Friars Minor as guardians of the shrine and its revered image.

The Franciscan friars were to guard the holy image for more than 400 years.

Within the church, which is grand in every detail, is the small pieta enthroned beneath a marble canopy which is so elaborate that it naturally captures the attention of those just entering the church.

The image is a mere 18 inches high, carved in wood and polychromed. Our Lady is clothed in red with a blue mantle and white wimple. Her Son's body lies across her lap in a lifeless attitude. The shrine is located above the three altars that are arranged in something of a circle. The Communion rail is so situated that the communicants may kneel in a complete circle around the shrine.

Of interest in the church is a wall from 1659 which depicts not seven, but eight Sorrows of Our Lady, the eighth being the departure of Our Lord from the house of His Mother.

During the Thirty Years' War the Swedish soldiers sacked the church and stole everything of value from the treasury, but left the image unharmed. Again, when Napoleon's troops visited the area, they likewise left the statue untouched. It is thought that the Virgin Mother's sorrowful expression at the death of her Son touched the hearts of the desecrators, who respected nothing but the image of Our Lady of the Vineyards.

The shrine is visited daily by pilgrims from both near and far, but the number is especially large on September 15, the Feast of Our Lady of Sorrows.

— 32 —

COMFORTER OF THE AFFLICTED

Kevelaer, Germany
1641

The original village of Kevelaer, located a few miles north of Dusseldorf, was destroyed by fire in the sixteenth century. Renegade soldiers who harassed the place, as well as the miseries of the Thirty Years' War, discouraged interest in the area, but in the year 1641 an unusual event was to introduce a grand renewal.

It was during the Christmas season of the year 1641 that an itinerant peddlar named Hendrick Busman, who lived in the adjacent town of Geldern, was traveling the deserted moors where the village of Kevelaer formerly stood. The history of the shrine and the miraculous image began during one of his journeys when he stopped to pray before a wayside cross. We should perhaps allow the merchant to introduce himself and explain what occurred. A portion of the minutes of the Synod of Venio is translated as follows:

> I am Hendrick Busman. I am espoused with Mechel Schrouse, who ages some 50 years. I have sustained my living with her by means of small merchandizing and have thus been caused severally to go here and there in the pursuit. Hence I was underway around Christmas in the year of Our Lord 1641, having come from Weeze, then being near the place known as Kevelaer. At this point stands a cross at the wayside. There I heard a voice which said unto me: "At this place shalt thou build me a chapel."
>
> On this I felt great amazement and looked to all sides, but beheld no one. I continued on my way and put all thoughts of this voice from me. Seven or eight days later I again travelled the same road and at the designated place I a second time perceived the aforesaid voice with the same words. I heard the voice, which issued

> from the direction of the wayside cross both loud and clear. A third time I again heard the voice.
>
> This caused me great sorrow, considering my humble circumstances and meager means. Notwithstanding, I had been charged with this duty and I determined to make daily a small saving from my petty income in order to build the shrine.
>
> Subsequently one month before Whitsuntide there came to my aforementioned spouse Mechel by night a vision in blazing light of a shrine containing a picture of that same nature as she had noticed in the hands of two soldiers some time previously. These soldiers had carried with them two paper pictures of Our Lady of Luxembourg. . .and had tried to sell them to Mechel. On hearing the price asked, however, she declined to make the purchase.
>
> On this account I myself was strengthened in my beliefs, so I sent forth my wife to discover the whereabouts of the soldiers and the picture. They had left the pictures to a lieutenant of the army who was at that time in prison in Kempen. Mechel went to him and solicited of him one of the pictures. . .
>
> Everything I have said has truly happened and is reality. I, Hendrick Busman, verily swear to this on my oath. . .to the Glory of God and the Holy Mother and Virgin.

After his wife obtained one of the pictures, Hendrick began at once to arrange for the construction of the shrine, ". . .in that manner as had been seen by my wife in the vision."

Meanwhile, the thrice-heard voice and the vision became widely known. The Carmelite nuns at Geldern heard the reports and asked that the picture be temporarily entrusted to them, and for 24 hours they kept a reverent vigil before it. When the print was returned to the Busman cottage, the stream of visitors who wished to venerate the holy image was such that the tranquility of the home was greatly disturbed. For this reason Hendrick asked the Capuchin Fathers to temporarily enshrine the image in their chapel. Here, too, the great crowds of people visiting the image were such that the Fathers had to request that it be taken as soon as possible to the shrine that Hendrick was preparing for it.

The shrine that the poor trader built was a tall, thick pillar of bricks with a roof and a deep niche. In preparation for its enshrinement in Kevelaer, the picture was glued to a board that was cut in the shape of the niche into which it was to be fixed.

The parish priest of Kevelaer, Johannes Schink, accepted the holy image when it was brought to him in solemn procession on June 1, 1642 and it was he who installed the picture in its shrine. He soon found himself unable to minister to the huge crowds that were visiting it. In answer to the pastor's urgent request, the bishop delegated three Oratorian priests to assist him.

The heavenly Mother quickly rewarded the love and veneration that was showered upon her humble portrait. The blind, deaf, dumb and crippled were cured, as well as those laboring under various diseases and injuries. So many wonders were performed during the first five years that an investigation was ordered by the vicar-general of the diocese. After a thorough investigation and the taking of depositions, countless incidents were declared to be miraculous. Confirmation of the miracles brought even larger crowds to the little shrine.

After Hendrick and his wife fulfilled the task given by Heaven, they quietly retreated into history. But before his death on March 14, 1649, Hendrick was gratified at seeing the huge crowds that venerated the little picture. He was not to be forgotten, however, since his name and that of his wife were inscribed centuries ago on a plaque that still remains at the base of the original shrine. Another, much larger plaque, is located on the outside wall of the sanctuary that now encloses the original shrine. This plaque gives his name once more and gives him credit as the originator of the devotion to the Comforter of the Afflicted.

The original brick pillar was left untouched and exposed to wind and rain for a number of years. Eventually the importance of the shrine required a more impressive structure. The present sanctuary, consecrated in 1654, encloses the original shrine which is located behind the altar upon which the miraculous image is now enshrined. Located in a beautiful square known as Kapellenplatz (Chapel Square), the sanctuary is known as the Chapel of Grace or the Chapel of Mercy. The structure is hexangular in shape and is surmounted with a quaint-shaped roof and a squat little steeple. Built into one side is a large window through which the image may be easily viewed day or night by the people kneeling in the square and by those sitting on the benches that have been provided for visitors.

Also located in the beautifully shaded, cobble-stoned Kapellenplatz is a building called the Candle Chapel, or the Pilgrim's Church. It is here that the early pilgrims gathered and pilgrimages ended. In this chapel are countless giant candles, some 10 feet tall, that serve as ex-votos. Here also is found a curious array of different heraldic shields, which have been left during the past 300 years, each blazoned with the arms of some diocese, parish or guild.

The Basilica of St. Mary is also found in the square and was built expressly to meet the needs of the huge press of pilgrims who arrive in great numbers annually between May 1 and November 1.

During the French Revolution, all processions and pilgrimages were suppressed. In the interest of safety the miraculous image was concealed in a cavity in the tower of the parish church. Reopened in 1802, the sanctuary was roofed with copper plates while the exterior was restored and the interior artistically embellished.

The attention of every visitor is directed to the miraculous image which is a faded paper print, a mere five inches in height and three in width. It depicts the miraculous statue that is revered in Luxembourg. (See Chapter 66). The paper print depicts the crowned Virgin, who holds a scepter in her right hand while supporting the Child Jesus with her left. Behind her, on her right, is the city of Luxembourg, while on the left is depicted the Luxembourg Chapel of Mercy. Protected behind glass in a costly golden frame, the print is now surrounded with golden angels, trails of golden roses, golden medals, chains and jeweled ornaments, all contributed by grateful recipients of the heavenly Mother's benevolence. Many of these ornaments were donated by members of royalty. A diamond and jeweled crown was positioned above the picture's frame when the Comforter of the Afflicted was honored with a papal coronation in 1892, the 250th anniversary of the shrine.

Although the first visitors to the shrine were the poor and unlettered, many wealthy and learned persons soon found their way to the miraculous image. These included King Frederic William I, who was the father of Frederic the Great, King Frederic William IV; various dignitaries of both Church and State; and Pope John Paul II.

With the possible exception of Altötting some 60 miles east of Munich, Kevelaer may be regarded as the most frequented of all Marian shrines in Germany, since more than half a million pilgrims visit there each year.

SURROUNDED BY EX-VOTOS, or tokens of appreciation for favors granted, the miraculous image of the Blessed Virgin Mary known as Comforter of the Afflicted is visited in Kevelaer, Germany, today—as it has been for three centuries—by pilgrims from all walks of life. A faded paper print measuring a mere 5 x 3 inches, depicting the miraculous statue of Our Lady and the Child Jesus that is revered in Luxembourg, is surrounded by a golden frame, golden angels, roses and medals, and jeweled ornaments.
(Right) This painting by Karl Wenzel depicts the picture of mercy.

THE CHAPEL OF MERCY at Kevelaer is captured in this copper-plate engraving from the early nineteenth century. The shrine contains the miraculous little picture shown on Page 126. Pilgrims view the image through a large window built into one side of the structure.
(Next Page) Here is a clear rendering of the miraculous image of the heavenly Mother, Comforter of the Afflicted, and her Son. In 1641, a humble merchant named Hendrick Busman was thrice directed by a voice to build a chapel near Kevelaer. Based on a vision received by his wife, Mechel, a print of Our Lady of Luxembourg was sought out and construction of the shrine began. Huge crowds soon visited and asked for favors. Cures abounded, and countless incidents were declared to be miraculous.

CONSOLATRIX AFFLICTORVM ORA PRO NOBIS
Vera Effigies Matris IESU Consolatricis afflictorum in agro suburbano Luxemburgi Miraculis et Hominum Visitatione celebris, Anno 1640

— 33 —

THE IRISH MADONNA OF HUNGARY

Györ, Hungary
1697

The extraordinary miracle of the Irish Madonna of Hungary is not a legend, but is a reality based on facts and the testimony of reliable witnesses.

The picture was hanging in the Cathedral of Clonfert, in the diocese of Tuam, Ireland, when, in 1649, Oliver Cromwell invaded Ireland with 10,000 Englishmen. Among other objectives, his campaign was meant to eliminate papal influence and establish a Protestant interest in the country. When the religious persecution began, Bishop Walter Lynch of Clonfert and some of his priests were arrested. To prevent the Irish Madonna from falling into the hands of those who would destroy it, Bishop Lynch smuggled the picture out of Ireland and kept it in his possession. The bishop, together with some members of his group, escaped in 1652 from the island known as Innisboffin, where they had been imprisoned. They dispersed to various countries, where they were warmly received.

Bishop Lynch and the portrait spent some time in Belgium and in Portugal. Later he traveled as far as Hungary. There he was joyously received by the bishop of Györ, who appointed him as his auxiliary. The Irish bishop learned the Hungarian language and worked 10 years among the faithful. Although he seemed content, he was nevertheless longing to return to his native country. When he learned that the persecution in Ireland had subsided, he prepared for the return journey. The picture was meant, of course, to return with him, but Our Lady had other plans.

Before the date of his departure, the Irish bishop became desperately ill. On his deathbed he bequeathed the picture to the Bishop of Györ, who subsequently had the body of his Irish friend buried in the crypt of the cathedral.

The people of Györ quickly adopted the picture of the Madonna. It was especially welcomed because the arrival of the portrait coincided with a series of victories over the Turks.

During the years many souls have come from throughout Hungary to pray before the Madonna for personal and national needs and to thank Our Lady for the disasters that were prevented through her intercession.

The portrait of Our Lady and the Infant Christ is charming. The Child lies asleep on a pallet, His crowned head on a fluffy pillow, His two arms resting atop the fold of a covering. The Blessed Virgin also wears a crown and appears to be kneeling beside the Child. With her hands folded in prayer, Our Lady looks serenely down upon her slumbering Babe.

While the Hungarians enjoyed peace and plenty during the year 1697, the Irish were afflicted with great hardships and religious persecution. In that year the Parliament passed an edict that ordered the expulsion of all priests from the territory of Ireland and the British Isles. Churches were confiscated and all traces of the Catholic religion were to be eliminated. A national Irish church was established and only members of this church were permitted to serve as ministers at funerals.

On March 17 of that year, St. Patrick's Day, as thousands were attending Holy Mass in the Cathedral of Györ, the eyes of the Madonna began to shed tears and blood which ran down the canvas to the image of the sleeping Jesus. The Irish Madonna was weeping for her suffering children. The people who had been attending the Holy Sacrifice, as well as those who were summoned to witness the miracle, took turns in gathering around the portrait while the priests repeatedly wiped the face of the Madonna with a linen cloth that is still preserved in the Cathedral.

To further examine the miracle and the possible source of the blood and tears, the portrait was taken down from the wall and removed from its frame. No explanation could be given for the phenomenon, which continued for more than three hours.

Before long not only Catholics, but also Protestants and Jews flocked to see the miracle. Thousands witnessed the event, and many of these gave testimony of what they saw. A document signed by a hundred people bears the signatures of the governor of the city, its mayor, all its councilmen, the bishop, priests, Calvinist and Lutheran ministers as well as a Jewish rabbi. All volunteered their signatures to the document stating that they had witnessed an undeniable miracle.

The miracle of Our Lady weeping blood and tears on St. Patrick's Day in 1697 for her suffering children in Ireland left a deep impression on the people of Hungary down to the present day. At all times, but especially in times of disaster, the people flock to her shrine in order to gain strength and hope in the midst of crisis. By virtue of this portrait, the Madonna has linked two nations whose people have suffered for their faith and freedom.

WEEPING BLOOD AND TEARS. The year 1697 brought hardship and religious persecution to the Irish, and on St. Patrick's Day of that year, the portrait pictured above (which was located in Hungary) shed tears and blood. The painting had been bequeathed to the Bishop of Gyor by an Irish bishop forced from his homeland because of persecution of Catholics. The miracle continued for more than three hours and was witnessed by thousands. This portrait has been chosen by Our Lady to link the people of two nations, Hungary and Ireland, both of which have struggled for the right to practice their faith.

— 34 —

OUR LADY OF GRACES

Cork, Ireland
Fourteenth Century

Perhaps the smallest of all the miraculous images is this three-inch, fourteenth-century ivory statue of the Blessed Mother.

Its history relates that a piece of wood brought in by the tide was found on the bank near the town of Youghal. Some fishermen wanted to take it since the wood seemed to be of an unusual kind not grown in the area, but the wood proved to be exceptionally heavy. It is said that ten horses were unable to move it. Eventually the rising tide dislodged it and bore it a little further along the way toward the Dominican monastery of Youghal. Two of the religious found it there and brought it to their cloister. During the night the prior of the monastery had a strange dream in which he was told that an image of Our Blessed Lady was concealed in the wood. The image was subsequently found and was reverently enshrined.

The image was the object of special devotion to the faithful who flocked from all parts of Ireland to venerate it. The blessings and graces generously distributed by the Mother of God prompted the religious to change the name of the monastery from Holy Cross to Our Lady of Graces.

Because of its diminutive size, the daughter of one of the Geraldines decided to make it more prominent by placing it in a specially designed shrine. For this purpose a silver case was made. It was richly decorated with floriated ornaments and was surmounted by a cross. In front were folding doors which, when open, displayed the sacred image. On the inside of one door was a crucifix; on the other was the figure of a saint. The case bore the following Latin inscription which translates, "Pray for the soul of Honoria, daughter of James Fitzgerald, who caused me to be made. A.D. 1617."

It is reported that from the time of the image's discovery, miraculous powers have been uninterruptedly ascribed to Our Lady of

Graces. As long as it was possible, the Irish people made pilgrimages to the monastery of Youghal.

During the dark days of persecution, nuns and monks were dispersed from their cloisters. Sacred vessels, vestments and other religious objects were usually sent to the safety of other houses of prayer. It is believed this is the reason the holy image is now found in St. Mary's Dominican Church in the city of Cork, Ireland.

Among the many instances of cures and graces obtained by prayers offered in honor of the image was that of Mr. Michael O'Callaghan, father of a bishop of Cork. As a votive offering of thanksgiving for his miraculous recovery, he donated a new shrine which bears the inscription: "Michael O'Callaghan and family devoutly returning thanks to Saint Mary of Graces, 1872." During the solemn Triduum conducted in St. Mary's in 1895, the image of Our Lady of Graces was installed in this new shrine above the altar of the Rosary.

During the Triduum, the Very Rev. Canon Keller of Youghal revealed that the image was known to Pope Leo XIII, who sent his best wishes and prayers.

Canon Keller also spoke of the great devotion and confidence in the Blessed Virgin Mary which prevailed in Ireland. We are told that:

> He did not know a nation in all the pages of the history of the church where the Catholic Faith had been more steadfastly adhered to, or where great suffering or sacrifices were made for the Faith than in Ireland. Meanwhile churches were levelled to the earth, shrines were burnt and altars overthrown, but the figure of Our Lady of Youghal was always saved.

He also revealed that he envied them in their possession of the statue which had been discovered in his city of Youghal.

In addition to the discovery of the miraculous image, the city of Youghal is also known as the home of the Elizabethan explorer and adventurer Sir Walter Raleigh, who was once the mayor of the city. Local legend has it that Sir Walter Raleigh planted the first Irish potato in the garden of his home.

The monastery at Youghal has totally disappeared, but the ruins of the church where the image was first enshrined may still be seen.

— 35 —

OUR LADY OF HEALING

(Our Lady of Waterford)
Waterford, Ireland
Seventeenth Century

In the city that is regarded as the world's largest crystal factory, in a tower that is the only remnant of the thirteenth-century Franciscan Friary known as St. Saviour's, is enshrined a small oaken figure of the Blessed Virgin that is known locally as Our Lady of Waterford or as Our Lady of Healing.

The history of the statue begins with the Reverend Nicholas Fagan, an Irishman by birth, who took the habit of religion in the famous Cistercian Abbey of Farrara in Castile, Spain, in the latter part of Queen Elizabeth's reign. After some years he was sent back to Ireland. He managed to preserve his life and engage in apostolic labors, in spite of being exposed to many dangers. More than once he was beaten and wounded by his enemies.

Reverend Fagan was very intent on promoting devotion to the Blessed Virgin as a powerful means of restoring and strengthening the Catholic Faith in Ireland. For this purpose he brought with him from Seville an image of Our Blessed Lady, which he enshrined in the hospital of St. John in the city of Waterford. Don Gaspar Jongelino relates in his work entitled, *Propora di S. Bernardo,* that "Large numbers of Catholics devoutly visited the image where Our Lord, through the intercession of His Blessed Mother, worked many and astounding miracles at the shrine."

One of these miracles involved a certain man who lived in the county of Kilkenny, whose arm had been withered from birth so that he was unable even to move it. One night in a dream, it seemed as though the Mother of God appeared to him and suggested that he journey to Waterford and visit her image which was then preserved in St. John's Hospital. The vision promised that if he did so, his arm would be fully restored. On awakening he decided to comply with the suggestion. Later that same day he arrived in Waterford.

He first visited the Reverend Nicholas Fagan so that he could tell him the reason for his visit, but the priest suggested that he wait until the next day, when he would celebrate Holy Mass and recommend his cure to God.

The next morning the man and a considerable number of Catholics assembled in the oratory, where Reverend Fagan offered the Holy Sacrifice. At the moment of the Elevation, the man realized that his hand and arm were suddenly and perfectly cured. Not wishing to cause a disturbance at that moment by declaring what had happened, he held his peace until the end of the Mass. He then raised his arm, now as healthy and whole as the other, and proclaimed his cure to all present.

Another miracle that occurred, but one which is of an entirely different nature, involved a certain person of the neighborhood who seemed from all appearances to practice his faith, but who, in reality, lived a very disorderly life. The man had stolen some necklaces of great value and was soon placed under suspicion. When he was accused of the crime, he swore his innocence under oath. To further prove his innocence he decided to hear Mass at St. John's oratory before the holy image. Accompanying him were several people who had witnessed his taking the oath. During the Holy Sacrifice the necklaces fell at his feet. Finding himself detected, he confessed his crime. The Reverend Fagan is said to have given him a severe scolding.

— 36 —

PROTECTRESS OF THE ROMAN PEOPLE

(Salus Populi Romani)
Rome, Italy
c. 352

A certain Roman aristocrat named John was blessed with an abundance of the world's wealth and was distinguished by a family of notable ancestors. He was happy in his marriage, except for his childlessness, which Heaven would not correct despite his many prayers. Accepting this disappointment with Christian resignation, he and his wife prayed that the Blessed Mother might designate an heir so that they might bequeath their immense fortune and property to one of Our Lady's own choosing. Since the patrician and his wife placed their fortune in Our Lady's hands, Heaven's decision was indicated in a miraculous fashion on the morning of August 5, about the year 352.

Tradition reveals that after a warm summer night, the rays of the morning sun fell upon Mount Esquiline where a carpet of snow had fallen within certain limits in the form and size necessary for a church, and no more. The unexpected brightness alerted the people, who journeyed to the spot. The snow remained intact, despite the heat. Informed during the night by means of a dream, both the patrician and Pope Liberius had been told of Our Lady's intentions for the property. Upon awakening the patrician hurried to the site, while the Pontiff, wanting to emphasize Our Lady's wishes, went to the area in solemn procession.

When told that Our Lady indicated by the snowfall the exact location of a church she wished to have built, the people staked off the area. When the work was completed, the snow immediately disappeared. The patrician lost no time in providing all the money necessary to defray the cost of the building, which was completed two years later. For many years it was known as the Basilica Liberiana, after the name of its consecrator.

In the early part of the following century Pope Sixtus III rebuilt portions of the basilica with greater magnificence and enriched it with silver articles and adornments for which it was then known as the Basilica Sixti. Because of its size and splendor it was eventually known as St. Mary the Greater or St. Mary Major. It received other names as well, including the Church of St. Mary of the Snows and the Church of St. Mary of the Crib, to commemorate the venerable relic which was later deposited there.

Whether the ancient story of the foundation of this basilica is truth or unfounded legend, it seems that Pope Benedict XIV wanted to settle the matter by proclaiming, "It must be acknowledged that nothing is wanting to enable us to affirm with moral certainty that the prodigy of the snow is true."

In looking for an image of Our Lady which would both adorn this sanctuary and inspire devotion in the hearts of the faithful, Pope Liberius selected a venerated picture that hung in the pontifical oratory. It had allegedly been brought to Rome by St. Helena (who had rescued the Holy Places of Palestine and the Relics of the Passion).

The holy image was painted on a thick cedar slab and measures nearly five feet high by three and a quarter feet wide. The Madonna is wrapped in a gold-edged mantle of dark blue which covers her head, shoulders and arms. Her features are depicted in the true Greek style. The Child Jesus is held upon her left arm. As He gazes upward at His Mother His right hand is extended in blessing, while His left clasps a book. Haloes surround the heads of both Mother and Child, and both still wear the crowns given to them by Pope Gregory XVI.

The Popes have always had a tender devotion for this famous picture of Our Lady. Popes Symmachus, Gregory III, Adrian, Leo III, Paschal I and Clement VIII have prayed before the image. Benedict XIV was always present on Saturdays for the singing of the Litany, and Paul V was carried on the eve of his death to the Blessed Virgin's chapel for a final prayer before his beloved image of Our Lady. Pope Pius IX is said to often have made midnight visits to the shrine. Other popes through the ages have honored the miraculous image and have donated articles and architectural additions to adorn the Madonna's basilica.

St. Stanislaus Kostka is said to have favored this image, and St. Ignatius Loyola said his first Mass here on Christmas night, 1538. Another first Mass was offered on April 3, 1899 by the newly ordained Eugenio Pacelli, who was to visit the basilica many times—especially 40 years after his ordination, when he was Pope Pius XII.

St. Francis of Borgia, third General of the Society of Jesus, was the first to petition the Pontiff for the authority to reproduce the image. Copies made from this reproduction have in turn become miraculous. The Jesuit house at Ingolstad possesses a copy, which more than once has spoken in order to settle the vocations of those who were in doubt.

During the pontificate of St. Gregory the Great (590-604) a plague viciously attacked the people of Rome, killing entire families. The pontiff fervently prayed to the Blessed Mother. During the Easter festivals he carried her image in solemn procession. Arriving at Hadrian's Mausoleum (now called San Angelo), an angelic choir was heard singing the joyful Resurrection hymn:

Regina coeli, laetare, alleluia;
Quia quem meruisti portare, alleluia;
Resurrexit sicut dixit, alleluia.

Without hesitation, the holy Pontiff added:

Ora pro nobis Deum, alleluia.

After the Pontiff spoke these words there appeared above Hadrian's Mausoleum an angel, believed to be St. Michael, who replaced in his scabbard the sword of vengeance which he had held over the city. In commemoration of this vision, Pope Alexander VI caused the figure of an angel in white marble to be placed on the summit of the building.

The miraculous painting has also been carried in procession by other Popes, the last time by Pope Gregory XVI in 1837 when Rome was visited by a cholera epidemic. The prayers of the Pope and the people were acknowledged by Our Lady when the epidemic promptly ended. In thanksgiving, the Pope affixed two crowns of gold and jewels to the picture, one for the Mother, the other for the Son. These crowns replaced the crowns of silver which had been offered by various people in former times beginning with Clement VIII. All of these, unfortunately, were lost during some of the numerous political disturbances to which the city had been so often subjected.

St. Gregory the Great regarded the basilica of St. Mary Major with special affection and loved to offer the Holy Sacrifice there.

One Easter Sunday, at the words of the Mass, *"Pax Domini sit semper vobiscum,"* he heard a celestial voice sing the response, *"Et cum spiritu tuo."* In commemoration of this marvel, when other Popes officiated in the church, the choir remained silent at this part of the Holy Mass.

It was Pope Paul V (1605-1621) who arranged for the building of a magnificent Lady Chapel. On January 27, 1613 the miraculous painting was removed from its original shrine above the high altar for placement in this special chapel. The Pope indicated that the image deserved a splendid chapel of its own, because ". . .ancient records testify that it has always been distinguished by the devotion of the faithful, and that many and wonderful miracles have proceeded from it."

Recent excavations reveal that a great deal of the brick and mortar suggest fourth-century work, while other bricking suggests architectural changes made during the time of Sixtus III (432-440). Mosaics from the time of Pope Liberius (353-366) still decorate the church. Other decorative embellishments in the nave remain as Pope Sixtus III left them. It is suggested that the embellishments and improvements made by Pope Sixtus III were regarded by him as a memorial to the success of the Council of Ephesus, held in 431, during which the Nestorian heresy was defeated when the Blessed Virgin Mary was officially proclaimed the Mother of God.

St. Mary Major (Santa Maria Maggiore) is one of the four major basilicas in Rome, and it is one of the largest Catholic churches in the world. It vies with Santa Maria Antiqua in being considered the first church in Rome to be consecrated to Our Lady. Its fame extends throughout the whole Church. The feast of its dedication is liturgically commemorated on August 5.

On this feastday each year, the glorious anniversary of the origin of *Santa Maria Maggiore* is celebrated with the utmost pomp and splendor. A touching and lovely custom of long ago is still observed. During Mass and Vespers, in commemoration of the miraculous shower of snow that indicated the site and size of the basilica, a shower of jasmines and other white flowers falls from the dome of the chapel in which the image is kept. The flowers likewise recall the graces which are lavishly scattered by the hand of Mary over the hearts of those who are devoted to her.

The image of Our Blessed Mother bears a name that differs from the magnificent church in which it is enshrined. Owing to the miraculous cessation of plagues and the answered prayers of her devotees, the image is affectionately known as *Salus Populi Romani*, Protectress of the People of Rome.

THE HOLY IMAGE of Our Lady pictured above was chosen by Pope Liberius to adorn the sanctuary of the Church of St. Mary of the Snows, or St. Mary Major, located in Rome. The painting, on a thick cedar slab measuring five feet high by three and a quarter feet wide, is said to have been brought to Rome by St. Helena.

— 37 —

OUR LADY OF OROPA

Oropa, Piedmont, Italy
Fourth Century

Described as the most popular place of pilgrimage in the region of Piedmont, the sanctuary of Our Lady of Oropa is found in the beautiful panoramic regions of northern Italy, just north of Biella and some 35 miles northeast of Turin. The founding of the sanctuary which houses the wonderworking statue of Our Lady is credited to St. Eusebius (d. 370), who was the first bishop of Vercelli and the first in the West to unite the clergy into a monastic way of life.

It was while visiting Jerusalem that St. Eusebius was inspired to discover three statues of Our Lady which had been buried under some ruins. Upon leaving Jerusalem, he visited his native town of Cagliari in Sardinia. Here he left one of the three figures. The second he gave to a hermitage he had established at Crea in the Monferrato district of Italy. The third, which was considered the finest, he kept and eventually enshrined in a hermitage chapel at Oropa. It was here that he spent much of his time before his holy death.

During the fifth and sixth centuries the heresy of Arianism infected the church. Arius, a priest of Alexandria, taught that Jesus was not the equal of the Father or true God, but merely a creature much more perfect than other creatures. Those who opposed this heresy were severely persecuted. During this time of trial the faithful found courage and strength by frequenting the hermitage shrine of Our Lady of Oropa, which had earlier become a popular place of pilgrimage.

Already, at this early time in the shrine's history, Orsi (the Biellese chronicler) wrote about the great concourse of pilgrims and what he called "stupendous miracles," which were performed as a result of prayers offered to Our Lady of Oropa.

It is recorded that the Canons of the shrine at one time decided to remove the Black Madonna to their church some distance away.

Half a mile from the shrine, at the bottom of the hill, the procession stopped. The figure had become too heavy to move and could be lifted only when it was decided to take it back to the shrine. The spot is now marked by a chapel called the *Capella Del Transporto.*

When Biella was smitten by the plague in 1599, the community vowed to build a great church for Our Lady of Oropa. The plague ceased, and the vow was honored by the building of a church which enshrined the Eusebian chapel built by the original hermits. The little primitive chapel was situated under the dome, somewhat resembling the free-standing holy chapel of Einsiedeln. The whole was arranged so that a pilgrim might enter the Eusebian Chapel by the original door or peep through the old window at the miraculous statue within.

Preserved above the little altar is the statue of Our Lady, which is about three feet in height. Carved of cedar wood, the most noticeable feature is that the hands and faces of both Mother and Child are jet black, not with age, but deliberately colored by the original carver. Our Lady is shown standing. On her left forearm is the Holy Child, raising His hand in benediction. The figures are elaborately dressed, as befits their royal station. On the head of the Madonna rests a unique triple crown representing three coronations, those of 1620, 1720 and 1820. A great golden halo of 12 diamond stars represents the fourth coronation of 1920. In this Our Lady of Oropa is unique, having been honored with four papal coronations.

A strange phenomenon has been observed through the centuries. Although protected by glass, dust nevertheless accumulates through crevices and by degrees covers the figures, robes, crowns and jewels. It has been carefully noted, and closely studied, that never has a particle of dust fallen upon the faces of Mother or Child. It is said that no explanation can be advanced to account for this unusual condition.

Because of the wonders worked at the shrine, the Holy See in 1856 requested a list of the various maladies that had been miraculously corrected. The recorded miracles of Oropa numbered more than 500.

The shrine of Oropa is surrounded by a veritable city of buildings and activity. There are buildings containing offices for the conducting of business; other buildings for the care of pilgrims;

as well as a medical bureau, shops, restaurants, chapels and a museum of fine religious art.

In addition to the grand pilgrimages and the many miracles worked at the shrine, including the phenomenon of the respectful dust, Oropa has still another distinction. A tablet at the shrine records that it was here that Marconi, "In the summer of 1895, while contemplating the Biellese Alps from the heights of Oropa, bethought him that man might find a new energy in space, and the means to a new method of communication." Marconi later invented the radio and it was from Oropa, under Our Lady's patronage, that he sent the first radio message to the Vatican.

— 38 —

THE MADONNA OF CONSOLATION

(La Madonna Consolata)
Turin, Piedmont, Italy
Fifth Century

Believed to have been painted in the middle of the fifth century, the icon of The Madonna of Consolation is enshrined high atop the main altar of the church known throughout Turin as the magnificent Santuario della Consolata.

Because of its age, the facts concerning the early history of the icon are not exact, but two paintings in the Sanctuary tell the traditional story of its discovery. In one painting, which apparently represents a night-time scene, a woman is directing a man's attention to a radiant light that glows atop a heap of stones. The second painting depicts the icon atop the stones and a bishop in full episcopal vestments pointing to the portrait. Altar servers and a kneeling man and woman surround the bishop.

An antique processional standard also depicts the bishop and the discovery of the icon. Beneath the painting on the standard is the date of the discovery: June 20, 1104.

The miraculous icon depicts the Madonna with a pensive expression. Dressed in golden-edged dark blue garments, she holds the Child Jesus on her left arm while her right hand rests gently on her chest. The Child Jesus, wearing a green tunic and a red mantle, imparts a blessing with His right hand, while the left clasps the left thumb of His Mother. An unusual detail of the icon is the ring worn on the Madonna's right hand. The other adornments consist of a star on her right shoulder and another atop her veil. A headband under the veil is also embellished with stars.

The miraculous nature of the portrait is proved by walking through the Galleria Degli Ex-voto, which is a long, wide hallway attached to the Sanctuary. Covering the walls on both sides of this hallway are hundreds of framed rectangular paintings depicting a cure or a favor, all of which represent symbols of gratitude. One of the more detailed is dated 1670; another is dated 1702.

The Sanctuary of the Madonna is quite interesting in that it was constructed on the site of a tenth-century monastery of St. Andrew the Apostle and is actually two connecting churches. Upon entering, one discovers the oval *"Aula di sant'Andrea,"* the "Room of St. Andrew," which represents the antique church of the Saint. This leads to, and is connected to, the *vano esagonale,* or the hexagonal room which is the sanctuary church of Our Lady. Radiating from here are four large, impressive chapels. The main point of interest in the sanctuary is, of course, the main altar with the miraculous painting of the Madonna of Consolation. Here countless pilgrims throughout the years have knelt in adoration and supplication. Originally designed and built by Guarini between 1678 and 1703, the sanctuary was sumptuously restored in 1903.

City officials in 1706 proclaimed the Madonna of Consolation patroness of the city, and in 1714 an annual feast and procession of the Madonna were inaugurated. The date assigned for this observance was June 20, the anniversary of the icon's discovery atop the heap of stones. Every year a large procession is held in which an almost life-size silver statue of Our Lady of Consolation is carried through the streets on a flower-covered platform. Attending are many clerics and men in uniform, together with countless people of the city. Donated by Queen Maria Cristina in 1832, this silver statue replaces the original one, which disappeared at some point in time.

One of the chapels in the hexagonal church is dedicated to St. Joseph Cafasso (d. 1860), who labored among the convicts and lectured in moral theology at an institute in Turin. He was also the spiritual director of St. John Bosco. Atop the altar in this shrine is a painting of the Saint preaching to members of the clergy. Under the altar is a reclining statue representing the Saint, which contains his relics.

On one side of the sanctuary is an eleventh-century Romanesque belfry; on the other side is a tall Corinthian column topped by a statue representing the Madonna of Consolation. This monument is a symbol of thanksgiving erected by the city of Turin in recognition of the sudden cessation of a cholera epidemic in 1835. The sudden dismissal of the epidemic must have been quite extraordinary and miraculous, since a huge painting dated 1835 (which is kept in the city hall of Turin) depicts Archbishop Luigi Fransoni sitting before the altar of Our Lady, accepting from two clergymen a votive offering of thanksgiving. Also depicted in this large painting are other clerics and a number of formally dressed men representing city officials who are standing near the steps of the altar.

Various Popes have recognized the sanctuary, especially Pope Pius X, who elevated the Sanctuary to the dignity of a pontifical basilica in 1906. More recently, Pope John Paul II visited the sanctuary on April 13, 1980, during his pastoral visit to the City of Turin.

Among the many persons who have visited the shrine of the miraculous icon are some who were later raised to the honors of the altar, including: St. Joseph Benedict Cottolengo, St. Joseph Cafasso, St. John Bosco, St. Leonard Murialdo, Bl. Sebastian Valfre, Bl. Federico Albert, Bl. Anna Michelortti, Bl. Clement Marchisio, Bl. Michele Rua, and the Servant of God, Luigi Boccardo.

Our Lady of Consolation is the patroness of a religious order founded in 1901 by Fr. Joseph Allamano. Called the Consolata Missionaries, the priests, brothers and sisters of the missionary order spread the gospel among the poor of Africa, South America, Europe, Asia, Canada and the United States.

(Right): A view of the altar of the magnificent Santuario della Consolata in Turin, Italy, which enshrines the miraculous painting of the Madonna of Consolation.

ANCIENT AND MIRACULOUS, the image of the Madonna and Child pictured above was found atop a heap of stones on June 20, 1104. It is believed to have been painted in the fifth century.

— 39 —

OUR LADY OF MONTE VERGINE

Monte Vergine, Campania, Italy
1119

The Mount was famous in ancient times for the temple dedicated to Cybele, who was worshiped as the nature goddess and the mother of the gods. Atop the ruins of this temple now stands the monastery church containing an ancient Byzantine portrait of the Queen of all nature, and the true Mother of God, the Blessed Virgin Mary.

The sanctuary owes its existence to St. William of Vercelli (1085-1142). At the age of 15, this saint embraced a life of great austerity and in 1119 fixed his residence in solitude upon this mountain located between Naples and Avellino. Known as Monte Virgiliano (in memory of Virgil, who is supposed to have consulted the priests at the temple of Cybele), St. William changed the name to Monte Vergine, Mount of the Virgin. Here he was favored with many supernatural gifts, including an apparition of the Blessed Mother holding the Divine Child in her arms. The mission entrusted to the Saint during this vision was to build upon this former stronghold of paganism a Christian temple dedicated to Mary so that, where the worship of the false goddess had once flourished, the cultus of the Blessed Virgin might be maintained.

When St. William completed the chapel desired by heaven, he dedicated it to Our Lady and enshrined in it a picture of the Mother of God giving nourishment to the Divine Infant. This tender portrait had been painted on a wooden panel, but is said to have lacked artistic merit.

Attracted to this haven of prayer were a group of pious young men who were the nucleus of a religious order which bore the name of Monte Vergine. Later the order was absorbed into the Benedictine Order, although the original members of Monte Vergine were permitted to continue wearing their white habits and the scapulars which they had adopted in respect to Our Lady's purity.

In the course of time the humble chapel of St. William was incorporated into a magnificent basilica. The picture of Mother and Child, which had remained in the original church, was removed in 1310 to make way for a more ancient portrait which was considered to be more beautiful and artistically superior.

According to tradition, this ancient portrait was held in great veneration at Antioch and was admired by Empress Eudoxia (d. 460), who gave it to her sister-in-law, St. Pulcheria, at Constantinople. When Baldwin II, the last of the Latin Emperors at Constantinople was dethroned, he escaped the city and took with him the time-honored picture of Mary Immaculate. Unfortunately, because of the painting's large size, the Emperor was unable to bring it away in its entirety. For this reason, the upper part of the portrait containing the faces of the Blessed Virgin and the Holy Child was cut off and carried into Italy. The portrait eventually became the property of Catherine of Valois and Philip of Anjou. In 1310 the lower portion of the portrait was added by Montana, an artist of Arezzo. It was then presented to the shrine of Monte Vergine, where it has been revered for almost 700 years.

Located above an altar in the transept, the larger-than-life-size-figure of Our Lady is seated on a rich throne. Her right hand embraces the Holy Child seated on her left arm. Both figures are richly vested, and both wear jeweled crowns. Attached to the picture are numerous chains of gold and jewels which were given as ex-votos. Also added to the picture are gems of great value including diamonds, rubies, emeralds and large pearls.

At the back of the throne-like chair on which Our Lady sits are diminutive figures of angels who wave golden censers. Other angels stand around the Virgin's footstool, singing and waving palms.

It is not the magnificent decorations of the picture which most impress the beholder, but the features of the Virgin Mother which are full of beauty and dignity. The eyes of the Virgin are large and dark and it is said that many who approach the picture with hearts full of sorrow and anxiety have experienced a calmness and restfulness of soul under the Virgin's steady gaze.

The miraculous nature of this portrait has been well established by virtue of the countless ex-votos which are attached to the walls of the chapel. Moreover, records reveal many wondrous interventions which have taken place.

One of these miracles was witnessed by countless pilgrims and the abbot himself, the Rt. Rev. Dom Victor Corvaia. It seems that the devotion of some pilgrims was expressed noisily with shouts and cries to the Blessed Virgin. But on one particular day, the voice of a distraught mother resounded louder than the others, so loud, in fact, that the abbot went to investigate. He found a mother kneeling in complete distress beside her child of three years. The sickly, deformed boy looked the image of death. From time to time she would lift him up to Our Lady, while pleading for a cure. Attracted to the scene were other pilgrims who murmured words of sympathy. The mother cried plaintively to Our Lady and finally ended her plea with the words, "Take him to yourself or else cure him." To the astonishment of everyone present, the child moved, wiggled from his mother's grasp and ran along the marble floor, completely cured. Weeping and shouting *"Evviva la Madonna"* ("Long live the Madonna"), the crowd's thanksgiving was joined to that of the grateful mother.

The pilgrimages at Easter and on September 7 and 8 are huge, with the participants often clothed in the festal attire of their individual provinces. The faithful climb the mountain while praying the Rosary and singing litanies and hymns, especially the *Salve Regina.* The road up the mountain is surrounded by scenery of exquisite beauty, but the pilgrim is only slightly distracted since the beauty he seeks is that of the Blessed Virgin as depicted in the miraculous portrait of Our Lady of Monte Vergine.

— 40 —

SANTA MARIA OF ARACOELI

Rome, Latium, Italy
Sixth Century

Conspicuous in its position atop the high altar of the Basilica of Santa Maria of Aracoeli is the celebrated portrait that is rivaled by the Madonna's portrait in St. Mary Major for the title of *Salus Populi Romani* (Salvation of the Roman People).

The image was painted on a block of beechwood and was thought to have originated in the eleventh century. Recent discoveries, however, place it as early as the sixth century and connect it with the early Byzantine monks who lived on the hill where the basilica is now located.

Its history reveals that when the people and the Roman Senate were intent on bestowing divine honors on Octavian Augustus (62 B.C.-14 A.D.), the Emperor became disturbed and fasted for three days. After this time the sky opened and, in a dazzling light, the Virgin Mary—standing atop an altar with the Child Jesus in her arms—descended, while a mysterious voice entoned the words, "This is the altar of the son of God." The Emperor prostrated on the ground, refused the honor contemplated by the people and built an altar to commemorate the vision. Around the altar was built a church that developed into the present basilica. An "Altar of the Legend of Augustus," embellished with mosaics and carvings in marble, is intact and displayed in the church.

While this legend is regarded by some as ". . .a myth to be regarded as a flower of history, the transformation of fleeting fact into eternal poetry," we find the legend included in the Universal Chronicles written in the second half of the sixth century. Without debating the legend's authenticity, it is known that a church dedicated to the Virgin Mary was already in existence there at the end of the fifth century. A group of Byzantine monks are known to have lived on the site, and in 883 there appeared the first signs of the spiritual sons of St. Benedict.

The basilica which honors this picture was built on the site of the ancient Capitoline fortress and symbolizes the triumph of Christianity over the pagan world. Built during the Benedictine period, it was called St. Mary's on the Capitol, but since the twelfth century it has been named Aracoeli (Altar of Heaven), in honor of the altar dedicated by the Emperor Augustus to the Son of God.

A papal bull assigning the church and monastery to the Franciscan friars is dated 1249. A century later, in 1348, the image was carried in procession through the streets of Rome on the occasion of a pestilence that visited the city. The short duration of the scourge was credited to the benevolence of the Mother of God.

During the same year, 1348, the stairway which leads to the basilica was constructed. It cannot be denied that the basilica was built atop a hill, since the steps number 124.

The prestige of the basilica is established by its possession of important relics in addition to the ancient portrait. The fifteenth-century statue of the Child Jesus, arrayed with innumerable golden trinkets, is kept in a chamber near the sanctuary. A chapel dedicated to the Empress St. Helena has an altar topped by a statue of the Saint. Beneath this altar is kept a twelfth-century wooden chest, elaborately carved and carefully sealed, that contains some of the Saint's relics.

The Vatican Chapter honored the miraculous image of Santa Maria of Aracoeli by crowning it in 1636, but it unfortunately lost this crown to the greed of Napoleon's troops in 1797. Its golden crown was restored in 1938. The Roman people were consecrated to the Immaculate Heart of Mary before this ancient image in 1949.

RIVAL PORTRAIT. This portrait of Our Lady, the Madonna of Aracoeli, "Salvation of the Roman People," rivals the painting also kept in Rome known as "Protectress of the Roman People." (See Chapter 38.) The image pictured above is believed to date back to early in the sixth century.

— 41 —

MADONNA DEL CARMINE

(Santa Maria della Bruna)
Naples, Campania, Italy
Thirteenth Century

When the Carmelite friars migrated from their peaceful mount in Palestine to settlements in Europe, it is believed that this portrait of the Virgin and Child was brought with them. When the religious settled in Naples during the middle of the thirteenth century, a convent and a small church was assigned to them. Here above the main altar they placed their treasured portrait of the Madonna del Carmine. From the beginning this portrait attracted the devotion of the people, and many miracles were granted. Unfortunately, this lasted only a few years before the bloom of their devotion began to fade.

This decline in attention began in 1268, when the young King Conradin of Naples was kidnapped by Charles of Anjou. A ransom was agreed upon, but when the child's mother, Queen Margaret, arrived in the harbor with a large treasure, she learned to her great distress that her child had been executed. Anxious to spend the treasure in some way upon her son, she removed his body from the small chapel that had been erected for his tomb, and had the remains interred in the church of the Carmelites. Determined to rebuild the Carmelite church on a scale of magnificence worthy of a royal mausoleum, the Queen had the church enlarged and redecorated. When this was completed, the portrait of the Mother and Child seemed too small and insignificant for the new memorial altar. On the Queen's orders the portrait was removed to a side chapel belonging to a Neapolitan family named Grignetti. Taking its place of honor was a larger picture of the Assumption.

Having lost its prestigious position, the portrait, in its side chapel, fell into comparative neglect for over 200 years. It was to be rescued in a marvelous fashion in the year 1500.

Since that year was a Jubilee Year, the devout Neapolitans decided to make a pilgrimage to Rome in order to share in the spiritual treasures that were so liberally dispensed in the Holy City. A large crucifix to be carried at the head of the procession was obtained from the church of St. Catherine. As they searched about for a picture of the Blessed Mother to take with them, someone suggested the portrait of the Madonna del Carmine.

After the Carmelite Fathers entrusted the portrait to the pilgrims, they set forth on their journey early on the morning of April 7. Along the way they intoned litanies, chanted psalms and sang hymns. After traveling only a short distance, their voices were heard by a poor, blind and deformed cripple named Thomas Saccone, who crawled to the roadside where the pilgrimage was to pass. Inflamed with a holy desire to join the procession and inspired to ask the Holy Mother for a cure, Thomas cried out for mercy and a healing as the image passed by. Immediately he felt a sudden glow penetrating his whole body. His limbs became straight, and he was infused with energy. Leaping up, Thomas thanked God and His holy Mother and joined the procession with deep fervor and gratefulness.

Occurring as it did in such a public forum, the miracle quickly became known to villagers along the way so that the sick and infirm were placed along the roads on which the procession was to pass. While the pilgrims were still many miles from Rome the miracles were reported to the Pope, who ordered an immediate inquiry. The authenticity and trustworthiness of these miracles was such that Pope Alexander VI greeted the pilgrims upon their arrival on April 13. It was he who decided that the miraculous portrait should be taken first of all to the basilica of St. Peter. After its placement, the Pope knelt and prayed before it. He incensed the portrait, blessed the people and encouraged the crowds to venerate the picture that had brought such marvels of healing. After five days of processions to other churches in the holy city, the pilgrims left for Naples on the 18th. Once again their path was bordered by crowds of sick people whose confidence in the Holy Mother was rewarded with miracles of healing.

While the procession was still a short distance from Naples, it was met by the Carmelites and the townspeople who now realized the value of the portrait that had been consigned for over 200 years to the shadows of a side chapel. When the portrait was restored to its place of honor above the main altar, another wave of healings served to further demonstrate the power of the Holy Mother—but this was to occur in a most unusual fashion.

Skeptical of the countless reports of healings, King Frederic II of Naples conceived a plan to test the power of the Heavenly Mother. His plan was so presumptuous that it must have amused Heaven. He ordered that on June 24 all the sick and infirm were to assemble before the image. Each was to bring a document, properly witnessed, giving their name, age, residence, and an exact description of their malady. On the day appointed, they surrendered their documents to the royal secretaries and assembled before the miraculous portrait. Witnessing the event was the royal family and important personages of the town. High Mass was celebrated while the choir of the royal chapel sang special hymns. At the *Gloria in Excelsis Deo,* the miraculous picture was unveiled. While the choristers swelled their voices in praise of God, the healthy members of the congregation shouted their devotion while the sick cried out in supplication. At once a ray of light descended and fell upon the face of the Madonna. It then reflected its brilliance on the assembled sick. It is reported that the instantaneous healing of each person was later authenticated against the documents they had presented to the royal secretaries.

A papal coronation of the miraculous portrait was celebrated in 1875 in the presence of Cardinals and Superiors of the Carmelite Order.

The miraculous painting of the Madonna del Carmine is also known as *Santa Maria della Bruna* because of the darkness of both Mother and Child. It is a tender portrait of the Child Jesus touching His cheek to that of His Mother. In a demonstration of His sweet love for His Mother He gently caresses her chin with His right hand, while clasping her veil with His left. Experts of the Museum of Capodimonte restored the painting in the year 1974. Now retouched and renewed, the Virgin Mother's clothing is dark blue trimmed in red. The Holy Child's garments are red, but of a different shade. The background is golden.

Situated above the main altar, the wonder-working portrait is enshrined and greatly revered in the Santuario del Carmine Maggiore in Naples. The portrait is especially honored during an annual festival held on July 16, the feastday of Our Lady of Mount Carmel.

PUT TO THE TEST: The miraculous portrait pictured above depicting Madonna del Carmine had been venerated for its holiness and healing powers for centuries before the skeptical King Frederic II of Naples conceived a plan to test the power of the Heavenly Mother. He ordered that all the sick and infirm assemble before the image with written documentation of their maladies. High Mass was celebrated and special hymns were sung, and when the miraculous picture was unveiled, a ray of light fell upon the face of the Madonna, reflecting its brilliance on the assembled sick. The instantaneous healing of each person was authenticated.

— 42 —

OUR LADY OF GRACE

Montenero-Leghorn, Tuscany, Italy
1345

Located on the western shore of Italy, Leghorn (*"Livorna"* in Italian) is a few miles south of Pisa and is a thriving seaport city of the Ligurian Sea. Just south of the city of Leghorn is Montenero, a beautiful mountainous area. Between the two is a channel where waters from melted mountain snow and that of heavy rains flow to the sea. The channel is named the Ardenza, and it was here that Our Lady of Grace was revealed.

The fortunate seer of this wonder was a poor crippled shepherd who was watching his flock beside the channel on May 15, 1345. Suddenly a spectacular light attracted his attention. Within the light was a beautiful portrait of Our Blessed Mother, which was surrounded by a number of small clouds. The whole area was wreathed in a heavenly fragrance. The poor shepherd gazed spellbound for a time until a voice urged him to lift the picture and carry it to the top of a nearby mountain of Montenero. At first he felt that his crippled condition would make the journey impossible, but reassured by the same voice, he lifted the painting and struggled with it up the mountain.

When he reached the summit the painting became unbearably heavy, so that the poor shepherd was forced to set it down. He then fell to the ground with fatigue. While he was resting he felt an unusual sensation in his crippled leg. He later said that it felt as though the leg "untied itself." Suddenly refreshed, he ran excitedly down the mountain, waving his crutch happily above his head and shouting his thankfulness to the Blessed Mother. At Leghorn he presented himself to the priests and reported all that had happened. The priests, for their part, were astounded at his cure and hurried to the mountain to examine the miraculous painting.

Because of the harsh climate atop the mountain, a shrine to protect the wondrous painting was immediately planned. This mountaintop chapel soon proved inadequate owing to the great number of people who heard of the shepherd's instantaneous cure and hurried to plead their needs before the miraculous portrait. The chapel was enlarged until today a magnificent church and a complex of buildings attest to its popularity as a major shrine dedicated to the Mother of God.

Another shrine was destined to rise at the place of the apparition beside the Ardenza where the crippled shepherd first saw the portrait. Known locally as *La Madonnina*, this small church is also known as The Chapel of the Apparition. Above its door and across the entire width of its facade is a large mosaic depicting the apparition: the shepherd, his sheep and the miraculous portrait surrounded by clouds and supported by angels.

Since the name of the shepherd is unknown, various theories concerning the origin of the picture have been advanced which give credit to one or the other painter. These claims have all been rejected, since it is said that the miraculous appearance of the portrait is beyond dispute.

The portrait of Our Lady of Grace has curious elements and is of great artistic interest. The full-length figure of the Blessed Mother is seated as though on a throne, except that her support is actually a large, fluffy, orange-colored pillow which is embellished with golden designs. Her dress is red; her mantle a rich blue. Both garments are bordered with gold. A golden halo, added later, has Gothic letters which read: *Ave Maria Mater Christi.*

The Child Jesus has a halo more ornate than His Mother's, of gold and red traced with a delicate golden design. The Child is seated on His Mother's left knee and is held gently by her left hand. He is dressed in a yellowish-orange garment which is also bordered with gold. The Child's right hand grasps the neckline of His Mother's dress; His left clutches the end of a golden cord.

Two curious features are noted. Perched on the Madonna's right wrist is a bird which seems to be chirping a song, much to the amusement of the Child. The other unusual feature is the cord held by the Child Jesus, which trails to the legs of the bird and is loosely fastened around both legs. This gentle restraint on the bird is open to several interpretations.

Also notable is the right hand of the Virgin, which seems ready to insure the balance of her Child—and yet is held as though in benediction. The prominent ears of both figures indicate, so we are told, their eagerness to listen to the appeals of the faithful.

The pilgrim who seeks the attention of both Mother and Child finds the miraculous portrait above the main altar of the church. In its marble altarpiece, the likeness of the holy pair is surrounded with a great burst of golden rays.

A number of marvelous events have testified to the Virgin's protective powers. When Leghorn was severely shaken by earthquakes on January 27, 1472, the people turned immediately to Our Lady of Montenero, and not one person perished. Today the anniversary of this favor is observed throughout the diocese with special services.

When Emperor Maximilian I in 1496 launched an expedition to destroy the seaport of Leghorn, the people again turned to Montenero. The Emperor's plans were defeated when a strong wind impeded the progress of the flotilla and confounded their plans.

St. Paul of the Cross experienced the protection of the Heavenly Mother when in 1750, while on his way to Pisa, he encountered a severe storm off Leghorn. With his ship in great danger of being capsized, he turned for help to the nearest shrine of Our Lady: Montenero. When all seemed lost, a great flash of lightning revealed that the ship was being steered by mysterious forces into the safety of still waters. The Saint considered this a miracle and lost no time in visiting the miraculous portrait to offer his gratitude. Near the altar hangs a votive plaque which shows St. Paul of the Cross kneeling in the midst of a stormy sea while praying to the holy image.

Other holy persons and illustrious pilgrims have visited the miraculous image, and many have left valuables as tokens of esteem or appreciation. Unfortunately, many of these have been stolen. Those that remained, together with other valued and curious adornments donated since the thefts, are attached to the painting on special occasions. There are so many of them that they actually clutter the holy image. On these feast days jewelled crowns are also attached to the portrait.

Our Lady of Grace was solemnly crowned on May 4, 1690 at the bidding of Pope Alexander VIII. Other Popes have also honored Our Lady of Grace. The church was raised to the rank of a minor basilica by Pope Pius VII in 1818, and in 1876 Pope Pius IX approved the feast of Our Lady of Montenero under the title of Our Lady of Grace. Pope Leo XIII authorized a Mass of Our Lady of Montenero, and in 1916 Pope Benedict XV granted it special indulgences.

The many favors granted to seamen led Pope Pius XI to designate Our Lady of Montenero as the Protectress of the Ligurian and Tyrrhenian Seas. Finally, Pope Pius XII declared Our Lady of Grace to be the principal patronness of the region of Tuscany.

One chronicler, after describing the beauty of the church, states that it is "...hopelessly overcrowded with ex-votos which smother the walls." The shrine itself declares that there is an "innumerable" quantity of ex-votos. This claim is not questioned since the shrine has a modern room, almost like a lengthy corridor, known as the Gallery of Ex-Votos, where ex-votos in paintings and medallions decorate the walls. In addition there are four smaller rooms known as the Antique Gallery wherein ex-votos actually clutter the walls. In one room especially, the ex-votos are in the form of countless paintings which depict the sea and various ships, all of which indicate the miraculous assistance of Our Lady, who exercises her power as the Patroness of the Seas.

CHAPEL OF THE ADORATION. The relatively small church pictured above is near the larger church and other buildings constructed upon the spot where, in 1345, a crippled shepherd first saw the miraculous portrait of the Blessed Mother known as Our Lady of Grace. Across the front is a large, colorful mosaic depicting the apparition.

PATRONESS OF THE SEAS. The walls of the one of the rooms in the shrine dedicated to Our Lady of Grace is covered with paintings which depict the sea and various ships, testimony to favors gained by seamen through prayers to the Blessed Virgin.

THE PORTRAIT of Our Lady of Grace shows her balancing on her knee the Child Jesus, who is apparently amused by a chirping bird perched on the Blessed Mother's arm. The prominent ears on both Mother and Child are sometimes interpreted to represent their eagerness to listen to the appeals of the faithful.

TOKENS OF GRATITUDE decorate the miraculous picture in the photograph above, visible evidence of the great veneration in which the image is held. One of the holy persons who has visited the shrine is St. Paul of the Cross.

— 43 —

OUR LADY OF BONARIA

Cagliari, Sardinia, Italy
1370

Because of its strategic location in the Mediterranean Sea, the Island of Sardinia has been the object of many conflicts. It was first occupied by the Phoenicians, next by the Carthaginians, the Romans and Vandals. In the eighth century it fell to the Saracens, until it was rescued by the Pisans and the Genoese. It came under the rule of Spain in 1323, but is now the property of Italy.

While it was still a fief of Aragon, Spain, the port of Cagliari in the southern part of the island of Sardinia proved to be invaluable as a pivot in the sea routes of the Mediterranean. The religious order known as the Mercedarian Order of Our Lady of Ransom, which was founded in Spain by St. Peter Nolasco and St. Raymond of Pennafort, saw the benefit of establishing a house of their order in Cagliari, the capitol city.

This plan was realized in 1330 by the Venerable Fra Carlo Catalan, a native of the city of Cagliari, who was given a piece of property for a house of the order. This property consisted of a low hill, close to the shore, which offered a magnificent view of the harbor.

The virtuous Fra Carlo, moved by a spirit of prophecy, foretold one day that a great storm would deliver a distinguished person to the monastery and that the arrival would be so spectacular as to move the people to a more serious practice of the virtues.

The event predicted by Fra Carlo took place on the feast of the Annunciation, 1370. Although the event seems too unusual for belief, it was investigated by a Canonical Process instituted in 1592 which was ordered by the Archiepiscopal Curia of Cagliari. The members of the Canonical Investigative Council inspected all the writings and monumental inscriptions from the time of the incident. There also exists a letter signed by the Viceroy of Sardinia which bears in its margin a note of the Royal Notary to the effect that the miracle was witnessed by a great number of people.

The miracle took place in this fashion: A ship laden with cargo was on its way from Spain to Italy when, without warning, it ran into a fierce hurricane off the Sardinian coast. To save the vessel, which was in danger of capsizing, the crew jettisoned the cargo, including a heavy chest which is today preserved in the sanctuary. The contents of the chest were unknown, but as soon as the chest touched the water the storm immediately ceased and the ship was becalmed, to the astonishment of passengers and crew. All on board were soon aware that it was the chest that had calmed the sea. Before long all the passengers and crew were watching the chest as it started to drift away. The journey of the chest was of such interest that some of the sailors got into a small boat and followed the chest as it drifted up the Gulf of Cagliari. It was washed ashore a few yards below the church of the Mercedarians.

The sailors attempted to lift the chest, but were unable to do so, even with the help of men who had watched from the shore. Finally a boy in the middle of the crowd suggested that they fetch some of the priests on the island. The chest was easily lifted by two of the priests, who carried it without difficulty into their church. There it was opened in the presence of a large number of people. Only one item was discovered within, a beautiful figure of Our Lady carrying the Christ Child.

Standing exactly five feet tall from the tip of the crown to its base, Our Lady is now dressed in a crimson tunic that is fastened at the waist with a wide belt. A mantle falls in graceful folds and is attached at the breast with a small brooch. The Madonna holds a plump, naked and beautiful Christ Child on her left arm while holding a long candle in her right hand. Attached to this candle, at the place where it is held in the hand, is a small silver model of a sailing ship. Formerly the Virgin Mother must have held a scepter, but since this is missing, she now holds the decorated candle. The Christ Child holds an orb in His left hand and looks downward at His Mother's right hand as though expressing an interest in the candle and the little ship. The Mother for her part is beautiful, but looks downward with a solemn expression.

A small ivory sailing ship was given to Our Lady in 1592. Carved all in one piece, this ivory model has a story all its own.

A pilgrim on his way to the Holy Land was forced to abandon his journey at Cagliari. He had intended to leave the ivory ship at the Holy Sepulcher as an ex-voto; instead, he offered it to Our Lady of Bonaria. It was hung from the ceiling by a string and was situated in front of Our Lady's shrine. It was soon noticed that the little ship pointed in the direction of the wind on the high seas, although the place where it dangled was away from the slightest draft. Experiments were made to test the prodigy, but it was always accurately renewed. This phenomenon proved to be of exceptional interest to the seamen.

A new altar was built in 1850. Someone at that time suggested that the ivory ship should replace the silver ship held by Our Lady. In order to affix it, a small hole had to be bored, but unfortunately, this caused the delicate ivory to crack in two. When it was repaired the ivory ship was once more hung from a cord beside the shrine of Our Lady.

These two miniature ships are not the only ones at the shrine. There are dozens of other tiny ships, as well as models and pictures which were given over a 400-year period.

Our Lady's shrine is located above and behind the high altar of the small Mercedarian church where she was first placed in 1370. Every day after Holy Mass gates are unlocked so that pilgrims may ascend by a narrow stair to the statue of Our Lady. They may pause to venerate it and then descend by the stairway on the other side.

During World War II a bomb fell nearby, but the shrine, only some 20 or 30 yards away, was unharmed.

St. Eusebius (d. 370), the martyr-bishop of Vercelli in Piedmont, was a native of Cagliari. It was perhaps through his influence that devotion to Our Lady was already well-established on the island in the fourth century. The devotion which flourished there through the years seems to have been rewarded by Our Lady with a gift of her miraculous image.

— 44 —

OUR LADY OF THE OAK

(Madonna della Quercia)
La Quercia, Latium, Italy
Early Fifteenth Century

Located some three miles from Viterbo, La Quercia was a neglected and almost barren area in the early fifteenth century, except for a vineyard owned by Mastro Battista Magnano Juzzante. Running through the vineyard was a road that led to the village of Bagnaia, and it was beside this vineyard road that thieves often waited for passing travelers. In the year 1417 Mastro Battista placed a picture of the Virgin Mary on an oak tree by the roadside at the edge of his vineyard. Perhaps he thought to discourage thieves, or his intention might have been to provide a wayside shrine for the relief and encouragement of travelers. We do not know his true intention, but we do know that the image remained on the tree, almost neglected, for 50 years. Finally it produced such wonders that a church, a monastery and a city developed around it.

An artist named Monetto had painted the image of the Virgin and Child on a flat red tile such as was then used to cover a roof. The image portrays a half figure of the Blessed Mother holding her Son between her two hands. The Virgin wears a blue veil; her Son a yellow tunic. The Child Jesus grasps the neckline of His Mother's pink robe with the left hand while holding a bird in His right. While the Child looks lovingly at His Mother, the Virgin (whose eyelids are slightly swollen) looks out toward her children who visit her shrine. The tile is chipped at the corners and at the bottom, but the wonder is that the colors are still vivid and the details sharp despite the ravages of weather during its 50-year exposure to the elements.

Travelers no doubt paused to pray before the image, much as they did beside other wayside shrines, but one visitor in particular is mentioned in the history of the portrait. He was Pier Domenico Alberti, a hermit from Siena whose hermitage was not far from the oak tree shrine. He often visited Viterbo, saying as he walked along, "Between Viterbo and Bagnaia there is a treasure."

Many people, after hearing the hermit, were driven by greed and began to dig in likely places along the road. Finding nothing, they finally asked the hermit to lead them to the place where the treasure was hidden so that they could benefit from its discovery. They argued that the hermit could not indulge in wealth, since he was bound by vows. It was then that the hermit took them to the oak tree and pointed to the treasure: the image of the Mother of God. The hermit then related what had occurred one night.

Aware that only an occasional traveler paused by the shrine, the hermit thought to remove the image to his humble dwelling, thinking that there he could spend considerable time in venerating the Holy Mother. For this reason he took the tile with him, erected it in his hermitage, prayed before it for a long time and then retired for the night. The next morning the tile was gone. It had mysteriously returned to its position on the tree.

A woman named Bartolomea also thought to venerate the image in her home and one day detached it from the tree and carried it away. That night she prayed before the image before retiring. On awakening the next morning, the tile was missing from the spot where she had placed it. Thinking that a member of the family had removed it, she searched for it throughout the house. When she could not find it, she remembered that a similar situation had happened to the hermit some years earlier. She ran to the oak tree and saw what she had already suspected—the tile had miraculously returned to its accustomed place.

Sometime later, she again took the tile home with her, but again the sacred image mysteriously returned to the tree. Bartolomea said nothing about the occurrence for fear that she might not be believed and that she might be accused of a crime for having taken the image in the first place. She held her secret until the month of May in the year 1467, when another miracle took place.

A certain horseman from Viterbo had enemies who one day took him by surprise outside the walls of Viterbo. Fleeing for his life, he made for the woods and rode furiously, with his enemies close behind him. At last overcome with fatigue, he caught sight of the large oak tree and the sacred image of Mary. He dismounted and threw himself before the image. Then, embracing the tree trunk, he placed himself under the Heavenly Mother's protection.

The enemies had him in view and saw him dismount and approach the oak tree. But when they dismounted to do him harm, they could not find him, despite a careful search among the vines and bushes. During their search the horseman had remained under the image, but he had become invisible to their eyes. Frustrated that they were unable to find him, the enemies finally departed. After giving thanks to Our Lady, the cavalier returned to Viterbo and told everyone of Our Lady's motherly protection. This miracle is depicted in a large painting found on the back wall of the sanctuary in the Basilica of La Quercia.

Once again the power of the Holy Virign was manifested when, in August of the same year, a vast area of central Italy was stricken by a plague known as the Black Death. After countless people had died, some survivors who feared that they too would die, remembered the miraculous tile. Driven by an inexplicable force, they ran to the oak tree to beg for healing from the miraculous Madonna.

An historian from Viterbo, Niccolo of the Tuccia, was present at the visitation, being then a Prior of the City of Viterbo. He recorded that 30,000 people visited the tile to invoke the protection of Our Lady. He also recorded that the plague ceased a few days later and that 40,000 arrived at the oak tree shrine to thank the Virgin Mary. Niccolo gave the names of 14 large cities represented during this act of thanksgiving, and then added that the people were from "many other neighboring towns." This miracle, together with many other miracles, was recounted throughout Italy, so that for many years La Quercia was second only to Loreto in popularity.

The donations left by these people were used in 1467 for the building of an altar and a small wooden chapel which was authorized by Pope Paul II on October 22. When donations continued to display the gratitude of the people, the chapel was enlarged into a church, which little by little developed into a magnificent structure that was consecrated by Cardinal Francesco de Gambara in 1577. A monastery, a cloister and a magnificent campanile were soon added.

Many Popes came to pray before the miraculous image, including Alexander VI, Julius II, Leo X, Clement VII, Gregory XIII, Benedict XIII, Gregory XVI, and Pius IX (who raised the church to the rank of basilica). Pope Pius V often visited the shrine and granted numerous indulgences. Pope Paul III made an annual pilgrimage to offer Holy Mass at the altar of Our Lady.

Other holy persons also offered their respects and prayers to the Lady of the Oak: St. Philip Neri, St. Charles Borromeo, St. Paul of the Cross, St. Ignatius of Loyola, St. Lucia Filippini, Bl. Rose Venerini, Colomba da Rieti, St. Hyacinth Marescotti, St. Camillus de Lellis and others.

The town that had been growing during the time the church was being built adopted the name of the oak, La Quercia. Many shops were established by craftsmen and tradesmen: stonecutters, painters, sculptors, leather workers, blacksmiths and others. Pope Paul III in 1593 had a beautiful street built which linked Viterbo to the Sanctuary. A little church was built along this street and a fountain was erected to provide refreshment for the weary pilgrim. Considering the influx of people who visited the shrine and those who decided to settle at La Quercia to be near Our Lady, we can speculate that some others, with unholy intentions, also came with them.

This can be seen by the desecration of the shrine on three occasions. Especially devastating was the theft that took place on Christmas evening in the year 1700, when thieves removed all the gold and silver from the church and stole the very jewels that adorned the holy tile—jewels that had been donated as tokens of gratitude for favors received. To overcome the sacrilege, the Madonna was crowned in 1706, having first been crowned in 1629 by the Vatican Chapter.

The church was somewhat abused by the French soldiers of Napoleon in 1800, then by the followers of Garibaldi in 1867. But the church escaped serious injury in a miraculous fashion on January 20, 1944, during World War II. After attacking the city of Viterbo, a squadron of 12 bombers made its way toward La Quercia. Arriving right above the town, the planes dropped their bombs. It seems Our Lady had her protective mantle over the town, since the only building destroyed was a nursery which was empty just then because the nuns and the small children who stayed there had gone out for a walk. The three large pieces that remain of the bombs are kept behind the altar of the Madonna.

The shrine of the Madonna della Quercia is situated above the main altar of the basilica. Rising above the table of the altar is a sculptured background of Carrara marble which is considered to be the masterpiece of sculptor Andrea Bregno, who fashioned it in 1490. Adorned with angels and saints, the sculpture has an arched opening in the center. The miraculous image of Our Lady and her Holy Child is framed within this arch. Visible directly beneath the image is what remains of the oak tree on which the tile was originally placed nearly 600 years ago.

FRAMED WITHIN the beautifully sculpted marble arch shown above, the fifteenth-century miraculous image of Our Lady of the Oak continues today to console pilgrims.

WEATHER-WORN and nearly six centuries old, the painting shown above had been placed on an oak tree bordering a road that ran through a vineyard. The miraculous nature of the image was revealed when two different persons took the painting home with them, only to find that the image mysteriously made its return to its original position on the tree.

— 45 —

OUR LADY OF GRACE

(Madonna della Grazia)
Milan, Lombardy, Italy
Fifteenth Century

This miraculous portrait of Our Lady is found in the Baroque chapel which is located at the end of the north aisle in the Church of Santa Maria della Grazia. Considered to be the most venerated image of the Blessed Mother in the region of Lombardy, it was commissioned by Lodovico Sforza, a famous Renaissance ruler of Milan and Lombardy at the end of the fifteenth century. Tradition and recorded facts relate that when frequent epidemics of the plague devastated the lands along the Po River, the epidemics stopped before they reached Milan. It was everywhere noted that this occurred after the image was enshrined.

The same Lodovico Sforza entrusted Leonardo da Vinci with the task of decorating one of the walls of the monastery that was attached to the church. The result was the famous Last Supper which is found in the refectory of the former Dominican monastery.

Both the monastery and the church suffered during the French Revolution when the refectory, with its famous painting, was used as a stall for horses. The monastery and church also suffered damage during World War II from aerial bombardment.

PLAGUE PREVENTION. Frequent epidemics of the plague ravaged Italy during the fifteenth century, but the Milan area was protected by the portrait seen above. The miraculous image is located in the church of Santa Maria Della Grazia.

— 46 —

OUR LADY OF GOOD COUNSEL

Genazzano, Latium, Italy
1467

Visitors to the Santuario Madonna del Buon Consiglio are alerted to the church's treasure by way of a Latin inscription above the main entrance which translates:

> In the year of the Incarnation, 1467, on the feast of St. Mark, at the hour of Vespers, the image of the Mother of God, which you venerate in the marble chapel of this church, appeared from on high.

The history of the portrait is closely aligned with that of Genazzano, a small town located about 30 miles southeast of Rome. As early as the fifth century, Genazzano donated a large part of its revenues to Pope Sixtus III (432-440) for the restoration of the Roman basilica of Our Lady of the Snows, which is also known as St. Mary Major. As a gesture of appreciation, the portion of Genazzano that had contributed the most was endowed with a piece of property on which was eventually built a church dedicated to Our Lady of Good Counsel. In 1356 the church was entrusted to the care of the Augustinians who had been in Genazzano since 1278.

With the passage of time the church became decrepit and ill-kempt. During the year of the miracle, 1467, a local widow named Petruccia de Geneo felt herself called to spend her meager funds on needed repairs. Her friends and neighbors thought her plan presumptuous and declined to support her praiseworthy endeavor. After the widow had spent all her money on repairs, work had to be halted due to the increased cost of both materials and labor. When the people saw this, they scoffed and ridiculed her, laughingly calling the unfinished work "Petruccia's Folly." Her efforts were nevertheless rewarded in a marvelous manner.

On St. Mark's Day, April 25, 1467, the entire population of the city was participating in the yearly festival in honor of the Saint. At about 4 o'clock in the afternoon the merrymakers began to hear the strains of exquisite music. Then, while they silently gazed at the sky for the source of the singing, they saw, in an otherwise clear sky, a mysterious cloud that descended until it obliterated an unfinished wall of the church. Before the thousands of awe-struck revelers, the cloud parted and dissipated, revealing a portrait of Our Lady and the Christ Child. This was resting on the top of the unfinished wall that was only a few feet high. It is said that the church bells of the city rang of their own accord, attracting people from outlying areas who hurried to investigate the untimely ringing. Petruccia, who had been praying in another area, rushed to the scene when she heard the bells and fell down in tears before the miraculous image.

The provincial of the Augustinian order, Ambrogio da Cori, recorded that:

> All of Italy came to visit the blessed image; cities and towns came in pilgrimage. Many wonders occurred, many favors were granted. . .The very beautiful image of Mary appeared on the wall without human intervention.

So great was the number of healings that a notary was appointed to make a register of the more important cases. This record, which is still preserved, notes that from April 27 until August 14, 1467, 171 miracles occurred.

Because of these miracles and the attention given the image, an investigation was initiated by Pope Paul II. Two bishops were sent as commissioners to examine all that pertained to the portrait and the miracles. These were Bishop Gaucer of Gap in the Dauphiny and Nicholas de Crucibus, Bishop of Lesina, a Dalmation diocese. The details of their findings are said to be preserved.

The miraculous portrait was first called the Madonna of Paradise from the manner of its arrival, but this title was soon changed as a result of information secured from two refugees who arrived in Genazzano from Albania, a country that was then being terrorized by the Turks. The men testified before the papal delegation that they had seen the very same image in a church in the Albanian town of Scutari only a few weeks before. The commission of inquiry established that a portrait of the Madonna that had been venerated in the church at Scutari was indeed missing. Where the picture previously had been located, there remained an empty space the exact size of the portrait. With the origin of the picture confirmed, the portrait was renamed Our Lady of Good Counsel after the church where it had been miraculously relocated. Even today, when the Albanians visit the portrait, they refer to it as "their" Madonna and call her Our Lady of Scutari or the Madonna of the Albanians. They maintain to the present day that the portrait spontaneously left their church when Albania was invaded by the Turks.

Measuring approximately 15-1/2 inches by 17-1/2 inches, the painting is a fresco executed on a thin layer of plaster or porcelain not much thicker than paper. One writer describes it as a fresco painted on a material resembling egg shell. It has been established that the removal and transport of such a fragile material from the wall of the Scutari Church could not have been successfully accomplished by human hands.

Although it is behind glass that is secured in a golden, gem-encrusted frame, neither the frame, the glass nor anything else actually touches the portrait. It is said to rest on its base, unsupported in any other way so that a thread can be passed in front of the portrait, around the top, and behind it. The portrait actually defies gravity and has done so for over 500 years.

The portrait is a charming and delicate rendition of the Madonna and Child. Their cheeks touch, and the Child's right arm is around His Mother's neck. His left hand holds the neckline of her dress. The tunic of the Child is red; the Mother's tunic is green. The ivory-colored mantle that covers the head and shoulders of the Madonna is also draped on the shoulder of the Child. Mary's chestnut hair is said to be arranged in a Roman style. The aureole of the Madonna is golden while that of the Child is red, in the same shade as His tunic. The Madonna seems half-turned toward her Son and half-turned toward the faithful in what is suggested as a double interest. A curiosity exists in that the face of the Madonna appears sad when viewed from an angle, but when one stands before her she appears to smile.

Church authorities have noted that the cheeks of the Virgin seem to change shade from red to pink, as if to awaken the emotions of the viewer. It is a recognized fact that the color of the portrait acquires various tones in different periods of the year, even though it is protected by glass against humidity and the effects of the environment.

Pope Urban VIII, who at first disbelieved the legend regarding the portrait's miraculous appearance, was finally so convinced of the truth and reality of the Genazzano tradition that he made a pilgrimage there in 1630 to pray for the cessation of a plague that was then scourging Italy.

In 1777 the Sacred Congregation of Rites added its recognition of the legend by approving a Proper Office commemorating the history of the shrine. This was to be used by the Augustinian Order, whose members faithfully served the church and the miraculous image of the Madonna.

The widow, who humbly set in motion the restoration of the church that was to occasion wonders and miracles, lived to see not only the church completely restored, but she also saw the erection of a splendid monastery. After her death she was given the great honor of being buried in the chapel of the Madonna.

The shrine of Our Lady has been visited by countless pilgrims throughout the centuries, with the church and the portrait remaining secure for 500 years. During World War II, however, a bomb fell on the basilica, crashed through the roof and exploded on the floor of the sanctuary, doing terrible damage. The main altar was literally obliterated. The altar of the Madonna, only a few yards away, remained intact—and the fragile image remained miraculously unaffected.

PETRUCCIA'S FOLLY. A poor widow named Petruccia de Geneo was ridiculed in 1467 for spending her meager money on repairs to the basilica of Our Lady of the Snows (St. Mary Major). Scorn turned to wonder when the portrait above miraculously appeared from a mysterious cloud that descended onto one of the church's unfinished walls. Records state that 171 miracles of healing have taken place as pilgrims have come from all parts of Italy to visit the blessed image.

DEFYING GRAVITY. The miraculous image of Our Lady of Good Counsel is pictured in its holy surroundings, the altar of the Santuario Madonna del Buon Consiglio in Italy. For over 500 years, the portrait has been positioned so that it rests on its base, unsupported in any other way. Executed on a thin layer of plaster-like material, the image could not possibly have been removed by human hands from the church wall where it first appeared.

— 47 —

MADONNA OF THE TEARS

(Madonna delle Lagrime)
Trevi, Umbria, Italy
1485

The painting of religious portraits on the outside walls of homes, especially those of stucco, was customary during the fifteenth century as it is today in many European cities. In Trevi this artwork was assigned to students of a nearby school conducted by Pietro Vannucci, a master painter.

The modest home of Diotallevi d'Antonio Santilli, located on the road between Spoleto and Trevi, was similarly decorated when a portrait of the Madonna was painted on the outside wall on October 4, 1483, the feastday of St. Francis of Assisi.

The miracle of the tears took place two years later, on August 5, 1485. On that day a passerby noticed moisture on the wall and discovered that it originated from the eyes of the Madonna. These were no ordinary tears, but those of blood. One can only imagine the excitement this event created. Neighbors flocked to the house to see the prodigious occurrence of bloody tears falling from the eyes of a Madonna painted on a stucco wall. News spread quickly to people in nearby villages; they likewise hurried to the house to see the miracle of the bloody tears. Disbelievers and skeptics came and were convinced. Many of these doubters and others received spiritual graces and miracles of healing.

A notary of Trevi was alerted and he, too, rushed to the scene. He described the prodigy in writing and recounted all the miracles that he witnessed. His document, as well as other official records that were made by the municipal authorities, can be found in the archives of the City of Trevi.

Also preserved is another contemporary account of the miracle and the origin of the shrine. This was written by Fr. Francesco Mugnoni, an Olivetan, who resided a short distance from the house of the miracle.

The reason for the tears was a matter of great concern and speculation until it was finally decided that they represented the sympathy of the Madonna for the pestilence which for years had tormented the territory around the city of Trevi.

On August 21, 1485, one week after the start of the miracle, the first Holy Mass was offered in the small chapel that had been hastily erected near the wall of the Madonna. Permission was soon received for a daily Mass to be offered in this little improvised chapel. Because space was inadequate from the start, plans were soon made to replace the chapel with a magnificent building worthy of the Mother of God. Monies were collected, and work was begun on March 27, 1487.

The community entrusted the building to Antonio Marchisi of Settignano. The magnificent portal and stonework were designed and executed by John di Giampietro of Venice. The interior was beautified with the paintings of Pietro Vannucci, who conducted the school of art in Trevi. The sculptures are credited to Giovanni of Carrara.

When the church was completed, the portion of the wall that was covered with the portrait of the Madonna was cut from the wall of the house and removed to the church, where it now receives the admiration and attention of the Madonna's devotees.

Soon a house for religious was built near the church. First entrusted to the Olivetans, it was later occupied in turn by various religious orders.

Always regarded as the patroness of the city, the Madonna of the Tears was officially designated as such on July 26, 1846.

The shrine has been enriched with many ex-votos which signify the numerous benefits conferred upon the people of the city and visiting pilgrims through the intercession of the Madonna of the Tears. One of the most outstanding of these tributes is a relief in silver depicting the City of Terni, which was presented in thanksgiving for the deliverance of that city from the plague.

The feast of the Madonna is celebrated on the Sunday after Easter.

TEARS OF BLOOD issued in 1485 from the eyes of an image of the Madonna painted on the wall of a modest home. The wall covered with the miraculous portrait was later cut from the house and removed to the church constructed by Our Lady's devotees.

MADONNA OF THE TEARS. Above is a close-up view of the miraculous portrait of the Blessed Virgin Mary and her divine Son which expressed supernatural sympathy for those suffering from the plague.
(Right.) The church of the Madonna of the Tears, located in Trevi, Italy.

FLANKED BY ANGELS, the image of Our Lady and the Child Jesus has been enriched with many ex-votos conferred by grateful pilgrims.

— 48 —

MADONNA DELLA GUARDIA

Genoa, Liguria, Italy
1490

Italians affectionately call Genoa "The Superb," not only because of its architectural magnificence, but also because it is regarded as the greatest seaport in Italy. Its location between the Gulf of Genoa and the sharp slopes of the Apennines produces a beautiful setting. It is likewise an interesting city, with its medieval churches and ornate marble palaces of Renaissance times. To the historian the city is known as the boyhood home of Christopher Columbus; to the hagiographer it is renowned as the home of St. Catherine of Genoa, whose incorrupt body lies in the church dedicated to her memory.

Just north of the city, atop a tall mountain known as Monte Figogna, are numerous church buildings and the shrine of Madonna della Guardia. On the mountain, in the year 1490, a shepherd named Benedict Pareto was grazing his flock when his attention was drawn to a brilliance which surrounded a woman holding a child on her arm. As the lady approached him, Benedict Pareto felt compelled to kneel.

After the Lady assured him that he should not be afraid, she introduced herself: "I am the Queen of Heaven and have come to you with my Divine Son for this reason: that through you there may be built a church on this spot, to be dedicated in my name."

After Benedict protested that he had no money with which to build a church, the Lady calmed his confusion with the words, "Trust me, Benedict. The money will not be lacking; only your own good will is needed. With my aid all will be easy."

After the Lady departed and Benedict recovered from the sweetness and beauty of the apparition, he experienced a great urgency to report the event to his parish priest and began to run excitedly down the mountain path. On the way he met his wife, who was performing her daily chore of bringing his noonday meal. After learning of the apparition she blamed the event on the heat of the sun and began to ridicule him, warning him not to mention the apparition to anyone.

The next day Benedict went about his work as usual, but when he climbed a fig tree looking for fruit he fell and broke a number of bones. According to the history of the shrine, he was carried home, received the Last Sacraments and felt an overwhelming regret for having failed to share Our Lady's request with those in a position to provide what she wanted. As soon as he experienced this grief, Our Lady once more appeared to him and again requested a shrine at the place of her first appearance. Benedict Pareto is said to have been instantaneously cured.

When his neighbors, who knew the severity of his injuries, heard of his cure, they listened to his story and contributed to a fund authorized by the parish priest for the building of a small oratory on Monte Figogna.

Benedict Pareto's apparitions are said to be beyond dispute. Among the many reasons given is the certainty that the oratory was in use in 1507. By the year 1530 it had been replaced by a larger chapel which was in the care of the Masseria, a group of lay people who served as guardians of the shrine. This group included many members of the Pareto family, including two of Benedict's sons.

Following the Council of Trent, the Bishop of Navarra visited the sanctuary in 1582 to enforce regulations formulated by the Council. After learning all he could about the history of the shrine, he formally rendered his approval and looked favorably upon an artistic relief located on the high altar which depicts the scene of the first apparition.

Another inquiry was conducted on May 27, 1604 by the Archdiocese of Genoa. Notarized by Andrea Mongiardino, the full dossier is preserved in the Genoa State Archives. Once again the history was approved. Permission for the publication of miracles was given, and devotion to the Madonna della Guardia was authorized.

One of the most outstanding miracles attributed to the Madonna took place in 1625 when Charles Emmanuel, Duke of Savoy, marched on Genoa with an army of 14,000 men. Fearing the worst, a saintly Capuchin laybrother, Fra Tomaso da Trebbiano, exhorted the people to have confidence in the Madonna della Guardia and to offer prayers at her shrine. They immediately complied and fervently petitioned the Madonna for protection. The next day, when the Duke attacked with his soldiers, he was roundly defeated by a small band of peasants who had been sent into battle with the blessing of their parish priest. The victory was everywhere accepted as a miracle of the Madonna della Guardia.

As a symbol of gratitude for this victory, a marble statue which depicts Our Lady as she appeared to Benedict Pareto was placed in a chapel on the mountain which marks the actual site of the first apparition.

Another statue, regarded as the original, is found in the wayside chapel of St. Pantaleon on the mountainside. In addition to these two statues, there is still another, which is the one most sought after by pilgrims. This is found above the high altar in the church on Monte Figogna. It was this statue that was given a formal coronation in 1894 as commanded by Pope Leo XIII, and it is this wooden representation of Our Lady that was credited with numerous miracles which are exemplified by thousands of ex-votos which decorate the walls of the church. Always illuminated, the shrine of Our Lady is reached by stairs on either side of the sanctuary. Pilgrims ascend to pray at the feet of the Madonna and to admire the many jewelled tokens donated by grateful recipients of her favors.

The shrine has been recognized by many Popes throughout the years who have granted special indulgences to the members of the associations and confraternities organized in honor of Our Lady. These Popes include Clement XIV, Pius VI, and Pius XII.

One of Genoa's native sons who had a particular devotion to Madonna della Guardia was elevated to the Chair of St. Peter as Pope Benedict XV.

— 49 —

OUR MOTHER OF PERPETUAL HELP

Rome, Latium, Italy
1495

The documented history of this wonder-working icon begins in the year 1495, when the image was highly reverenced in a church on the island of Crete. At that time it was already considered of great age, with some writers placing its origin at either the thirteenth or fourteenth century. It was afforded every measure of devotion because of the number of favors granted to those who prayed before it.

Most writers agree that the painting came into the possession of a wealthy merchant in the late fifteenth century. Some writers claim that the merchant stole the painting. One claims that he obtained it through honest means, while still another reports that the merchant and others fled Crete with the painting when Crete was threatened by the Turks. Whatever the reason, it is known that the merchant carried the painting with him to Rome, and that he became seriously ill. Before he died he requested that the painting be placed in a church as soon as possible. Contrary to his request, the painting remained in private hands until 1499, when it was escorted in a solemn procession to the Church of St. Matthew on the Esquiline Hill. A tablet which hung for many years beside the portrait told of this procession and noted that, "In this manner, the picture of the most glorious Virgin Mary was enshrined in the church of St. Matthew the Apostle, on the 27th of March, 1499, in the seventh year of the Pontificate of our most Holy Father and Lord in Christ, the Lord Pope Alexander VI."

Our Blessed Lady seemed eager to make known the virtues of her image by way of a miracle that was performed during this procession. A man who had been paralyzed for some time was immediately cured when the image passed in procession near the house in which he lay.

For the next 300 years the image hung in St. Matthew's church, where innumerable favors were granted to the people who prayed in its chapel. With members of the Augustinian Order as its guardian, the image was known by various names: Our Lady of St. Matthew, Our Lady of Never-failing Help, Our Lady of Ever-enduring Succor, and finally, Our Mother of Perpetual Help.

In 1798 Marshal Berthier, under orders from Napoleon Bonaparte, invaded Rome and forced Pope Pius VI into exile in France. One writer reports that Berthier's successor, Massena, destroyed almost 30 churches, including the Church of St. Matthew. Thankfully the priests had had time to remove the miracle-working image of Our Lady. For several years it found refuge in the Church of St. Eusebius. It was then placed in the Church of St. Mary of Posterula, where it was hung in a side chapel and was all but forgotten for almost 40 years. The image had at least one devoted admirer, an elderly lay-brother, Augustine Orsini, who was particularly devoted to it and often told its history to whomever would listen. One of those who was keenly interested was a young altar boy, Michael Marchi.

When Pope Pius IX in 1853 requested that the Redemptorists establish a house in Rome, they chose a property on the Via Merula, which was located between the Lateran and St. Mary Major. While the church was being built, one of the priests, Fr. Edward Schwindenhammer, mentioned that he had found a reference which revealed that their new church was being erected adjacent to the site where once had stood a church which enshrined a miraculous image of the Blessed Mother. One of the priests replied that he knew the history of the image and the exact location where it could be found. The priest was the former altar boy, Michael Marchi. On learning of the portrait's whereabouts, the Redemptorist General, Fr. Nicholas Mauron, gained a private audience with the Pope. The Holy Father listened to his plan to have the portrait returned to the site where it had been enthroned for almost three centuries. Pope Pius IX then recalled that as a small boy he had once prayed before the miraculous image while it was in the Church of St. Matthew.

In compliance with the wishes of the Pope, the image was given by the Augustinians to the Redemptorist Church of St. Alphonsus. Our Lady's triumphal return to her chosen site took place on April 26, 1866. During this translation two noteworthy cures took place: one was the healing of a boy who was seriously ill with meningitis; the other miracle involved a young girl who received the use of her paralyzed leg.

Never has a portrait of the Mother of God been given as much papal attention as this image received from Pope Pius IX. Not only did he pray before the image as a boy, but he also approved its translation. His approbation of the image was acknowledged on June 23, 1867, when the icon was crowned by the Vatican Chapter. The ceremony was conducted by the Latin Patriarch of Constantinople, whose presiding was indicative of the icon's popularity among Eastern Rite Christians.

Pope Pius IX also fixed the feast of the image for the Sunday before the feast of the Nativity of St. John the Baptist, and by a decree dated May, 1876, he approved a special office and Mass for the Congregation of the Most Holy Redeemer (the Redemptorists). When confraternities were erected throughout Europe, the Pope combined them in 1876 into one Archconfraternity of Our Lady of Perpetual Help and St. Alphonsus. The Pope's name was the first in the register of the archconfraternity, and he was among the first to visit the portrait in its new home.

Devotion to this wonder-working icon spread rapidly to the United States. In 1870, when the Redemptorists were asked to establish a mission church in Roxbury, not far from Boston, they dedicated their small church to the Mother of Perpetual Help. They received from Rome the first copy of the portrait, which had been touched to the original. Since then more than 2,300 copies that had been similarly touched to the original have been sent to other houses of the Order.

The United States also takes credit for inaugurating the Tuesday night devotions to the Mother of Perpetual Help. Devotions that first took place at St. Alphonsus (Rock) Church in St. Louis, Missouri, on Tuesday nights, were quickly adopted by churches of the Order and by other churches, and took the form of a perpetual novena, a practice that is now observed worldwide.

A study of the portrait is necessary to understand its historical and artistic qualities. Although its origin is uncertain, it is estimated that the portrait was painted sometime during the thirteenth or fourteenth centuries. It is painted in a flat style characteristic of icons and has a primitive quality. All the letters are Greek. The initials beside the Mother's crown identify her as "Mother of God." Those beside the child, "ICXC," are abbreviations meaning "Jesus Christ." The smaller letters identify the angel on the left as "St. Michael the Archangel." He is depicted holding the lance and spear with the vessel of vinegar and gall of Christ's Passion. The Angel on the right is identified as "St. Gabriel the Archangel." He holds the cross and the nails.

When this portrait was painted, halos were not commonly depicted. For this reason the artist rounded the head and veil of the Mother to indicated her holiness. The golden halos and crowns were added much later. The Madonna in this portrait is out of proportion to the size of her Son since it was Mary whom the artist wished to emphasize.

The charms of the portrait are many, from the naivete of the artist, who wished to make certain the identity of each subject was known, to the sandal that dangles from the foot of the Child. The expression of the Child Jesus is haunting as He grips the hand of His Mother while gazing sideward at the instruments of torture held by the Angels. Above all, the expression of the Madonna evokes a sadness on the part of the viewer. With her head gently touching that of her Son, and while surrounded with the instruments of her Son's future sufferings, she seems to gaze plaintively—as though seeking compassion from those who look upon her.

Countless miracles attributed to the image extend from the time of its documented history in 1495 through the years until the present day. These seem to give ample testimony and proof of the portrait's favor with the Mother of God.

The miraculous portrait is still enthroned on an altar in the Church of St. Alphonsus in Rome. The ruins of the Church of St. Matthew, where the image was reverenced for almost 300 years, are found on the grounds of the Redemptorist monastery.

COUNTLESS MIRACLES are attributed to Our Mother of Perpetual Help, pictured above upon the altar in the Church of St. Alphonsus in Rome.

MIRACULOUS CURES have issued for several hundred years from the image of Our Mother of Perpetual Help, pictured above. Never has a portrait of the Mother of God received as much papal attention as this image elicited from Pope Pius IX. In the painting, the Madonna's head gently touches that of her Son; she seems to gaze plaintively at those who look upon her. (See Page 197 for further explanation of the portrait's elements.)

— 50 —

SANTA MARIA DE LIBERIS

(Saint Mary of the Liberated)
Cascia, Umbria, Italy
Sixteenth Century

A painting known locally for its wonder-working assistance during plagues is found in the city made famous in the Catholic world by St. Rita. Named *Santa Maria de Liberis,* it is first mentioned in the will of Francesco Benenati, which is dated 1520. In the will Francesco made provision for a large candle to be given periodically to the chapel on the hill dedicated to Our Lady.

This first chapel dedicated to Santa Maria de Liberis was constructed on the property of the Augustinians during the sixteenth century as the result of the terrible plagues that afflicted the area during the years 1505 to 1525. This was one of many shrines named "*Ad Pestem*" which were especially built for the convenience of those who frequently prayed for a healthy resistance to the disease and for the recovery of those already afflicted.

In the church of Our Lady is an altarpiece painted by Padre Agabiti (1470-1540) which was completed in the fifteenth century. The Madonna is depicted as the main point of interest, but also depicted are St. Rita as well as Bl. Simon Fidati, Bl. Giovanni da Chiavano and Bl. Ugolino, all natives of Cascia and all members of the Augustinian Order.

The portrait of the Madonna and Child became extremely popular among the people and was visited by large crowds. In 1571, when the governor of Cascia, Sebastiano Rutiloni, visited the chapel he was greatly impressed by the number of pilgrims and arranged for an extra door to be made for the easy movement of Our Lady's many visitors.

The Augustinians and representatives of the community of Cascia met in 1579 to arrange for the construction of a larger church to better accommodate the people. When the work was begun authorization was received from Roberto Menardi, vicar of the Archdiocese of Spoleto, to transfer the altarpiece containing the holy image to the church of St. Augustine until the new church was completed. The altarpiece with its miraculous image was later returned to its original site.

Pope Gregory XIII, in recognition of the miraculous image, granted the extraordinary privilege that every Mass offered before the altar of Santa Maria de Liberis by a member of the Augustinian Order would release a great number of souls from Purgatory.

The Archbishop of Spoleto, Mons. Lorenzo Castrucci, gave permission in 1630 for a procession to take place on the eve of the Assumption. The holy image was then carried through the streets of Cascia in petition for the city's protection when a new and terrible epidemic threatened the territory.

The miraculous image was later transported to the Church of St. Rita when repairs were needed at the Church of Santa Maria de Liberis. The church of Our Lady eventually fell into ruins, and only the walls indicate the place where countless people pilgrimaged to seek the Madonna's powerful protection.

— 51 —

OUR LADY OF CAPOCROCE

Frascati, Latium, Italy
1527

Rome is only 15 miles from Frascati, which is on the northwestern slopes of the Alban Hills. The town is known for its healthy climate, its beautiful scenery, its white wine and its handsome villas which date from the sixteenth and seventeenth centuries. But the child of Mary is intent on more than these interests, since the first notable structure one sees when entering Frascati by the highway from Rome is the church which harbors the miraculous image of Our Lady of Capocroce.

The fresco of Our Lady and Child decorated a small area of the wall surrounding a vineyard which was situated a short distance from the present location of the church. The portrait was there for many years, encouraging the passerby to pause for a prayer or a hasty ejaculation. Its history was unknown, nor was there any special reason for inquiring about it, until the year 1527, when the town was jolted by an event that raised the portrait from a casual interest to one of celebrity.

The occasion was introduced when a struggle existed between Emperor Charles V and the French monarch, Francis I. In an effort to bring about peace, Pope Clement VII made the tragic decision to ally himself with the French. The Emperor became furious. Encouraged by the imperialists, the people plotted trouble for the Pope. In addition, the imperial army in northern Italy, infuriated by lack of pay and longing for plunder, marched south. They burst into Rome, sacked the Vatican and desecrated St. Peter's. One source reports that 18,000 infantrymen, 3,500 horsemen and an undetermined number of others were bent on wreck and ruin. Mainly Spaniards, Italians and Germans, they entered Rome and raised fury for two months. Pope Clement VII sought refuge in Castel Sant'Angelo, where he heard the agonizing screams of his poor flock.

Finally the plunderers looked toward the cities close to Rome, and in particular toward the beautiful city of Frascati. Because the city provided a panoramic view of the countryside, the approach of the ruffians was visible when they were still some distance away. While the officials of the city planned a desperate resistance, terrified women gathered their children and made for the churches to plead for protection from the Mother of God.

The fierce yells of the soldiers and ruffians sounded over the mountainside as they approached the city, but as they reached the portrait of the Virgin and Child on the wall, those in the front ranks halted abruptly. The lips of the painted Virgin opened, and coming forth was a voice of irresistible power and authority. The shouts of the advancing thieves quieted as the voice commanded: *"Indietro, fanti! Questa Terra e mia!"* "Back, soldiers! This land is mine!" Not one man dared to disobey the command. Turning around in utter confusion, they rushed from Frascati toward Rome in a state of shock and terror.

Following the prodigy of 1527, extraordinary veneration was accorded the miraculous image. At the entrance to the town a chapel was built for its enshrinement, and it was here that an incalculable number of spiritual and temporal favors were dispensed by Our Lady of Capocroce. This first chapel was a plain, modest one which soon grew too small to accommodate the increasing numbers of Mary's clients. A Eucharistic miracle, occurring in 1611, led to the building of the present, more beautiful church.

In that year, a pious and wealthy Roman priest, Jerome de Rossi-Cavoletti, was offering the Holy Sacrifice at the altar of the miraculous painting. Just after the Consecration of the Sacred Host, It left his hand and disappeared. The priest looked for It with great diligence. He questioned the servers, but could not find It. He examined his conscience, but he could not discover guilt or irreverence. Finally he turned his eyes on Our Lady's picture and prayed for relief of his distress. As he gazed he heard an interior voice sweetly chiding him: "Jerome, you are rich in the goods of the world. Look at this humble chapel. Is it worthy of the Queen of Heaven?" He immediately vowed to replace the humble structure with a large and beautiful church in honor of Our Lady of Capocroce. After he had made the vow, the Sacred Host reappeared upon the altar. The priest accomplished his vow and even added a large rectory for the clergy who would be charged with the care of Our Lady's shrine. The new church was consecrated in 1613.

A century later, in the year 1713, another prodigy attested to the Blessed Virgin's special care for her children of Frascati. While a great many people were assembled in the church kneeling before the miraculous picture, suddenly the silence was broken by a cry of warning issuing from the venerated picture. "Flee! Flee!" Since the voice was insistent and full of authority, the people immediately obeyed and rushed from the church. As soon as the last person crossed the threshold, the whole roof fell in. Our Lady's warning had preserved all of her clients from serious injury and many from certain death.

It was during the same year, on October 28, 1713 that the image of Mother and Child was afforded a signal honor when the Vatican's Chapter of St. Peter visited the shrine. Amid the enthusiastic rejoicing of the people, magnificent golden crowns were placed atop the heads of Mother and Child.

Still another prodigy is recorded of this miraculous portrait. Italy, it seems, as well as the rest of Europe, was to experience at the end of the eighteenth century frightfully evil days of sacrilege, impiety, and violations of human and divine laws. As though to assure her devoted children of her continued protection against these evils, Our Lady of Capocroce, in the presence of an immense throng of spectators, alternately opened and closed her eyes. It has been conjectured that by closing her eyes Our Lady meant to shut out the spectacle of the world's iniquity; by opening her eyes she bestowed a sign of her loving compassion and protection on her faithful children gathered around her shrine. This miracle occurred in 1796.

Throughout the centuries Our Lady's protection for the City of Frascati has proven the truth of her words, "This land is mine." To the Blessed Virgin alone do the citizens attribute their preservation from the earthquakes that have troubled neighboring districts. Their immunity from the terrible scourge of cholera is also credited to Our Lady of Capocroce. At the turn of the century, when Albano, only four or five miles from Frascati, as well as the surrounding territories lay prostrate under this disease, only one town was absolutely untouched by the epidemic—Frascati.

Once again the Chapter of St. Peter gave evidence of their devotion to the Virgin of Capocroce when in 1863 they placed two angels in gilded copper above the miraculous picture. The angels held over the head of Our Lady a large crown denoting her heavenly queenship and her reign over the hearts of the people.

The horrors of war unfortunately touched the land of Mary when on September 8, 1943 an aerial bombardment damaged most of Frascati. The church of Our Lady remained undamaged, but on January 29, 1944 another bombardment reduced the church to a heap of ruins. The portrait had thankfully been removed for safekeeping. After the war, the building of another church was begun. Finally, on May 2, 1954, when the building was completed, the beloved painting of the Madonna and Child was restored to the place of honor where it has been venerated ever since by the people of Frascati. They are privileged, indeed, in the possession of the miraculous image of Our Lady of Capocroce.

"**BACK, SOLDIERS!** This land is mine." Citizens of the city of Frascati, Italy were saved from plunderers in 1527 when the fresco of Our Lady and Child (pictured above) ordered them to go back. The renegades retreated in utter confusion.
(Right.) The desire to venerate Our Lady of Capocroce brings the faithful to the church pictured here, which was built in 1954. Another church had been located on the same spot, but was ruined by bombing during World War II.
(Page 208.) PRESERVATION FROM EARTHQUAKES and cholera has been attributed by Frascati residents to Our Lady of Capocroce.

VIA DI
S. ROCCO

— 52 —

OUR LADY OF MONTALLEGRO

Rapallo, Liguria, Italy
1557

Meaning "Happy Mount," this shrine of Our Lady is situated on a mountain overlooking the resort town of Rapallo and its gulf. Approximately 15 miles southeast of the great port city of Genoa, Rapallo's gulf also opens into the Ligurian Sea. But unlike the many shrines of Our Lady located on the shores of Italy which are consecrated to the Queen of the Sea, that of Montallegro has a different dedication.

The shrine owes its origin to one, Giovanni Chichizola, who was making his way home through the mountains behind Rapallo on July 2, 1557. Coming upon a cool, shady spot, he paused for his noonday rest. The sound of a sweet voice calling his name startled him into alertness. There, standing close beside him, was a beautiful lady surrounded by an intense light. With a reassuring smile the vision addressed Giovanni with the words: "Do not fear, Giovanni. I am Mary, the Mother of God. Go and tell the people of Rapallo of my appearance." The vision then directed his attention to a small picture propped against one of the rocks where he had been resting.

"Tell the people that this picture was brought here from Greece by angels. I leave it here in token of my love for them. Fast on Saturday." The vision then disappeared as if carried away in a cloud.

Giovanni was filled with happiness as he looked upon the painting, which depicted the Blessed Virgin at her death and Assumption. His first reaction was to pick up the picture and carry it to Rapallo, but he found it impossible to remove the picture from the rock. Giovanni then called to other peasants who were nearby to come see his treasure. While he told them his wondrous story, they discovered that a trickle of water was starting to flow from the same rock against which the picture stood—a place which until that moment had been perfectly dry.

Giovanni left the blessed picture in the charge of his friends while he ran to the city. The priests to whom he told his story were skeptical, but because of Giovanni's excitement they reluctantly followed him to the place of the apparition. There they saw the picture which none of the peasants could lift, and the spring which had mysteriously appeared.

One of the priests raised the portrait without difficulty and carried it in procession to the parish church, where it was carefully locked up pending further investigation.

The next day the painting was missing from its locked enclosure, but was found on the mountainside at the place where Giovanni had originally found it. This could mean but one thing: Our Lady wanted her image to remain on the mountain, and that it should be protected by a chapel.

The people at once began to plan for a chapel and the more permanent church that would come later. A herculean task confronted them, since hundreds of tons of solid rock had to be removed to provide a level place for construction, and building materials had to be dragged up the mountain to a height of some 1,900 feet. Nevertheless, a year after Our Lady's apparition, the church was ready for consecration.

Painted on wood, the miraculous picture measures 6-1/2 by 5 inches, with the upper part slightly rounded. Our Lady is shown lying on a bier which is covered with a red pall and surrounded by a number of small flowers. Our Lady is clothed in a brown robe. Her feet are bare, and her head is surrounded by a halo. Behind the bier is a figure representing the Blessed Trinity. A large aureole represents the Beatific Glory into which Mary was admitted. St. Peter, vested in Greek episcopal vestments, stands at Our Lady's head, while at her feet a group of saints linger in a mournful attitude. Archangels Michael and Gabriel are also depicted.

In the basilica which replaced the original chapel, the celebrated picture is enshrined in a pavilion behind the high altar.

Preserved in the State Archives of Genoa are important documents relating to the inquiry made in 1558. Given before Msgr. Falceta, the Archbishop's Vicar-General, the documents pertain to the questions asked of Giovanni Chichizola and the observations of Msgr. Falceta.

Records also reveal that Our Lady's intervention brought about deliverance from the plague in 1579, 1590 and 1630. On these and other occasions, the people saw to it that Our Lady was thanked by means of votive plaques, hundreds of which still hang in the basilica. The ex-votos became so numerous that galleries were built to accommodate them. These additions to the sanctuary soon proved inadequate, since the plaques multiplied to such an extent that even the cloister and sacristy were covered with them.

The Sacred Congregation of Rites, in 1739, granted the plea of the city of Rapallo to name Our Lady of Montallegro as its patroness. Once again the shrine found acceptance with the Vatican when Our Lady of Montallegro was crowned in solemn ceremonies on July 7, 1767 by the Bishop of Ajaccio, Corsica.

And what became of the rock upon which the miraculous picture rested at the time of the apparition? It is found almost concealed at one side of the altar. And what of the water from the miraculous spring? A white marble trough with a faucet is provided for those who want to drink the water or collect it in bottles. Just above the faucet is a small door through which the rock is visible. Also seen here is the small cavity which is the actual source of the water.

— 53 —

OUR LADY OF SORROWS

Rho, Lombardy, Italy
1583

One year before his death, St. Charles Borromeo (d. 1584) heard a strange story that originated at Rho, a small city about 15 miles from Milan. Since the Saint was the Cardinal-Archbishop of Milan, he felt an obligation to send representatives to investigate the alleged miracle that had occurred in his archdiocese. This miracle involved a portrait of the Sorrowful Mother depicted in a seated position, with the crucified Body of Our Lord reclining on her lap. The portrait was already regarded as miraculous when St. Charles visited and prayed before it in the year 1570. The group that investigated learned the following facts regarding the more recent wonder involving the portrait.

Two peasant farmers, Gerolamo De Ferri and Alessandro Ghioldi, had stopped in the church at Rho on April 24, 1583 to pray before the ancient image of Our Lady of Sorrows, known affectionately as *"l'Addolorato"* ("The Griever"). Being familiar with the image, they were surprised to see that the eyes of the Madonna were swollen, as though the image had been crying. Thinking that they might be mistaken at the change, they drew near the portrait. At that moment tears of blood started to drip from the eyes. Deeply overwhelmed at seeing this, and grieved at the anguish of the Sorrowful Mother, they nevertheless alerted others to witness the miraculous event. It is not recorded in historical accounts just who used a handkerchief to wipe some of the tears from the portrait, but it is known that he suspected that the blood might be drops of paint that had melted in the heat. But when the linen was removed, it was stained with blood; moreover, all who examined the linen handkerchief affirmed that the tears were unmistakably composed of blood.

It is not known exactly how long the bloody tears flowed from the eyes of the Madonna, but it is certain that the church soon became crowded with excited parishioners who witnessed the event and quickly spread the news to Milan and surrounding villages. News of the event soon reached St. Charles Borromeo, who dispatched his representatives.

Carlo Bascape, the man in charge of the episcopal investigation, spent three weeks at Rho studying the event, while a notary took depositions from 40 witnesses. Bascape then reported back to the saintly Archbishop, and he, in turn, sent the depositions to Rome.

Rome was swift in replying, and St. Charles Borromeo lost no time in journeying to Rho. There he announced to the delighted people that the miracle was officially declared to be authentic. The Saint then knelt in prayer before the portrait. When he stood up, he turned to those who filled the overcrowded church and promised that he would build a noble basilica worthy of the Mother of God and her miraculous portrait. The following year, on March 4, 1584, St. Charles honored his pledge by laying the first stone for this basilica. Eight months later the people were grief-stricken at the death of their saintly Archbishop.

On the third centennial anniversary of St. Charles Borromeo's death, a large bronze statue depicting the Saint was erected in the square before the basilica. Dressed in episcopal robes, with a mitre on its head and a crozier in its hand, the statue stands facing the basilica which the Saint had arranged to be built in honor of the Mother of God.

The basilica is decorated with splendid carvings and priceless paintings. There are several large side chapels, one being dedicated to St. Charles Borromeo. Elsewhere, the Saint is depicted in adoration before the miraculous portrait.

The custodians of this magnificent basilica are the Oblate Missionaries of Rho, also known as the *Missionari dell'Addolorata,* the Missionaries of the Griever. Their founder was the Reverend Giorgio Maria Martinelli (1655-1727), who was declared Venerable by Pope Paul VI.

Kept in the sacristy of the basilica is a tabernacle-like safe. Reverently kept there is a large silver reliquary. In the center of this, visible behind a crystal oval, is the linen handkerchief which is stained with the bloody tears of the Madonna.

The miraculous portrait has, of course, the place of honor in this beautiful basilica, being situated above the main altar. Here the Madonna's many visitors recall not only the miracle, but also the reason for the bloody tears of the grieving Mother.

The yearly anniversary of the miracle (April 24) is observed with impressive ceremonies and much celebrating by the people of Rho, while the feastday of the Sorrowful Mother (September 15) is commemorated more solemnly.

PRECIOUS TEARS. A linen handkerchief stained with the tears of blood shed by the Madonna, Our Lady of Sorrows, in 1583 is kept today on the altar of the magnificent basilica of Rho, pictured on page 215.

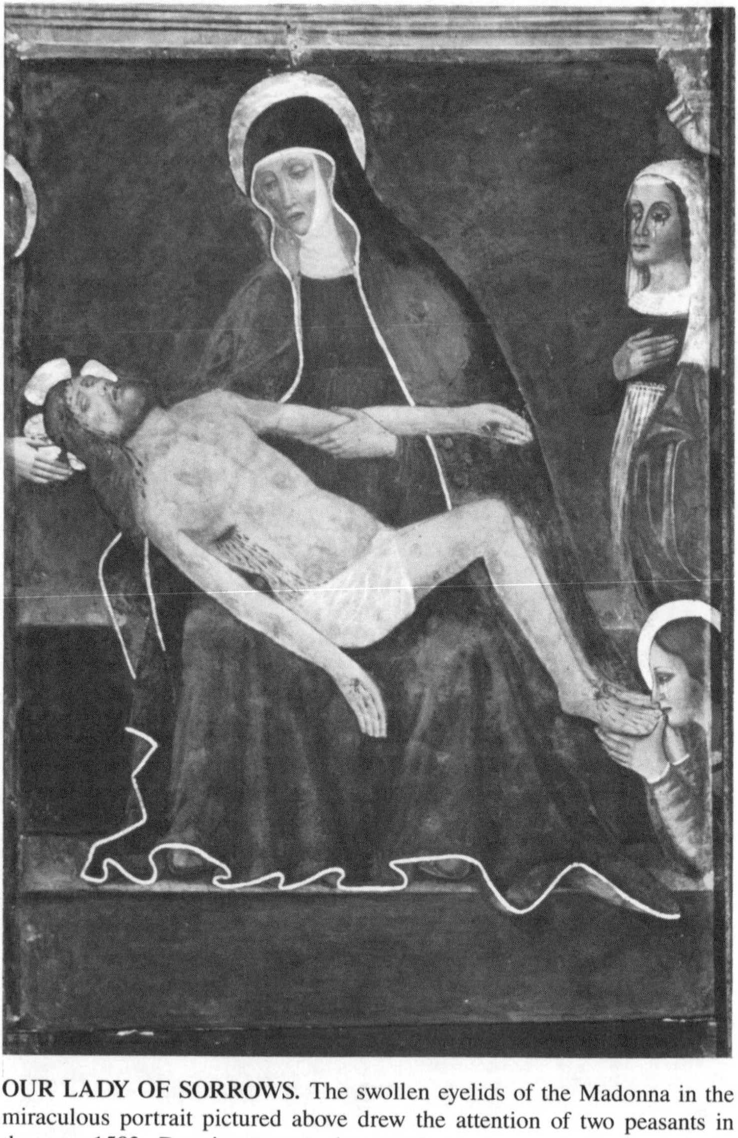

OUR LADY OF SORROWS. The swollen eyelids of the Madonna in the miraculous portrait pictured above drew the attention of two peasants in the year 1583. Drawing nearer, the men became overwhelmed when the Sorrowful Mother's eyes shed tears of blood.

PRECIOUS RELIC. The linen handkerchief which is stained with the bloody tears of Our Lady of Sorrows is kept in the silver reliquary pictured above. The people of Rho observe the miraculous event on April 24 each year with celebrations and impressive ceremonies. A more solemn commemoration is held annually on September 15, the feastday of the Sorrowful Mother.

— 54 —

OUR LADY OF CONFIDENCE

Todi, Umbria, Italy
Seventeenth Century

When the great Italian painter Carlo Maratta (1625-1713) was only 25 years old, his work was so well received that he was brought to Rome by Cardinal Albrizio and the governor of his home district of Ancona. After his introduction to Pope Alexander VII he received many commissions, which brought him great recognition throughout Europe. He was eventually knighted by Pope Clement XI in the year 1704 and was made court painter by Louis XIV during the same year.

Known for his portraits, especially those of the pontiffs, he was also the portrait painter of the Blessed Virgin Mary. His religious pictures are said to be "marked by a certain strength and nobility, coupled with a gracious harmony." We do know that one of his portraits of the Blessed Virgin has become widely known, not so much for its artistic merit as for its benefit to the soul.

This portrait of Our Lady of Confidence came into the possession of Sister Chiara Isabella Fornari (1697-1744), a young nun of the Poor Clare Convent at Todi, Italy. It is believed that the artist himself presented the portrait to the young nun.

Because of this picture, Sister Chiara Isabella and the sisters of her community were drawn to a deep and intimate relationship with Our Lady, who showed her approval through unusual cures and conversions.

Our Lady once indicated her liking for the portrait by appearing to Sister Chiara Isabella. During this apparition the Blessed Virgin promised the nun that she would grant a particular tenderness and devotion toward herself to everyone who venerates her image in the picture of Our Lady of Confidence. Combined with the aspiration, "My Mother, my confidence," this devotion has proven especially efficacious.

In compliance with a number of requests, copies of the portrait have been made. One of these was placed in the small students' chapel of St. Mary's Seminary at the Lateran Basilica in Rome. During World War I, over 100 seminarians who were forced into the armed services of Italy returned home safely. This favor was attributed to Our Lady of Confidence, and it was this favor which prompted the seminarians to crown both Mother and Child with diadems of gold and jewels.

While a student at the seminary, Pope John XXIII became a devotee of Our Lady of Confidence. He frequently visited the portrait and honored it still more by offering his first Mass in its presence. Afterward, he continued his visits to Our Lady of Confidence and offered Mass there, especially on the second Sunday in Lent, the feastday of Our Lady of Confidence.

Venerated in Italy for over 200 years, the picture is a simple one of Our Lady holding the Child Jesus. The Babe is especially attractive as He points a finger toward His Mother, the source of graces and confidence.

SALVE FOR THE SOUL. This portrait of the Blessed Virgin Mary, painted by Carlo Maratta (1625-1713), is widely known for its benefit to the soul. In an apparition to a nun in the late 1600's, Our Lady promised a particular tenderness toward herself to all who venerate her image, known as Our Lady of Confidence.

— 55 —

ADVOCATE OF SINNERS

(Santa Maria della Grotta)
Cava de'Tirreni, Campania, Italy
1654

A certain place in Italy was said to be infested by evil spirits when Don Federigo was passing by in the year 1654. Whether it was a product of his imagination or not, Don Federigo believed he encountered some of these spirits at the mouth of one of the natural caves which are common in the area. With the caves located on the side of a hill, the narrow path in front of the caves is a dangerous one, since on the other side is a precipice which drops some 120 feet into a valley. Located four miles northwest of Salerno, it is because of these many caves that *Cava de'Tirreni* derived its name.

Before Don Federigo passed that way again, he decided to place the spirit-infested cavern under the protection of the Madonna. Since the cost of a statue or painting was beyond his means, he fastened inside the entrance of the cave a little print which represented the Blessed Virgin and the Child Jesus. Above the head of the Virgin was a dove and hovering angels; on her right side was St. Paul, the first hermit, while St. Onofrius was on her left. The title of the picture was "Advocate of Sinners." Formerly known as the *Grotta degli Sportiglioni* (Grotto of the Bats), in time the cave adopted the name of the picture and came to be known simply as *Avvocatella* (Advocate).

A truly astounding fact is that this simple print remained for a period of 48 years where Don Federigo had placed it, being uninjured all that time by time or moisture.

At the end of the 48 years, in the year 1702, Fra Angiolo Maria di Majuri, a lay brother of one of the Franciscan monasteries in Cava, prepared a little niche in the cave for the painting of a fresco which would duplicate the little picture. At the same time he encouraged the neighbors to burn a lamp before it, and since he maintained a great devotion to the Mother of God, he frequently prophesied that the cave, which was once the haunt of evil spirits, would become the place where the Mother of God would dispense the goodness of her liberal hands.

In time, one of the priests of the monastery arranged for an altar to be placed before the painting. He also arranged for a lamp to be kept burning and for litanies and other devotional exercises to be frequently recited there.

One of the most outstanding miracles attributed to the Advocate of Sinners, which was also duly witnessed, occurred on May 19, 1703. A poor man named Antonio Casaburi, with his six-year-old son, was leading his donkey along the path by the cave. The donkey, which was laden with corn, stepped too close to the edge of the road and fell over, carrying the boy with him. During the 120-foot fall, the father cried loudly to *Santa Maria dell'Avvocata.* Then, in the company of three others who had witnessed the accident, Antonio climbed down to the spot, only to find the animal quietly grazing while the boy busily worked at collecting the scattered grain. Both were completely unharmed.

When the miracle was reported by the father and the three witnesses, multitudes of people hastened to the grotto. The crowds became so large that travel on the narrow path became extremely dangerous. For this reason ecclesiastical authorities decided to enlarge the area and erect a spacious chapel. With the monies so liberally donated by the pilgrims, the work on the new chapel progressed quickly.

When the new chapel was almost completed, a new bishop was appointed for the area. It was this bishop who meant to learn for himself the truth of the many miracles and favors reported at the shrine. Theologians were gathered for this investigation, and the shrine was boarded up to prevent access to the miraculous image.

Fourteen days later, when the miracles were accepted by theologians, the barricades were removed and the *Avvocata* was once more available to receive the pleas of the faithful.

The first Mass celebrated in the new church took place on September 7, 1704. The celebrant was a priest of 70 years who had himself received a miracle at the hands of the Blessed Virgin.

A short distance from the shrine is the Benedictine abbey of *La Trinita della Cava,* which is of great historical interest. Founded in 1011, the abbey has an eleventh-century crypt, a twelfth-century marble pulpit, and fourteenth- and fifteenth-century frescoes.

The cathedral is likewise a place of great interest, but the place most dear to the hearts of residents and neighbors alike is the shrine of *Santa Maria della Grotta,* where the miraculous image awaits the many visitors who turn with confidence to their advocate before the throne of God.

— 56 —

ST. MARY OF THE SEVEN VEILS

Foggia, Puglia, Italy
1732

St. Alphonsus was 36 years old and had been a priest for only six years when, in the year 1732, he experienced the first of a long list of miracles and visions. It was also the year in which he founded the Congregation of the Most Holy Redeemer, which is also known as the Redemptorist Order.

The Saint's success at preaching missions was well known to the Bishop of Foggia, who invited St. Alphonsus in February of 1732 to preach a novena in honor of Our Lady. St. Alphonsus was eager to perform this service, having heard that in Foggia there was a miraculous picture of Our Lady which the year before had become animated to reveal a beautiful young girl of thirteen or fourteen years of age.

When not preaching the novena or hearing confessions, St. Alphonsus spent his time before this miraculous portrait, sometimes spending hours in deep contemplation. One day as he approached the altar on which the portrait was hung, he fell into an ecstasy that lasted over an hour. On this occasion the Blessed Mother appeared to him. Later, the Saint commissioned a painting which depicted the Blessed Mother as he had seen her.

When he returned to Naples after the novena, the news of the apparitions was already well known, and this sparked an outcry of criticism by his superiors, friends, religious organizations and well-known prelates. Plans were formulated to obstruct the Saint's intention to form the new Congregation of the Most Holy Redeemer. The most bitter of all the criticisms was that voiced by his great-uncle, Canon Gizzio, who declared that Alphonsus was "...not guided by God, but by the fanciful dreams of a nun." Alphonsus replied simply, "I beg to say that I am not led by visions, but by the Gospel." Another time, in the presence of noted churchmen, Gizzio bitterly remarked that Alphonsus was "brainless, a worshipper of himself."

Forty-five years later, in 1777, Alphonsus, then a bishop, traveled to Foggia for the solemn crowning of the miraculous image. It was then, with the integrity and authority of his episcopal office supporting him, that he effectively silenced his critics by giving this official statement concerning the apparition:

> Alphonsus Maria de' Liguori, bishop of St. Agatha of the Goths and rector major of the Congregation of the Most Holy Redeemer: To all and each who shall see or read these our letters, we make it known and testify in the word of truth with an oath, that in the year seventeen hundred and thirty two, in the city of Foggia. . .several times and on different days we saw the face of St. Mary the Virgin. . .Her appearance was that of a young girl of thirteen or fourteen years, and she moved to the right and left. . .not as if in a picture, but as though sculptured, or of flesh and blood. And at the same time that she was seen by us, she was equally perceived by all the people gathered to hear the sermon.

The Redemptorist Order every year commemorates this vision as a special feast of the Blessed Virgin of Foggia.

The miraculous image that became animated is kept in the cathedral of Foggia. The oval painting is found in a tall rectangular frame. The backing of the frame, known as the Sacred Table of the Virgin of the Seven Veils, is ornamented with a monogram of the Madonna and flowering vines. When not on exhibit, the image is kept in an ornamental silver shrine which is in the form of a tabernacle. Angels support the golden crown presented by St. Alphonsus in 1777.

The cathedral is proud to identify the portrait as "St. Mary of the Seven Veils, Protectress of Foggia, which appeared to St. Alphonsus de' Liguori."

A MIRACULOUS IMAGE of the Blessed Mother as she appeared to St. Alphonsus in 1732 is kept in the frame pictured at right. The backing of the frame is known as the Sacred Table of the Virgin of the Seven Veils.

— 57 —

MOTHER OF DIVINE LOVE

Rome, Latium, Italy
1740

The ruins of a castle first known as *Castello del Leone,* now known as the *Castel di Leva,* is found on the *Via Ardeatina* just outside Rome. Although the castle is in ruins, a part of the wall that surrounded the castle still stands. In the western part of the wall is a gate tower, the wall and tower being made of tufa bricks. Over the archway of this tower hung for almost two centuries a portrait which was given the name, "Mother of Divine Love."

The artist is unknown, as is the date of its origin, although the image is thought to have been painted in the fourteenth century. What is known for a certainty is that the portrait was given in 1570 by Monsignor Cosimo Giustini to a charitable organization known as the Conservatory of St. Caterina della Rosa. For reasons which are unknown, the image was positioned on the tower, where it was left unprotected against the ravages of the weather.

The image was venerated only in the wintertime, when shepherds visited the lonely image to recite a Rosary while their sheep grazed nearby. Except for the shepherds, the place was solitary and neglected when the miracle of 1740 took place.

In the spring of that year a pilgrim was walking on the *Via Appia* toward Rome. Thinking that he could shorten his journey, he took another route and then lost his way. When he saw farm buildings in the distance, he headed in that direction in the hope that someone could tell him the shortest route to Rome. Suddenly, to his horror, a pack of growling sheepdogs appeared from behind a cluster of bushes and bolted toward him. Panic-stricken, the pilgrim started to run while the dogs drew nearer and nearer. He was at the point of being attacked when he saw the image of Our Lady on the nearby tower. Instinctively he shouted, "Madonna, help me!"

Immediately, an invisible force seemed to hold the dogs back, and in another moment they were calmed. They soon turned and went peacefully away, leaving the pilgrim safe. The Madonna had, for the first time, intervened at *Castel di Leva.* This was to be the first of a long sequence of graces and favors.

The chronicles of the time report that the pilgrim told as many people as he could about the miracle. Soon these people and others journeyed to the Madonna at *Castel di Leva* to beg for her heavenly intervention. Devotion to the Virgin Mary spread so quickly and gained such popularity that an historian of the time wrote, "Night and day pilgrims come continuously and receive much grace."

During the time that the miracles and graces were being distributed by heaven, Pope Clement XII died and Rome was awaiting the election of his successor. On August 17, Pope Benedetto XIV was elected. One of his first acts was to send Friar Giovanni Antonio Guadagni, a Discalced Carmelite, to investigate the activities at *Castel di Leva.*

The Friar's report was so favorable that a decision was made to remove the image from the tower for enshrinement in the nearby church of *Santa Maria ad Magos,* which was located in a place named Falcognane. This church was subordinate to the Basilica of St. John Lateran.

Because of the spiritual value of the portrait, there arose a dispute between St. John Lateran and the Monastery of St. Caterina della Rosa over its ownership. The Roman Rota Court was eventually called upon to settle the matter. On March 8, 1743 the court decided in favor of the monastery and ordered that the image should be brought back to *Castel di Leva* as soon as a church could be built for its enshrinement.

When the church was at last completed, the miraculous image was transferred from Falcognane on Easter Monday, April 19, 1745. The records of the church reveal the names of the priests who officiated at the ceremony and the names of the confraternities which took part. In the procession were two bands of musicians, as well as a detachment of Papal Grenadiers.

The solemn consecration of the church took place during the Holy Year of 1750. On March 31 of that year Cardinal Rezzonico dedicated the church and the high altar to Our Lady of Divine Love. Cardinal Rezzonico was the Bishop of Padua and was known as an exceptionally holy man. When Pope Benedict XIV died, Cardinal Rezzonico was elected Pope, with the name Clement XIII.

A problem soon arose concerning the need for a priest to spiritually assist the people and to organize the spiritual life of the shrine. Since a priest could not be found who was willing to stay permanently at the shrine, a Parochial Vicar was assigned in 1802. This priest did not live at *Castel de Leva,* but only stayed there during the pilgrimage season, which traditionally started on Easter Monday and ended in July. During the rest of the year the shrine was practically abandoned, although the Madonna continued to attract pilgrims to her altar.

Because the shrine was frequently empty, it attracted thieves who robbed it of its valuables on June 2, 1930. It was then that Don Umberto Terenzi, a member of the Roman clergy, was made Rector of the shrine. After enjoying the beauty of Rome and its ceaseless activity, he found his new assignment to be lonely and uninteresting. Finally, he decided to appeal to his superiors for a transfer. He was on his way to Rome with this intention in mind when his car overturned at a bend in the road just below the shrine. Invoking the name of Our Lady, he escaped without injury. Accepting this as an indication from Our Lady that he ought to remain at the shrine, he returned to the little church and remained there for the rest of his life. A small sign indicating the place of Don Umberto's accident is located on the right side of the last bend of the road leading to the shrine.

During the first year of Don Umberto's pastorate, the shrine grew in importance. A regular bus service was established between Rome and the shrine, a white statue of Mary Immaculate was erected on top of the church and a new bell was blessed and installed. In the next few years the shrine was designated the parish church of the area. A school was established and an order named the Daughters of the Madonna del Divino Amore was organized. Eventually a railway station was built, as were a post office and a police station.

The importance of the shrine was noted in 1935 when 3,000 soldiers recommended their safety to the Madonna before leaving for the Ethiopian war. Each of the 3,000 warriors returned safely, in spite of the dangers they had encountered.

During World War II the sacred image was transferred to Rome for safety. This move was prudent, since the area around the Madonna's shrine became the target of endless bombings during the winter of 1943-1944. This took place because the name *"Castel di Leva"* appeared on military maps; it is said that the Germans mistakenly believed that the name indicated a military installation. But in spite of all the bombings in the immediate area, the shrine remained safe and untouched.

The first refuge of the Madonna's image during the war years was in the Roman basilica of San Lorenzo in Lucina. When the war drew nearer to the Holy City, Pope Pius XII asked that the Pentecost Novena and the following Octave services be celebrated with special solemnity to implore the *Madonna del Divino Amore* for the safety of Rome. When this refuge proved too small to accommodate the crowds who prayed there for the end of the war, the image was transferred to the Basilica of Sant'Ignazio.

While General Alexander's tanks were attacking the enemy in the streets of Rome on June 4, 1944, Sant'Ignazio Church was crowded with people who dedicated themselves to the *Madonna del Divino Amore* by "a solemn vow of the salvation of Rome." They promised to lead a Christian life, to embellish the shrine at *Castel di Leva* and to create a charity and religious organization there in her honor. It is reported that with unexpected suddenness, the German resistance collapsed and the Allied troops were able to liberate the city that very evening, June 4, at 7:15 p.m.

The people were filled with wonder at the abrupt end of the fighting, and Winston Churchill himself wrote in *From Teheran to Rome* (page 225) that the taking of Rome occurred in an unexpected manner.

The Roman Observer in its June 12 and 13, 1944 issues wrote:

> Tens of thousands of people gathered [in Sant'Ignazio] to pray for the Pope, for Italy, for Rome and for peace; processions of devout and disciplined pilgrims—many of them barefooted, family groups, institutions and school children came endlessly to the main entrance to give thanks to the Virgin Mary, to kiss the painting as the custom had always been, to feel reassured in order to face the difficulties of life.

Among the pilgrims on June 11, 1944 was Pope Pius XII. With Don Umberto Terenzi at his side, the Pope spoke to the crowd gathered in Sant'Ignazio and offered the Madonna his gratitude for the safe deliverance of Rome.

On the feast of the Sacred Heart, June 14, Cardinal Machetti

Salvaggiani ordered a special thanksgiving service to be celebrated in every parish church of the city during which the "Vows of Rome" were to be renewed.

Amid a great crowd of people, the holy image of the *Madonna del Divino Amore* was carried back to *Castel di Leva* in a grand procession on September 12, 1944.

The vow of Rome was kept. The people applied themselves to Christian living, they embellished the shrine and, with Don Umberto's assistance, a charity organization was established which aids many local interests, as well as foreign missions.

Before his death in 1974, Don Umberto founded the *Madonna del Divino Amore's* Daughters Congregation and the Oblate Sons of the *Madonna del Divino Amore* Congregation. Both congregations have as their motherhouse the shrine of the Madonna. When Cardinal Ugo Poletti received the vows of both congregations in 1975, he called the shrine "a spiritual treasure."

The shrine was likewise praised by Pope John Paul II, who visited *Castel di Leva* on May 1, 1979. After praying before the image of the Madonna, the Pope said, "I also wished to come in pilgrimage to this blessed place, to kneel at the feet of the miraculous image, represented enthroned with the Child Jesus in her arms and the dove over her as the symbol of the Holy Spirit."

Along many of the streets of Rome are found niches that enclose reproductions of the miraculous painting. These exemplify the devotion which the people have for the holy image—a devotion manifested by the Roman people on every Saturday night from Easter to October. During these "nightly pilgrimages," the people gather at midnight at the *Axum Obelish* and walk in procession along the *Via Appia Antica* and the *Via Ardeatina* toward the shrine, where they participate in the celebration of an early Mass.

This weather-worn and somewhat faded painting, which was visited only occasionally by shepherds, now accepts the tributes of countless pilgrims who implore Heaven for graces and blessings through the intercession of the Mother of Divine Love.

IMAGE IN AN ARCHWAY. In one of the many miracles of the portrait of Our Lady known as "Mother of Divine Love," the Blessed Mother answered the plea for help of a pilgrim who was being attacked by sheepdogs.

MOVED TO A CHURCH in 1745, the miraculous image, "Mother of Divine Love" has been carefully guarded for centuries. During World War II the sacred portrait was moved to Rome, where thousands of people prayed before the image.

— 58 —

REGINA SANCTORUM OMNIUM

(Queen of All Saints)
Ancona, Marches, Italy
1796

Overlooking the Adriatic Sea on the western coast of central Italy is Mount Guasco, which proudly serves as the foundation for the Cathedral of Ancona. Dedicated to St. Cyriacus, the first bishop of the area, the cathedral is the home of a miraculous painting which became famous in 1796.

On June 25 of that year the eyes of the Madonna, depicted in the painting, were discovered to be filled with tears. This was interpreted as the Virgin's sadness at the calamities that were being inflicted upon the Church by Napoleon. After causing untold hardships for Pope Pius VI, Napoleonic troops overtook Rome in 1797. Although aged and sick, the Pope was forcibly taken prisoner and carried over the Alps to France, where he died in exile in 1799. His statue, in a kneeling position, was placed in the Basilica of St. Peter at the entrance of the crypt.

The miraculous picture of the Holy Virgin was solemnly crowned by Pope Pius VII on May 13, 1814, under the title *Regina Sanctorum Omnium.*

— 59 —

MATER ADMIRABILIS

(Mother Most Admirable)
Rome, Latium, Italy
1844

St. Francis of Paula, General of the Order of Minims, founded in Rome during the fifteenth century a monastery known as *Trinita dei Monti*. Much later, in the year 1828, when the Minims decided to abandon the property, Pope Leo XII expressed the desire that it should be offered to the religious of the Sacred Heart. The *Trinita dei Monti* then became a school and a center of devotion to the Sacred Heart.

A young French girl, Pauline Perdrau, a student at the school who later became a religious of the order, petitioned Mother de Coriolis, the superior of the house, for permission to paint a fresco of Our Lady in a niche of the corridor that surrounded the cloister. The Superior was hesitant. Although Pauline was known to be talented, the girl knew nothing of fresco painting or the techniques required for preparing the wall to successfully accept the application of paint. Despite her misgivings, the Superior granted Pauline's request. The year was 1844.

Pauline is known to have worked six to seven hours a day on the painting. Thirteen hours were spent on the face alone. When the painting was completed, the wet paint was thought to be too vivid and was left to dry under a protective drape. When the curtain was removed some days later, the paint appeared in the lovely shades that are admired today. Pauline considered it a miracle and a special sign of Our Lady's answer to her constant prayers that the face of the Blessed Virgin appeared more comely than Pauline's meager talent could have produced.

The fresco depicts the Virgin in a most charming fashion. It is this author's opinion that it is among the most beautiful of the miraculous images of the Virgin Mary. Pictured amid marbled walls and floor and with a colorful landscape at her back, the Virgin is seated with a distaff on her left and a lily in a vase on her right. A full spindle is in her right hand that rests casually in her lap. A footstool supports one foot, while a basket of books is positioned near the other. Brown hair is seen beneath the white veil that is also draped around her shoulders. Her mantle is white, while her dress is a lovely shade of pink. Twelve golden stars encircle her head, which is modestly inclined.

Because of the marbled surroundings, some thought the portrait depicted the Virgin of the Temple, but the symbol of purity by the Virgin's side dictated the title of the image: The Madonna of the Lily. The name was changed on October 20, 1846, two years after its completion, when Pope Pius IX visited the school. Standing before the fresco the Pontiff exclaimed, *"Mater Admirabilis,"* or "Mother Most Admirable," the title that has endured ever since.

During the same year of the Pope's visit, the first of many miracles credited to the portrait took place when the Reverend Blampain, a missionary of the Congregation of the Holy Heart of Mary, recovered the power of speech which he had completely lost during an illness. Because of this miracle and many others that followed, Holy Mass was celebrated before the image according to the permission given by Pope Pius IX. Indulgences were granted to those who prayed there, and the Feast of *Mater Admirabilis* was authorized for October 20 in commemoration of the Pope's visit.

Among the many pilgrims who have visited the shrine of *Mater Admirabilis* have been several Saints: St. Madeleine Sophie Barat, St. John Bosco, St. Therese of Lisieux, St. Pius X, St. Vincent Pallotti and Bl. Aloysius of Orione.

Copies of this miraculous fresco are kept in the Convents of the Sacred Heart. One of these copies was favored by Josefa Menendez, a member of the Society of the Sacred Heart of Jesus (d. 1923), who received numerous visions of Our Lord and whose cause for beatification has been introduced. Josefa Menendez tells that on August 10, 1920, "I went into the oratory of *Mater Admirabilis* to ask our Blessed Lady to help me to console her Son. When I reached the chapel (at Les Feuillants), I suddenly found myself in the presence of Jesus. . .He drew me to His Heart and let me hear harmonies such as I had never heard here below. . ."

Others, too, have benefited spiritually after imploring the help of the Admirable Mother. Graces have been generously distributed, especially those that affect the interior life. These have helped many to realize the foibles of this life and the value of life eternal.

The miraculous image is found in Rome at the *Instituto S. Cuore,* which is located in the Piazza Trinita dei Monti.

MATER ADMIRABILIS, or "Admirable Mother," is the name bestowed upon this portrait of Our Lady by Pope Pius IX in 1846. Prior to that time it had been known as "The Madonna of the Lily," the lily in the picture symbolizing Our Lady's purity.

— 60 —

MOTHER OF MERCY

Rimini, Emilia, Italy
1850

Located on the shore of the Adriatic Sea, Rimini is both an ancient city rich in history and a modern seaside resort. It is also a fine port for the fishermen whose catches supply the picturesque fish market in the Piazza Cavour. Rimini's history dates to the Roman occupation, when it became a stronghold at the junction of the Via Emilia and the Via Flaminia. Traces of the Roman occupation remain in the Bridge of Tiberius (which, an inscription reveals, was completed in A.D. 21) and in the Arch of Augustus (built in 27 B.C.).

Little known outside this historic and interesting city is a miraculous painting of Our Lady entitled "Mother of Mercy" which is enshrined in the Church of St. Clare. The portrait was kept in the church for many years as an artistic embellishment until it attracted citywide attention for its reputation for the miraculous. The event that thrust it to the forefront took place in the year 1850, when the eyes of the painting were seen to repeatedly open and close. One can only imagine the great stir this phenomenon caused among the people. Clergymen were called to witness while crowds filled the church to satisfy their curiosity. The movements of the eyes did not occur only that day, but actually continued at intervals for several months, giving everyone an opportunity to study and examine the marvel at all times of the day and from every angle. Everyone who doubted was convinced.

While the phenomenon was beyond dispute, it still seemed practical to conduct at least one experiment for the record. So it was that a test was devised. The witnesses included four laymen of sterling reputation and three holy and learned priests. After obtaining permission, they gathered in the church on the night of December 9, 1850. To quote one author who explained it:

MIRACULOUS FRESCO. Painted in 1844 by a young French girl who later became a religious, the beautiful rendering of Our Lady shown above has been copied and revered by many who have been benefited spiritually, including Sister Josefa Menendez.

Preceding page: Mater Admirabilis. See page 234.
Above: Our Lady of the Pillar. See page 401.
Opposite: Our Lady of Good Counsel. See page 179.

238-3

Above: Our Lady Star of the Sea. See page 357.
Opposite: Our Lady of the Dew. See page 422.

Above: The Weeping Madonna of Syracuse. See page 249.
Opposite: Our Lady of the Pillar. See page 401.

Above: Mother of Divine Love. See page 226.
Opposite: Our Lady of Pompeii. See page 241.

238-9

Above: Our Lady of Altötting. See page 115.
Opposite: Madonna of the Tears. See page 185.

Above: Our Lady of Einsiedeln. See page 426.
Opposite: Our Mother of Perpetual Help. See page 194.

238-13

Above: Our Lady of Prompt Succor. See page 433.
Opposite: Our Lady of Kazan. See page 397.

Above: Our Lady of Guadalupe (Spain). See page 407.
Opposite: Our Lady of Akita. See page 257.

Above: Our Lady of the Rosary. See page 367.
Opposite: Santa Maria of Aracoeli. See page 154.

238-18

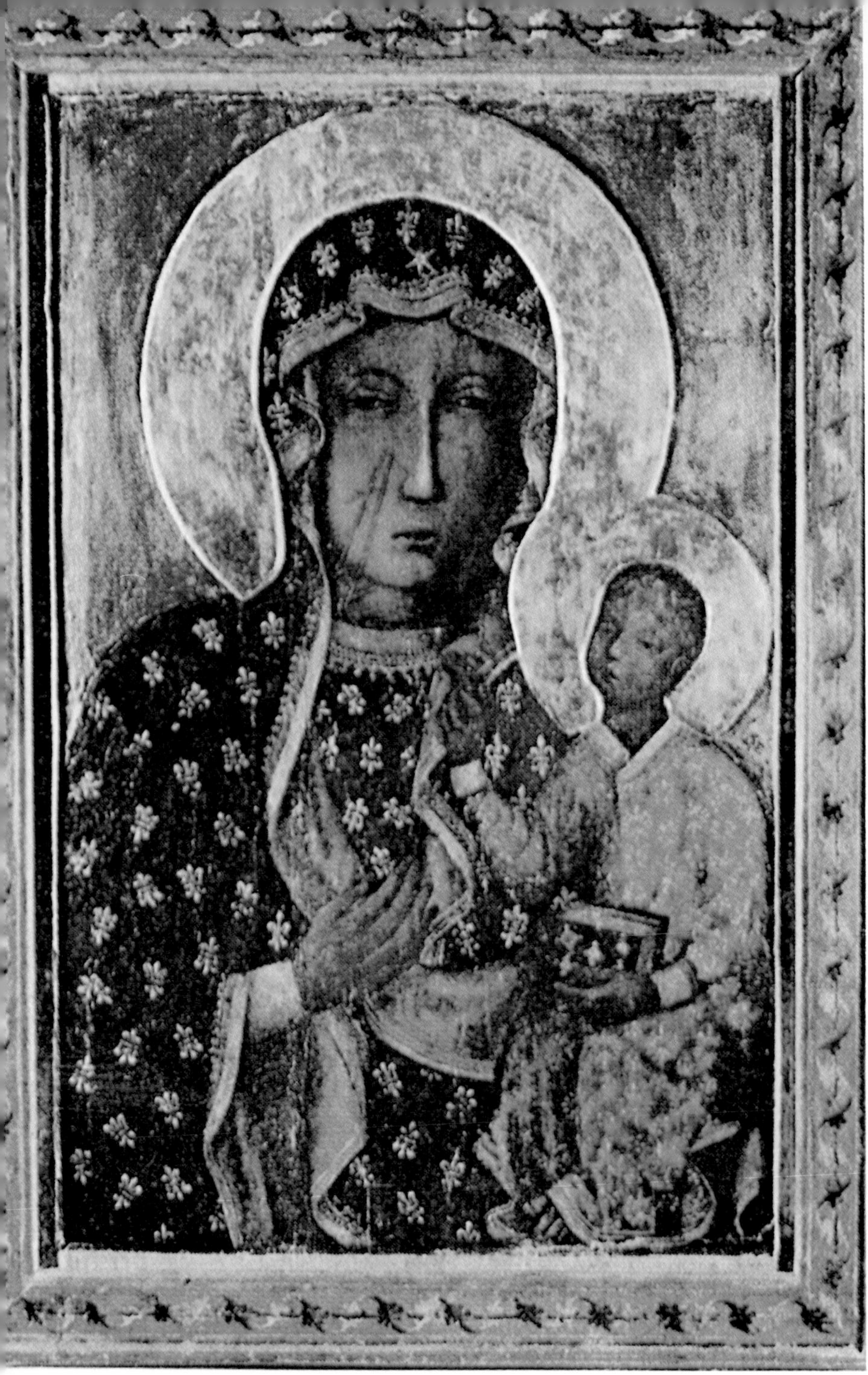

Above: Our Lady of Czestochowa. See page 380.
Opposite: Our Lady of Sorrows. See page 212.

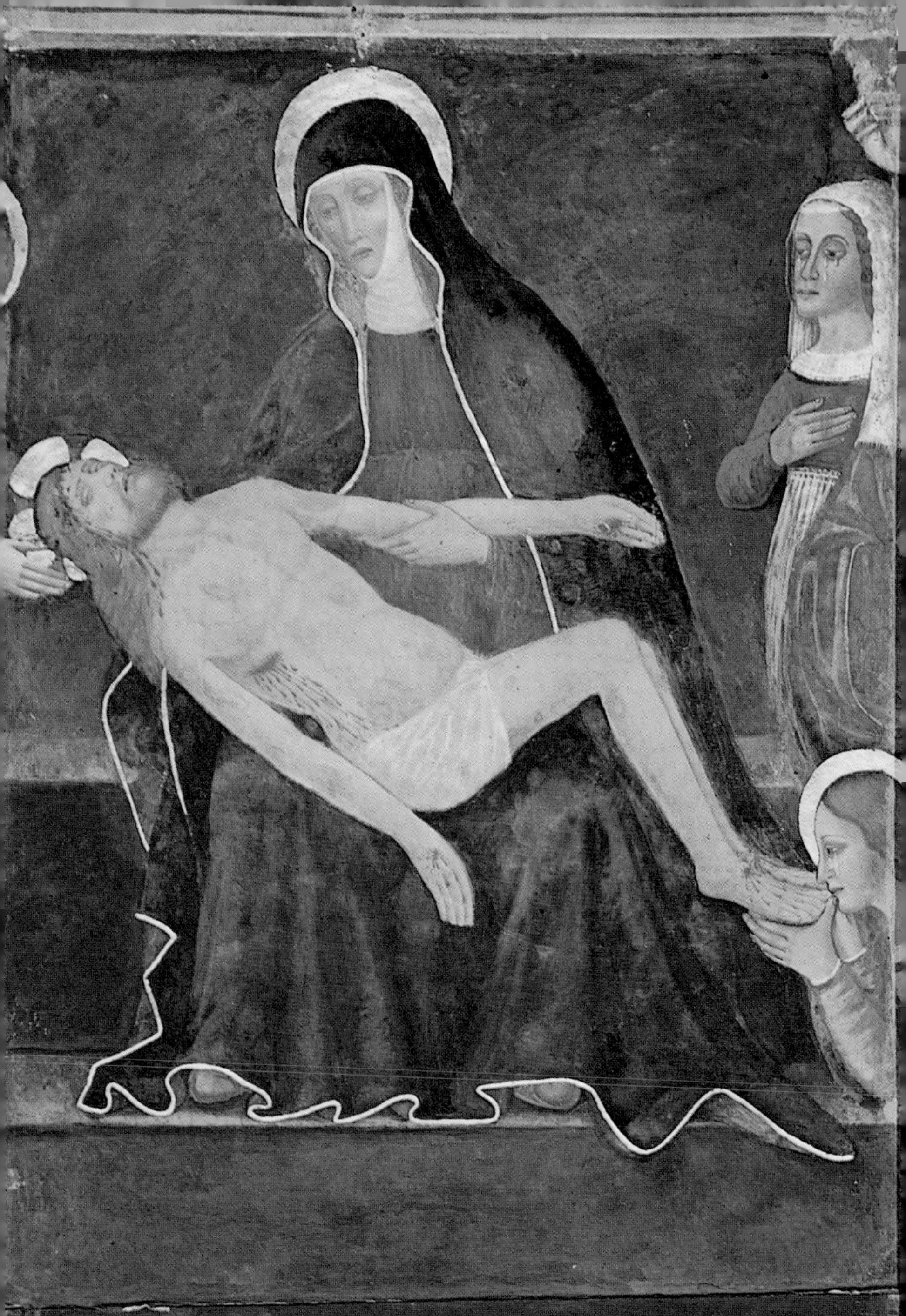

238-21

Above: Our Lady of Ortiga. See page 393.
Opposite: Our Lady of the Forsaken. See page 419.

238-22

Top: Our Lady of Confidence. See page 218.
Bottom: Our Lady of Capocroce. See page 202.
Opposite: Our Lady of the Holy Rosary. See page 56.

238-24

e: Our Lady of the Thorn. See page 101.
›site: Our Lady of Grace. See page 161.

238-26

Above: Our Lady of Ocotlan. See page 305.
Opposite: Our Lady of the Bowed Head. See page 12.

238-28

Above: Our Lady of Montserrat. See page 413.
Opposite: The Madonna of Consolation. See page 146.

Above: Our Lady of Guadalupe. See page 290. (Photo used with permission from Queen of the Americas Guild, Inc., P.O. Box 851, St. Charles, IL 61074.)

> By means of two needles fastened between the canvas of the picture and its frame, they stretched a thread horizontally across the painting, below the eyes of the Blessed Virgin. The line of this thread left no vacant space below the pupils whilst they were at rest; and the two spaces on either side became as it were two rudely shaped triangles. Thus, it so accurately defined the relations of the several parts of the eye to one another, that the least movement could not fail to be readily and certainly detected.

They all declared under oath that they first recited prayers of a novena, then, while singing the *Salve Regina,* at the words *Illos tuos misericordes oculos ad nos converte* (Turn thine eyes of mercy toward us), they saw quick and repeated movements of the eyes. They advanced closer and stared at the portrait. They each declared that they saw, among other movements, the pupils rise so far as almost to disappear under the upper eyelid, and again return to their original position.

When word of the phenomenon reached certain skeptics who had not witnessed the movements, the doubters suggested that those who believed so readily in the miracle either suffered from mental derangement or were somehow seduced by mass hysteria.

A certain physician of that day, Dr. Paley, in defense of the test and the movements which were observed by so many people, wrote: "It is in the highest degree improbable that the same derangements of the mental or visual organs should seize different persons at the same time—a derangement, I mean, so much the same as to represent to their imagination the same objects."

Eighteen years after the event, the Rev. Spencer Northcote published an account of the marvel. The good priest wondered how anyone could doubt the reality of the phenomenon, since it was witnessed:

> . . . not by one person but by many, by several hundreds and even thousands, by a whole city; they saw it not only separately, but together; not only by the light of lamps and of candles, but by the broad light of day; not only at a distance, but near; not once only, but several times; they not only saw it, but even, as we may most truly say, touched and handled it.

Agreeing with Rev. Northcote were all those who witnessed the movements and were edified and spiritually enriched by the experience.

— 61 —

OUR LADY OF POMPEII

(Our Lady of the Rosary)
Pompeii, Campania, Italy
1875

Pompeii has experienced tragedies and dismal times, but in more recent years the tragedies have been transformed into triumphs of Our Lady of the Rosary, and the unhappy times have been replaced by countless pilgrims who are the joyful recipients of miracles and graces.

One of the first tragedies to visit Pompeii occurred in the year 79 A.D., when Mount Vesuvius erupted with a vengeance. The volcano destroyed the Roman city and concealed it for centuries beneath volcanic ash. The city that developed about a mile from these ruins was also subjected to tragedy when it was ravaged in 1659 by a widespread epidemic of malaria that killed most of the population.

An ancient church that had been built before the epidemic was eventually demolished in 1740, and a smaller one was built as a replacement. Of the once-thriving parish, only a handful of people remained—and these were served by a tired and elderly priest. Finally, in addition to the various superstitions that gripped the people, they were additionally troubled and weakened by bandits who terrorized and pillaged. Pompeii eventually became known as "a most dangerous resort of bold and infamous robbers."

But Our Lady never abandons her children, and the most unlikely places have been chosen by her to display the wonders she can perform for those who are devoted to her. The instrument she used for her conquest of this unhappy city was Bartolo Longo (1841-1926), who would at first appear to be a most unlikely choice.

Educated in Naples to be an attorney, Bartolo was introduced to Satanism during his college days. After "ordination" as a priest in the church of Satan, he spent many years in the exercise of his office by preaching, officiating at the rites, publicly ridiculing the Catholic Church and her priests, and speaking against all matters relating to the Catholic religion. Longo was brought to Satan by bad companions; a good friend, Vincente Pepe, brought him back to God. Vincent eventually succeeded in placing Bartolo in the care of a Dominican friar, Alberto Radente, who helped him in the final stages of withdrawal from the sect.

After returning to the Sacraments, Bartolo decided to make reparation by joining a group of people who cared for the poor and the sick. A member of this group was Countess di Fusco, a wealthy widow who owned property near the ancient ruins. Commissioned by her to collect the rents, Bartolo saw for himself the desolation of the city and the spiritual poverty of the people.

One day in October 1872, while he paused in the fields near Pompeii, he began to reflect on his previous consecration as a priest of Satan. He tells us:

> I thought that perhaps as the priesthood of Christ is for eternity, so also the priesthood of Satan is for eternity. So, despite my repentance, I thought that I was still consecrated to Satan, and that I am still his slave and property as he awaits me in Hell. As I pondered over my condition, I experienced a deep sense of despair and almost committed suicide. Then I heard an echo in my ear of the voice of Friar Alberto repeating the words of the Blessed Virgin Mary: "One who propagates my Rosary shall be saved." These words certainly brought an illumination to my soul. Falling to my knees, I exclaimed: "If your words are true that he who propagates your Rosary will be saved, I shall reach salvation because I shall not leave this earth without propagating your Rosary." Like an answer to my promise, the little bell of the parish church of Pompeii rang out, inviting the people to pray the Angelus. This incident was like a signature to my firm decision.

Without delay, Bartolo organized a parish mission and invited a group of priests to speak about devotion to the Holy Rosary. To conclude the mission, he planned to exhibit a painting of Our Lady. He found an appropriate picture in a Naples shop, but unfortunately, he could not afford to purchase it. He was later informed that the picture was unsuitable, since Canon Law at that time required that a painting be executed in oils upon canvas or wood. The picture he had chosen was an oleograph on paper.

On his return home he shared his disappointment with Friar Alberto Radente, who told him of a painting that a nun named Mother Concetta had in her convent. Since she was willing to part with it, Friar Alberto encouraged Bartolo to ask for it. This painting had originally been discovered in a junk shop by Friar Alberto. He had purchased it for a mere eight carlins, or the equivalent of one dollar. The friar had given the portrait of Our Lady to Mother Concetta some time earlier.

When Bartolo saw this painting, he was extremely displeased by its pitiful condition and its historical and artistical flaws. He described the painting in this manner:

> Not only was it worm-eaten, but the face of the Madonna was that of a coarse, rough country-woman. . .a piece of canvas was missing just above her head. . .her mantle was cracked. Nothing can be said of the hideousness of the other figures. St. Dominic looked like a street idiot. To Our Lady's left was St. Rose. This latter I had changed later into a St. Catherine of Siena. . .I hesitated whether to refuse the gift or to accept. I had promised a picture unconditionally for that evening. I took it.

Bartolo was enticed into accepting the picture by Mother Concetta. She encouraged him with the words: "Take it with you; you will see that the Blessed Mother will use this painting to work many miracles." The words proved to be prophetic.

Since the painting was too large for Bartolo to carry back with him, he wrapped it in a sheet and gave it to a man who routinely drove his wagon between Naples and Pompeii. Not knowing the subject of the painting, the man arrived with the portrait positioned atop a load of manure that he was to deliver to a nearby field. In this inauspicious manner the Queen of the Rosary arrived in Pompeii.

The painting arrived on November 13, 1875. Every year the faithful observe the anniversary of the painting's arrival with special prayers and observances.

Two months after its arrival, in January of 1876, the picture's first restoraton was completed in time for the canonical foundation of the Confraternity of the Holy Rosary which had been organized by Bartolo Longo. Another restoration took place in 1879 by Maldarelli, a Neapolitan artist, who thought at first that the task was hopeless. Still another restoration is said to have taken place in 1965 by artists at the Vatican.

As a fitting shrine for this painting, Bartolo arranged for the building of a magnificent church. Its construction was funded by the pennies of the poor and the substantial gifts of the rich.

While it was being built, three outstanding miracles took place. The first involved a twelve-year-old child, Clorinda Lucarelli, a victim of fierce attacks of epilepsy. Distraught relatives of the child made a promise to help in the building of the proposed church if the child recovered her health. Clorinda was cured on the day the picture was exposed for veneration. Two doctors certified on oath that the cure was nothing less than miraculous.

A young woman, Concetta Vasterilla, who was dying in agony, was also cured when similar promises were made. During the day when the cornerstone of the new church was laid, May 8, 1876, Fr. Anthony Varone, who had received the Last Sacraments and was dying of a gangrenous condition, was likewise healed. He celebrated Holy Mass the following morning and acknowledged his miraculous cure from the pulpit on the feast of the Holy Rosary.

A month after the cornerstone was laid, another miracle took place when Madame Giovannina Muta was cured. She had been in the last stages of consumption when she was persuaded to make certain promises to Our Lady of Pompeii. On June 8, while Madame Muta lay in bed, she saw in a vision the picture of Our Lady of Pompeii—although she had never seen the picture in actuality. But as she gazed, Our Lady seemed to cast her way a ribbon on which was written: "The Virgin of Pompeii grants your request, Giovannina Muta." When the vision faded, Madame Muta was completely cured. Other marvelous miracles and favors have taken place which are far too numerous to mention here.

While the Sanctuary was being constructed, Bartolo turned his interest to helping orphans, writing books about the history of the Rosary and composing novenas and a prayer manual for use at the Sanctuary. While engaged in these activities Bartolo found time to marry the widow, Countess Mariana di Fusco, on April 1, 1885.

Together the couple spent their time and money in helping the many orphans who were entrusted to their care. They likewise helped candidates to the priesthood and religious life, Bartolo being credited with paying for the education of about 45 seminarians.

The church was consecrated by Cardinal La Valletta, Papal Legate for Pope Leo XIII, in May of 1891. In 1934, at the express command of Pope Pius XI, a great new basilica was begun. Completed in 1939, it was opened in the name of Pope Pius XII by Cardinal Magliones, Secretary of State to His Holiness. Pope St. Pius X had earlier expressed support for the Sanctuary and devotion to Our Lady of Pompeii.

The miraculous portrait of Our Lady of the Rosary is situated high atop the main altar of this artistically enriched sanctuary. In its golden frame, the colorful painting depicts the Blessed Mother seated upon a throne. On her knee is the Child Jesus, who is handing a Rosary to St. Dominic, while the Blessed Mother is handing a rosary to St. Catherine of Siena. Pope Leo XIII once stated, "God has made use of this image to grant those favors which have moved the whole world."

This once-discarded portrait, costing a mere dollar, which arrived in Pompeii under the humblest conditions, is now studded with diamonds and gems which were donated to Our Lady by her grateful clients.

It has been estimated that at least 10,000 pilgrims visit the sanctuary each day, but twice a year, on May 8 and the first Sunday of October, at least 100,000 pilgrims join in the solemn prayers which Bartolo Longo composed.

The former Satanist, the devout convert, respected lawyer and champion of the orphaned lived a long life of 85 years, dying on October 5, 1926. The tombs of Bartolo Longo and his wife are found in the crypt of the sanctuary.

The promise of the Blessed Mother that "One who propagates my Rosary shall be saved" was realized when Pope John Paul II affirmed the salvation of Bartolo Longo's soul at the ceremony of beatification which was conducted on October 26, 1980.

(Page 247). High atop the main altar of the basilica in Pompeii is found the miraculous painting that long ago had been purchased in a junk shop for the equivalent of one dollar.

MIRACLES AND FAVORS have taken place through the intercession of Our Lady of Pompeii, pictured above. The Blessed Mother, seated upon a throne, is depicted holding the Child Jesus on her knee. He hands a rosary to St. Dominic, and the Blessed Virgin places a rosary into the hand of St. Catherine of Siena. The portrait is embellished by diamonds and other gems donated by grateful followers of Our Lady.

A CLOSE-UP VIEW of the magnificent altar which houses "Our Lady of Pompeii."

— 62 —

THE WEEPING MADONNA OF SYRACUSE

Syracuse, Sicily
1953

This plaster sculpture, or plaque, which depicts the Immaculate Heart of Mary was mass-produced in a studio in Tuscany. It was then shipped with others of its kind to Syracuse, where it was purchased as a wedding gift. But after it had hung for a time in the humble home of the Iannuso couple, the plaque was singled out for the unexpected and prodigiously shed tears for four days.

The veneration paid this plaque in a church built especially for its exhibition was approved by three popes, but only after an ecclesiastical tribunal scrupulously studied the miracle and had the tears scientifically analyzed. It has been said by authorities that never was a miracle so thoroughly tested or so quickly approved.

The history of the image begins with its sculptor, Amilcare Santini, who modeled it in only three days "under artistic inspiration." It was made of plaster that had been dissolved in water and poured into a mold before it was turned out to dry in the sun. It was then sprayed with nitrocellulose varnish that made it shiny and suitable for painting. After it was colored, varnished and polished, ordinary screws were used to attach the image to a panel of black opaline. The panel measures 39 by 33 centimeters, the figure 29 by 22 centimeters.

The plaque was purchased as a wedding gift for Antonina and Angelo Iannuso, who were married March 21, 1953. They admitted that they were tepid and neglectful Christians, yet they hung the image with some devotion on the wall behind their bed.

Angelo was a laborer who had taken his bride to live in the home of his brother on Via Degli Orti 11. When his wife discovered that she was pregnant, her condition was accompanied by toxemia that expressed itself in convulsions that at times brought on temporary blindness. At three in the morning on Saturday, August 29, 1953, Antonina suffered a seizure that left her blind. At about

8:30, her sight was restored. In Antonina's own words:

> I opened my eyes and stared at the image of the Madonna above the bedhead. To my great amazement I saw that the effigy was weeping. I called my sister-in-law Grazie and my aunt, Antonina Sgarlata, who came to my side, showing them the tears. At first they thought it was an hallucination due to my illness, but when I insisted, they went close up to the plaque and could well see that tears were really falling from the eyes of the Madonna, and that some tears ran down her cheeks onto the bedhead. Taken by fright they took it out the front door, calling the neighbors, and they too confirmed the phenomenon. . .

Of the many visitors who examined the plaque at close range was Mario Messina, who was highly regarded in the neighborhood. After observing the slow formation of the tears he removed the plaque from the wall, examined it thoroughly and satisfied himself that the tears were not the result of an internal reservoir. After the plaque was dried, two tears immediately reappeared.

News of the phenomenon spread quickly throughout the city, bringing crowds that forced their way indoors and gathered in the streets around the house. The inspector of security, with the couple's permission, hung the plaque on the outside of the house to satisfy the curiosity of the people, but later, on seeing that the crush showed no sign of diminishing, the picture was taken to the constabulary in an effort to reduce the confusion. The image wept while outside the building and during its transport, but after 40 minutes at the police constabulary, when it did not weep, it was returned to the Iannuso home.

On Sunday, August 30, at 2:00 in the morning, the weeping image was placed on a cushion and displayed to satisfy the curious who had remained in the street throughout the night.

The image was nailed above the main door on Monday, and its tears were collected by the people on pieces of cloth and wads of cotton. During this time the curious were satisfied, the skeptics were convinced, and many of the sick were healed. Also during this day, to protect the plaque from falling, it was brought to an improvised altar outside the home of the Lucca family who lived directly across the street. Several hours later, after the recitation of the Rosary, it was returned.

Three priests visited the home during this time. One of them notified the Chancery, which assembled a group of distinguished clergymen, four men of science and three reputable witnesses, to comprise an investigative commission.

On the specific instructions of the chancellor, the commission gathered at the Iannuso home the morning of Tuesday, September 1 for the purpose of studying the phenomenon and collecting a sample of the tears for chemical analysis. The plaque was examined while it wept and while the liquid collected in the cavity formed by the hand over the heart. The commission examined the smooth finish and found no pores or irregularities on the surface. The backing was removed and the unfinished calcined gypsum was scrutinized and found in a dry condition, even though tears collected on the reverse.

Six coats of nitrocellulose colors were counted on the image; these were covered with a coat of nitrocellulose varnish. Using a sterilized pipette, a sample of tears was collected and placed in a sterilized vial that was taken to the provincial laboratory to be examined by doctors and chemists. One centimeter of liquid was obtained, about 19 to 20 drops.

Following this thorough examination, the image continued weeping for another 51 minutes, but at 11:40 in the morning the tears stopped, never to be repeated.

The sample of tears was compared scientifically with those of an adult and to those of a child. Following a detailed analysis, the conclusion reached by the doctors was that:

> . . .the liquid examined is shown to be made up of a watery solution of sodium chloride in which traces of protein and nuclei of a silver composition of excretiary substances of the quanternary type, the same as found in the human secretions used as a comparison during the analysis.
>
> The appearance, the alkalinity and the composition induce one to consider the liquid examined analogous to human tears.

The report was dated September 9, 1953 and was signed by Drs.

Michele Cassola, Francesco Cotzie, Leopoldo La Rosa and Mario Marietta.

Concerning this commission and the various investigations conducted, we must consider that the church is never in a hurry to pronounce her judgments on such occurrences and that she acts with maximum caution and prudent reserve and is ready to affirm miracles only after positive and unquestionable proofs have been extended. Nevertheless, sufficient proofs were apparently given, since a favorable judgment was rendered in a relatively short time.

The Archbishop of Syracuse visited the Iannuso home to examine the plaque and returned another day to recite the Rosary together with the crowd. Various monsignori visited the plaque, some of whom witnessed the weeping. Many cardinals expressed interest, while the Archbishop of Palermo, Ernesto Cardinal Ruffini, in a radio broadcast of December, 1953 stated:

> . . . After careful sifting of the numerous reports, after having noted the positive results of the diligent chemical analysis under which the tears gathered were examined, we have unanimously announced the judgment that the reality of the facts cannot be put in doubt.

Pope Pius XII, in a radio broadcast on October 17, 1954 said,

> . . .we acknowledge the unanimous declaration of the Episcopal Conference held in Sicily on the reality of that event. Will men understand the mysterious language of those tears?

The medical commission that was nominated on October 7, 1953 to examine seriously and scientifically the nature of extraordinary cures worked through the intercession of the Weeping Madonna of Syracuse, considered 290 cases of which 105 were of "special interest." These miracles were reported within a few years of the incident.

The first person to experience a miracle of healing was also the first to observe the weeping. From the time Antonina Iannuso first saw the tears, she recovered completely from severe toxemia and gave birth to a healthy son on December 25, 1953. Archbishop Baranzini officiated at the infant's Baptism.

The same astonishment experienced by the people of Syracuse at the time of the miracle was felt by those around the world who read about the occurrence in local newspapers, or heard about it on radio or television. It has been tabulated that reports even reached India, China, Japan and Vietnam. In Italy alone more than 2,000 articles appeared in 225 papers and magazines, while hundreds of articles appeared in 93 foreign newspapers in 21 different nations. Rarely is an event of religious interest given such worldwide attention.

That the events were the result of collective hallucination is rejected by authorities of the shrine where the image is now kept, since one, then two, then small groups and finally hundreds of people, including skeptics, viewed the event and the intermittent character of the weepings. The plaque was seen to shed tears in several locations inside the home and at three places outside; moreover, there was the tangible evidence of saturated cloths and cottons. Hallucinations are to be excluded because of the psychological state of numerous unbelievers who examined the image and even tasted the salty liquid. Moreover, photographs and motion-picture footage of the weeping cannot, of course, be hallucinated.

The question of condensation is likewise rejected since it would have covered the whole statue and would not have originated only from the corners of the eyes. Condensation would have collected on nearby objects as well, which did not occur, and if it had been present certainly would not have been salty.

The physicians and scientists who studied the event could offer no natural explanation for the occurrence and deemed it extraordinary in several documents.

The reliquary presented to Archbishop Baranzini on the occasion of the 50th anniversary of his ordination is of special interest since it contains the tears collected by the medical commission for their chemical analysis. The reliquary is comprised of three layers. The bottom contains, in addition to cloths that had been saturated with tears, one of the vials that contained the tears collected by the commission and cotton wool that absorbed some of the tears on another occasion. The second layer has four panels depicting the events. The third and highest layer has a crystal urn which holds another of the vials used for the collection of the samples. The tears within it are now crystallized.

The little house on Via Degli Orti 11, where the Madonna first shed her tears, is now an oratory where Mass is often celebrated.

The image itself is enshrined above the main altar of the *Santuario Madonna Delle Lacrima,* built specifically to accommodate the crowds that continually gather in prayer before the holy image.

Why did the Madonna weep? Many theories have been offered which remind us of the tears Mary shed at the foot of the Cross and of those shed by her during the vision of La Salette. During one of the visions of St. Catherine Laboure on July 18, 1830, St. Catherine noticed that the Virgin looked sad and had tears in her eyes. Perhaps we should pray the words engraved on the base of the reliquary, "Weeping Madonna, take from the hardness of our hearts tears of penitence." And we wonder with Pope Pius XII, "Will men understand the mysterious language of those tears?"

THE SANCTUARY of the Weeping Madonna of Syracuse. Engraved on the base of the reliquary are the words, "Weeping Madonna, take from the hardness of our hearts tears of penitence."

NEVER HAS A MIRACLE been so thoroughly tested, some maintain—or so quickly approved—as the plaster sculpture pictured above of the Madonna of the Tears, which shed tears for four days and which has brought about miraculous healings, at Syracuse, Sicily, August 29 to September, 1953.

The Weeping Madonna of Syracuse, Italy.

— 63 —

OUR LADY OF AKITA

Yuzawadai I Banchi, Soegawa, Akita-Shi, Japan
1973

A small group of devout women known as the Institute of the Handmaids of the Holy Eucharist were leading a quiet, hidden life of prayer in Yuzawadai on the outskirts of Akita when they welcomed into their novitiate Sister Agnes Katsuko Sasagawa, who was then 42 years old and a convert from Buddhism. When she entered on May 12, 1973, Agnes was totally and incurably deaf. Blessed by Heaven with various mystical favors, Sr. Agnes and her convent were to become so well known that their humble chapel would attract visitors from throughout the world.

The first extraordinary event at Akita took place on June 12, 1973—one month after the entrance of Sr. Agnes—when a brilliant light emanated from the tabernacle. This phenomenon occurred a number of times and was often accompanied by something like fog or smoke which gathered around the altar. During one of these illuminations Sr. Agnes saw "...a multitude of beings similar to angels who surrounded the altar in adoration before the Host." When this apparition took place, Bishop Ito was staying at the convent to conduct a week of devotions. Sr. Agnes dutifully confided to him the circumstances of this vision, as well as all the events and apparitions that followed. Bishop Ito and the convent's spiritual director, Rev. Teiji Yasuda, were witnesses to many of the events.

Sr. Agnes was also favored with visitations of her guardian angel. Asked to describe the angel, Sr. Agnes could only say that she had "a round face, an expression of sweetness...a person covered with a shining whiteness like snow..." The guardian angel confided various messages to the sister and often prayed with her, in addition to guiding and advising her.

During the evening of June 28, 1973, Sr. Agnes discovered on the palm of her left hand a cross-shaped wound 3 cm. long by

2 cm. wide, that caused excruciating pain. During the late evening hours of July 5, 1973, a small opening appeared in the center from which blood began to flow. Later, the pain would ease during most of the week except for Thursday nights and all day Friday, when the pain became almost unbearable.

During the early morning hours of the next day, July 6, 1973, the guardian angel appeared, telling Sr. Agnes: "...The wounds of Mary are much deeper and more sorrowful than yours. Let us go to pray together in the chapel." After entering the chapel the angel disappeared. Sr. Agnes then turned to the statue of Mary situated on the right side of the altar.

The statue had been carved from the hard wood of the Judea tree in 1965 by M. Saburo Wakasa, a Buddhist sculptor renowned in the area. Standing about three feet high, the statue is of Our Lady standing before a cross, her arms at her side with the palms of her hands facing forward. Beneath her feet is a globe representing the world.

When Sr. Agnes approached the statue, "I suddenly felt that the wooden statue came to life and was about to speak to me...She was bathed in a brilliant light...and at the same moment a voice of indescribable beauty struck my totally deaf ears." The vision asked various questions of Sr. Agnes and reassured her, "...Your deafness will be healed..." Our Lady then recited with her the community prayer that had been composed by Bishop Ito. At the words "Jesus present in the Eucharist," the vision instructed, "From now on, you will add TRULY." Together with the angel who again appeared, the three voices recited a consecration to the Most Sacred Heart of Jesus, TRULY present in the Holy Eucharist. Before disappearing, Our Lady asked that Sr. Agnes "pray very much for the Pope, bishops and priests..."

The following morning, when the sisters assembled for the recitation of Lauds, they discovered blood on the right hand of the statue. Upon a closer inspection they found two lines which crossed, in the middle of which was a hole from which the blood flowed. The wound exactly resembled that on the hand of Sr. Agnes except that, since the statue's hand was smaller, its wound was smaller in size. The wound bled on the Fridays of July during the year 1973, as did the wound on the hand of Sr. Agnes.

One of the sisters recorded her reaction concerning the wound on the hand of the statue: "It seemed to be truly cut into flesh.

The edge of the cross had the aspect of human flesh and one even saw the grain of the skin like a fingerprint. I said to myself at that moment that the wound was real. . ."

It was noticed that while the drops of blood ran the length of the statue's hand, which was open and pointing downward, the drops never fell from the hand.

The wound on the hand of Sr. Agnes appeared on Thursday, June 28. As predicted by the guardian angel, the wound disappeared on Friday, July 27 without leaving a trace.

The second message of Our Lady came on August 3, 1973, a First Friday, when the heavenly voice from the statue warned:

> . . .Many men in this world afflict the Lord. . .In order that the world might know His anger, the Heavenly Father is preparing to inflict a great chastisement on all mankind. . .I have prevented the coming of calamities by offering Him the sufferings of the Son on the Cross, His Precious Blood and beloved souls who console Him forming a cohort of victim souls. Prayer, penance and courageous sacrifices can soften the Father's anger. . .know that you must be fastened to the Cross with three nails. These three nails are poverty, chastity and obedience. Of the three, obedience is the foundation. . .

When Sr. Agnes was professed, she pronounced these three vows.

Although the wound on the hand of Sr. Agnes disappeared on July 27, the wound on the hand of the statue remained until its disappearance was noticed on September 29. At that time the statue emitted a brilliant light. The wound had remained for three months.

While it is a fact beyond dispute that the wounds in the hands of the statue bled, Bishop Ito advises that, contrary to some reports, ". . .the statue did not sweat blood or weep blood at any time."

During the course of the evening office of September 29, 1973, the whole community saw a resplendent light coming from the statue. Almost immediately the entire body of the statue became covered with a moisture resembling perspiration. Sr. Agnes' guardian angel informed her, "Mary is even sadder than when she shed blood. Dry the perspiration."

Five of the sisters used cotton balls to collect the moisture. These clumps of cotton were carefully kept and were soon noticed to have a fragrance which the nuns described as the scent of paradise. This heavenly fragrance continued to be perceived through October 15, 1973. When samples of the cotton were sent to the University of Akita for analysis, the conclusion of the scientists was that the liquid was of human origin.

The third and final message of Our Lady came on October 13, 1973, the anniversary of the great miracle of Fatima. Once again the statue of Mary gave off a celestial fragrance. Later in the day, while reciting the Holy Rosary, Sr. Agnes again heard the heavenly voice of Our Lady warning the world.

> . . . As I told you, if men do not repent and better themselves, the Father will inflict a terrible punishment on all humanity. It will be a punishment greater than the deluge, such as one will never have seen before. Fire will fall from the sky and will wipe out a great part of humanity, the good as well as the bad, sparing neither priest nor faithful. The survivors will find themselves so desolate that they will envy the dead. The only arms which will remain for you will be the Rosary and the Sign left by my Son. Each day recite the prayers of the Rosary. With the Rosary, pray for the Pope, the bishops and the priests.
>
> The work of the devil will infiltrate even into the Church in such a way that one will see cardinals opposing cardinals, bishops against other bishops. The priests who venerate me will be scorned and opposed by their confreres. . .churches and altars sacked; the Church will be full of those who accept compromises and the demon will press many priests and consecrated souls to leave the service of the Lord.
>
> The demon will be especially implacable against souls consecrated to God. The thought of the loss of so many souls is the cause of my sadness. If sins increase in number and gravity, there will be no longer pardons for them. . . Pray very much the prayers of the Rosary. I alone am able still to save you from the calamities which approach. *Those who place their confidence in me will be saved.*

Following Our Lady's message, the dazzling light that had engulfed the statue gradually disappeared.

Toward the end of May, 1974, another phenomenon occurred. While the statue's garment and the hair retained the look of natural wood, the face, hands and feet became distinguished by a dark, reddish-brown tint. Eight years later, when the sculptor came to see the statue, he could not hide his amazement that only the visible parts of Our Lady's body had changed color, and that the face itself had changed expression.

Still another phenomenon presented itself. On January 4, 1975, to the astonishment of the community and the Spiritual Director, Fr. Yasuda, the statue of the Virgin began to weep and did so three times that day. Also witnessing these lachrymations, in addition to members of the community, were Bishop Ito and a number of people who had joined the nuns for a New Year's retreat. In the 10 years following, scientific studies excluded any explanation other than the supernatural.

It was noticed that the tears collected on the inside edge of the eyes flowed down the cheeks, collected at the edge of the garment near the throat, rolled down the folds of the garment and fell upon the globe under Our Lady's feet.

Fr. Yasuda recorded in his book, *The Tears and Message of Mary,* that the statue:

> . . . had completely dried out during the years since it was made and little cracks had begun to appear. It is already miraculous if water would flow from such material, but it is still more prodigious that a liquid sightly salty, of the nature of true human tears, should have flowed precisely from the eyes.

Eventually, Bishop Ito arranged for Professor Sagisaka, M.D., a non-Christian specialist in forensic medicine, to make a rigorous scientific examination of the three fluids, although the Bishop did not divulge their source. The results of the tests were that: "The matter adhering on the gauze is human blood. The sweat and the tears absorbed in the two pieces of cotton are of human origin." Furthermore, the blood was found to belong to group B and the sweat and tears to group AB. Sr. Agnes belongs to group B.

A non-Japanese Jesuit priest from Sophia University in Tokyo was asked by Bishop Ito to conduct an examination. This unnamed Mariologist, now referred to as the Inquisitor, concluded that Sr. Agnes employed the occult practice of ectoplasm, that is to say, that Sr. Agnes was able to somehow "eject and transfer" her own blood upon the hand of the statue, and the same with the tears and sweat. When the Inquisitor was asked to explain how this could occur when Sr. Agnes was some 250 miles away visiting her family, or was asleep at the time of the events, the Inquisitor explained: "It is because another sister near the statue also possessed ectoplasmic faculties."

Unwilling to accept this opinion, the Bishop was advised by the Apostolic Nuncio to seek the assistance of the Archbishop of Tokyo in creating a commission of canonical inquiry. Unfortunately, the Inquisitor was named president of this group. Without any of the members visiting the convent to conduct a personal inquiry, the commission rendered an unfavorable verdict.

Still unwilling to accept a negative verdict to the events he himself had witnessed, Bishop Ito asked the advice in Rome of the Congregation for the Doctrine of the Faith, as well as the Congregation for the Propagation of the Faith. He was then advised to form another commission to study the events from the beginning. This commission rendered a favorable verdict regarding the supernatural aspects of the events.

The lachrymation of December 8, 1979 was filmed by a television crew at 11 o'clock at night. This film, taken on the feast of the Immaculate Conception, was shown on television to 12 million people throughout Japan. It is now shown by the nuns at the convent and was shown during news broadcasts throughout the world.

The sculptor of the statue, Saburo Wakasa, a citizen of Akita, was asked his reaction to the marvels that attended the statue. He replied:

> The statue of Mary was my first work connected with Christianity. Of my various statues, it is only with the statue of Mary at Yuzawadai that mysterious events occurred. . . I sculptured the whole statue of Mary, globe, and the Cross from the same piece of wood, so there are no joints. . .The wood from which I carved the statue of Mary was very dry and rather hard. . .

When questioned as to whether he regards as a "miracle" the reported shedding of tears from the statue of Mary, he replied, "Fushigidesu." (It is a mystery).

Another examination of the fluids was conducted by Karou Sagisaka, M.D. of the Department of Forensic Medicine, School of Medicine, University of Akita. The results were given on November 30, 1981 and revealed that: "The object examined has adhering to it human liquids which belong to the blood group O." Since the first analysis revealed that the blood belonged to group B and the sweat and tears to group AB, it has been established that the fluids belong to three different blood groups.

It is a medical fact that the blood, tears and sweat of an individual all belong to the same blood group. One fluid cannot differ in type from the other fluids of the same body. Since Sr. Agnes belonged to group B she could not have "ejected and transferred" blood or fluids belonging to group AB or O. The theory of the Inquisitor that Sr. Agnes exercised ectoplasmic power is therefore refuted.

On the feast of Our Lady of Sorrows, the statue cried for the last time. Two weeks later, Sr. Agnes' guardian angel presented a large Bible surrounded with a celestial light. The open Bible revealed the reference, *Genesis* 3:15. The angel explained that the passage had a relationship with the tears of Mary and then continued.

> There is a meaning to the figure one hundred and one. This signifies that sin came into the world by a woman and it is also by a woman that salvation came to the world. The zero between the two signifies the Eternal God Who is from all eternity until eternity. The first one represents Eve and the last the Virgin Mary.

The lachrymations number 101, and they took place at irregular intervals from January 4, 1975 until September 15, 1981. According to the records kept by the sisters, the number of persons witnessing the lachrymations went unrecorded on five occasions. However, all the other lachrymations were witnessed by no fewer than 10 persons, and other lachrymations were witnessed by various numbers of people, sometimes as many as 46, 55 and, for the last lachrymation, 65 people. Some of the witnesses were non-Christians and some were prominent Buddhists, including the mayor of the city.

As noted earlier, Sr. Agnes was totally and incurably deaf when she entered the community, having lost her hearing on March 16, 1973. Sister was able to speak, and understood spoken messages by lip reading. As predicted by her guardian angel, she temporarily regained her hearing on October 13, 1974. Deafness returned on March 7, 1975. Her hearing was permanently restored on May 30, 1982, as predicted by Our Lady during the first message of July 6, 1973. Both healings occurred instantaneously during Benediction of the Blessed Sacrament. Sr. Agnes is today in sound health, except for the rheumatism that has afflicted her hands.

A canonical law regarding the judgment of a Marian apparition was issued in 1978. According to a Vatican official: ". . .the authority to hand down a conclusion regarding the authenticity of any Marian apparition is given canonically to the ordinary (the bishop) of the local diocese where the apparition took place. . ."

In his pastoral letter dated April 22, 1984, Bishop John Shojiro Ito, the Ordinary of the Diocese of Niigata, wrote that having been given directives in this regard, "I authorize throughout the entire diocese of which I am charged, the veneration of the Holy Mother of Akita." The Bishop noted that the events are only a matter of private revelation, and are not points of doctrine. The Bishop also mentioned in his pastoral letter that he had known Sr. Agnes Sasagawa for 10 years. "She is a woman sound in spirit, frank and without problems; she has always impressed me as a balanced person. Consequently the messages she says that she has received did not appear to me to be in any way the result of imagination or hallucination."

Four years later, on June 20, 1988, during Bishop Ito's visit to Rome, the Sacred Congregation for the Doctrine of the Faith approved the contents of the pastoral letter.

Bishop Ito's official recognitions of the occurrences and the Madonna's messages were reported in the October, 1988 issue of the magazine *30 Days*. In the August 1990 issue, Cardinal Ratzinger is quoted as saying that "there are no objections to the conclusion of the pastoral letter." Cardinal Ratzinger has invited the Bishop to continue to inform him about the pilgrimages and conversions.

For more information, the reader is encouraged to contact the 101 Foundation, P.O. Box 151, Asbury, NJ, 08802-0151.

BRILLIANT LIGHT emanated from the tabernacle of a chapel near Akita, Japan in 1973. The wooden statue pictured above, situated on the right side of the altar, seemed to come to life, spoke to Sister Agnes Katsuko Sasagawa, and bled from a wound-type mark in the right hand. Other marvels followed, as when the statue became surrounded by resplendent light and gave off moisture that was analyzed by scientists to be of human origin. On October 13, 1973, the statue put forth a celestial fragrance and again spoke to Sister Agnes, invoking prayer and repentance. More phenomena followed, and between 1975 and 1981 the statue shed human tears 101 times.

— 64 —

OUR LADY OF DAWN

(Gate of Dawn)
Vilnius, Lithuania
Sixteenth Century

The historical monument and religious shrine which is known as the Gate of Dawn, or *Ausros Vartai,* is found in Vilnius, the capital city of Lithuania. In the first years of the sixteenth century, a great stone wall with nine gates and defense towers was built around the city. The Gate of Dawn, on the southeastern side of the city, was located near the Orthodox Church of the Most Holy Trinity. The Gate soon became a religious shrine when two paintings were hung on it, one depicting Jesus Christ, the other the Blessed Virgin Mary. This original painting of Our Lady sustained weather damage and was replaced by the one now treasured by the people of Vilnius.

Painted on eight oaken boards, the Blessed Virgin looks downward. Her hands are gracefully crossed at chest level. With only the face, neck and hands visible, the rest of the figure is entirely vested with intricately designed silver. The head of the Blessed Mother, which is inclined toward her right side, is covered with a silver veil and is surrounded by a golden halo that emits golden rays and stars.

According to the Carmelite Friar Hilary, who first recorded the history of the painting, the friars were particularly devoted to the painting of the Blessed Virgin on the Gate of Dawn. For this reason the Carmelite friars built a monastery in 1620 near the Gate. A year later, the friars began building a monastery church. At its completion in 1650, the church was dedicated to St. Teresa.

Twenty-one years after the completion of the church, the friars felt the need to express their devotion to the Mother of God by building a wooden chapel on the gate. Here they placed the painting, which was already covered with silver. It was during this time that the Blessed Virgin began to perform miracles for those who were devoted to her portrait. A Carmelite preacher recognized several miracles that took place during the transfer of the painting to the wooden chapel. Friar Hilary, the historian of the painting, recorded 17 other miracles that took place between 1671 and 1761. Although the Church declined to pass judgment on these miracles, the wonder-working powers of Our Lady of Dawn became widely known through the efforts of the Carmelites and the Jesuits.

While the miraculous nature of the portrait was still being considered by Church authorities, the newly consecrated bishops of Vilnius acknowledged their belief in the miraculous character of the painting by initiating a custom in 1688 whereby each joined a procession to the Gate of Dawn to pray for the Blessed Mother's guidance before assuming their episcopal duties.

When Vilnius suffered from a disastrous fire in 1715, the wooden chapel on the gate that was built by the Carmelites was unfortunately lost. However, before the flames reached the chapel, the Carmelites transferred the painting to the safety of the Church of St. Teresa. The painting was restored to its original site when a brick chapel was built for it in 1726.

The first official recognition of the miraculous painting occurred in 1773, when Pope Clement XIV granted an indulgence to all who worshipped at the Gate of Dawn.

When the Russians occupied Lithuania in 1795, they destroyed the wall that encircled Vilnius but, as though by a miraculous intervention, the Gate of Dawn shrine remained standing and untouched. When Friar Hilary's history of the shrine was reprinted in 1823, the miraculous painting became more widely known. The Carmelites at that time produced holy cards bearing the likeness of the venerated image. These they freely distributed to the faithful who wanted a small reproduction to keep in their homes. It is also recorded that 28 different reproductions of the portrait were painted by Polish, Lithuanian, German and French artists who wanted larger reminders of the miraculous image.

Our Lady of Dawn was greatly honored in 1927, when Pope Pius XI ordered its solemn crowning. This crown of precious metal is positioned atop the elaborate silver veil of the Madonna. Miniature angels on either side seem to assist in supporting the crown's weight.

Before World War II, the Holy Sacrifice of the Mass was offered every morning in the Gate of Dawn chapel. In the evening a litany and hymns were sung in praise of the Virgin Mary. The chapel was usually filled to capacity for these services, but was especially filled to overflowing on November 16, the Feast of Our Lady of Mercy. Often, when the chapel was filled with worshippers, many were obliged to kneel outside the chapel to express their devotion. Because of the busy pedestrian traffic, the street in front of the chapel was closed to all motor vehicles.

The situation was changed after the Russian occupation of 1944. The street was opened to vehicular traffic, religious processions were forbidden, and religious freedom at the shrine was curtailed. Convents, monasteries and religious schools were closed. Soon after Lithuania declared its independence from the U.S.S.R. in 1989, these religious houses were opened. Church services are once again freely celebrated.

For the third time in its history, Our Lady of Dawn was honored by the Vatican when in 1954 a stamp was issued which bore the likeness of the miraculous image. Four years later, the Lithuanian people installed a chapel in honor of the Gate of Dawn in the lower Basilica of St. Peter in Rome.

WONDER-WORKING POWERS are credited to the greatly venerated image of Our Lady of Dawn in Vilnius, Lithuania. The sixteenth-century painting was solemnly crowned by Pope Pius XI in 1927.

— 65 —

OUR LADY OF SILUVA

Siluva, Lithuania
1608

Lithuania is one of the three Northwestern countries on the shore of the Baltic Sea which recently escaped Russian domination. Throughout its turbulent history it has been conquered at various times by either Poland or Russia. In this troubled country, which has been dedicated and re-dedicated to the Blessed Mother, stands Lithuania's most important shrine to the Mother of God, that of Our Lady of Siluva.

Located in central Lithuania, Siluva was blessed with its first church in 1457 when Peter Giedgaudas, a wealthy Lithuanian noble, donated the wooden structure and the surrounding lands to the Catholic Church. A few years later St. Casimir, Prince of Poland, visited Lithuania on an important mission. Unfortunately, he became desperately ill and died there on March 4, 1484 at the age of 26. Burial was at Vilna, in the Church of St. Stanislaus, now the cathedral, where his remains are still found.

A tremor of desperation invaded the Church during the early sixteenth century when Lutherans attracted converts from among the nobility and the intellectuals. Calvinism also claimed its share of adherents in 1551. The peasants for the most part remained staunchly Catholic.

Since the people and land were ruled by Protestant nobles, Church properties were confiscated and given over to the various denominations. Everything Catholic was confiscated. When the church at Siluva was threatened in 1570, the pastor, Rev. John Halubka, had the foresight to collect some of the church's treasured articles including a few vestments, a favorite image of the Madonna and Child that hung above the main altar, and the church records. Placing them in a metal-covered oak chest, he buried it a short distance from the church near a large rock. This was providential, since the church was soon seized by Protestants.

Finally, in 1588, a new law was passed which gave Catholics the right to repossess church properties unjustly taken from them, but documents clearly proving previous ownership were required. For the church in Siluva, documents could not be found to prove that Peter Giedgaudas had given the land to the Church in 1457.

Whereas human efforts to find the documents failed, Heaven intervened to reward the faith of the people. So it was in the summer of 1608 that children, shepherding their flocks, saw a beautiful lady standing on a large rock. Holding a child in her arms, the lady wept bitterly. Startled by the vision, one of the children ran to a Calvinist teacher, Mikola Fiera, who promptly claimed it to be an apparition of the devil who was trying to draw people away from Calvinism.

News of the apparition spread. The next day, the area around the rock was crowded with the curious and the devout. While the Calvinist teacher was insulting and ridiculing the people for listening to the tales of children, the lady and her child once more appeared atop the rock, to the great surprise of all present. Momentarily taken aback by the vision, it was the teacher who ventured forward with a question for the lady: "Why are you weeping?" Sadly the vision answered, "Formerly in this place my son was adored and honored, but now all that the people do is seed and cultivate the land." Saying this, the lady and child disappeared. Although the Calvinists attempted to argue against the apparition, the people knew what they had witnessed, and all believed themselves privileged to have seen the Blessed Mother holding the Child Jesus. It is recorded that the teacher unexpectedly left Siluva shortly after the miraculous appearance.

When news of the apparition reached the Ordinary of the Catholic Church in the Diocese of Zemaiciu, the Bishop dispatched his representative, Canon John Kazakevicius, to thoroughly investigate and verify the reports. The Canon carefully questioned all who saw the apparition and recorded his findings.

A certain blind man of the village, on hearing of the apparition, remembered the metal-covered oak chest that the pastor had buried years before. History records that when the blind man was taken to the rock, his sight was immediately restored. He was then able to indicate the exact location of the chest, which was unearthed and examined. Inside was found the revered picture of the Virgin and Child, which was undamaged despite its many years underground. Also recovered were the vestments and the papers which proved ownership of the church property.

The Calvinists returned the land after years of negotiations in the courts. A new church was built, but since this soon proved inadequate for the large numbers of people who regularly paid homage to the miraculous image, a larger church was built which remained for 140 years. A stone church was built later, in 1786.

With the influx of pilgrims to Siluva, the Bishop had a small chapel built in 1663 over the rock of the apparition. A little over a century later the Bishop, with the approval of Pope Pius VI, formally approved the devotion paid to Our Lady of Siluva. Later, in 1886, a statue named "Health of the Sick" was placed atop the rock of the apparition. So popular was this shrine that a larger chapel was built in 1818—and still another in 1924.

For a few brief years, from 1918 to 1940, Lithuania was independent and devotion to Our Lady of Siluva flourished. However, in 1940 the Russians again absorbed the land into the Union of the Soviet Socialist Republic. Although Catholic services were forbidden, the Faith survived in the hearts of the people who met for secret services. Then, in 1989, Lithuania declared its independence from Russia. Church services once more are openly celebrated.

The image of the Mother and Child which was recovered in Siluva as the result of the Virgin Mother's appearance is credited with numerous miraculous healings and answers to prayer. With only the faces of both Mother and Child exposed, the painting is almost entirely covered with gold, except for small areas that are ornamented with silver. The folds of the Virgins' garments are embellished with intricate golden designs. Atop her veil is a crown; a smaller crown is worn by the Child Jesus. Golden rays extend behind the heads of each, while golden stars surround both figures. The Christ Child's golden right hand is raised in blessing, while the left hand holds a golden book.

The miraculous image is exposed only during public ceremonies. At other times it is concealed by a golden-framed painting depicting the apparition of the Blessed Mother standing atop the rock. Pointing to the earth with her right hand, the vision holds her Child on her left arm. Surrounding the rock are the shepherd children and their sheep. One of the children in the forefront of the painting faces away from the apparition while pointing it out to an elderly cleric, who gazes rapturously at the beautiful Mother and Child.

The Lithuanians who have immigrated to this country are said to feel honored and grateful for the chapel dedicated to Our Lady of Siluva which is found in the upper basilica of the National Shrine of the Immaculate Conception in Washington, D.C.

OUR LADY OF SILUVA, Lithuania, holding an image of the Christ Child, is pictured atop the rock under which important church documents had been hidden for 18 years during a time of religious persecution. An apparition of the Blessed Virgin and Christ Child called attention to the long-forgotten hiding place.

GOLD AND SILVER ornament the image of Our Lady of Siluva. Of the miraculous painting, only the faces of the Madonna and Child are visible. One of the Christ Child's hands is raised in blessing; the other holds a book.

— 66 —

OUR LADY, CONSOLER OF THE AFFLICTED

Luxembourg, Luxembourg
Seventeenth Century

Known officially as the Grand Duchy of Luxembourg, this independent country of 998 square miles is wedged between Belgium, France and Germany. The ownership of this Catholic country had been claimed at one time or another by either France, Austria, Germany or Spain. If the ownership of the land has been a matter of dispute throughout its history, the faith of the people has never been questioned, and their love for the Blessed Mother has always been forthrightly affirmed.

In the seventeenth century this devotion of the people to the Mother of God resulted in the Jesuits building a major church in Luxembourg, the capital city of the country. This church was consecrated to the Immaculate Conception, but the place that draws our attention is the shrine chapel of Our Lady, Consoler of the Afflicted. Built in response to an overwhelming demand, a Jesuit priest, Fr. James Brocquart, had this chapel built on the outskirts of the capital city so that people could pilgrimage there in a demonstration of love and devotion to their heavenly Mother. When the chapel was completed, the good priest enthroned a 38-inch statue. This image, carved of lime-wood, depicts the Virgin Mother holding the Christ Child on her left arm and a scepter in the right hand. With her hair falling in waves over her shoulders, the Virgin stands serene and dignified. The richness of its coloring and the brilliance of its gilding are said to have been little affected after 300 years of veneration.

The chapel immediately became a popular center of devotion where miracles were soon noted and favors granted. Fr. Brocquart, the founder of the shrine, was one of the first to experience a miracle of healing when he was miraculously cured of the plague. In 1627, a child who was dead from asphixiation was revived during the singing of the Litany of Our Lady, and hearing was restored to a child born deaf. By October 12, 1640, a list detailing 33 undisputed cures was compiled of those who had formerly been mute, blind or paralyzed. The Bishop of Trier recorded and authenticated many other cures between 1640 and 1647.

An official decree issued in 1666 placed the capital city of Luxembourg under the patronage of Our Lady, Consoler of the Afflicted. The next year, when Luxembourg was besieged during a dispute between France and Spain, a plot was discovered whereby the enemy intended to detonate part of the city's walls to gain entrance. It was widely believed that the enemy's plan was averted through the intervention of Our Lady. As a sign of gratitude, the Virgin was presented with a golden key to the city, which still hangs from the right wrist of the miraculous statue.

When French troops once again threatened the city, the Blessed Virgin foiled their attack with a miraculous rush of water which fell suddenly down a gorge of the Alzette River to prevent the enemy's advance.

In gratitude for Our Lady's motherly protection, the entire duchy was consecrated to the *Consolatrix Afflictorum.* People from throughout the duchy flocked to the capital for the grand celebration. It is recorded that 40,000 people received Holy Communion at the Mass of Dedication.

When the French Revolution burst upon Luxembourg, the city fell on June 5, 1795. Every church in the grand duchy suffered desecration to one degree or another, but the Chapel of Our Lady suffered the greatest insult by being destroyed. The beloved statue, however, was smuggled to safety and was secured by the Jesuits. It was eventually placed in the seventeenth-century church of the Immaculate Conception, where it remains to this day.

The devotion of the people is amply demonstrated each year during the Great Octave of 15 days, which is observed from the third to the fifth Sunday after Easter. This celebration commemorates the dedication of the capital city and the entire duchy to Our Lady. The Holy See approved a special Mass and Office for this yearly commemoration and granted extraordinary privileges for those who participate. During the Octave, special Masses are celebrated and a solemn renewal of the consecration is made. The most impressive activity is a lengthy procession of guilds and associations of workmen. With the miraculous statue carried in the procession on a dais and the Blessed Sacrament held by the bishop, choirs and bands provide appropriate music.

Usually enthroned above the main altar, the statue is removed during the Great Octave to a specially constructed altar which is beautifully decorated with flowers and silver lamps. The miraculous statue is always superbly dressed for the occasion, for nowhere, it is said, is a statue of Our Lady dressed to a greater effect than here. Her apparel for the occasion is chosen from her royal wardrobe which contains sumptuous dresses made by queens, princesses and royal duchesses. A choice is then made among the many lace veils which were the gifts of the most famous lace-making districts of Europe. There are also jewelry cases which contain a large assortment of crowns, scepters, orbs, brooches, necklaces, rings and medals of pearls and precious stones, all of which were donated by those who benefitted from the graces distributed by Our Lady, Consoler of the Afflicted.

During the years the church proved to be entirely inadequate for the many pilgrimages that visited the miraculous statue. Raised to the dignity of a cathedral, it has been carefully enlarged so that the additions are perfectly compatible with the old. Stained glass windows reflect many of the queenly titles given to Our Lady in her litany, while other windows depict the mysteries of her Rosary.

Although Luxembourg is a small country, the population is considered to be 98 percent Catholic. Many of these citizens have prayed in times of personal crisis before the miraculous statue and received consolation from a caring mother, Our Lady, Consoler of the Afflicted.

— 67 —

OUR LADY OF THE MOUNTAIN

Funchal, The Island of Madeira
Fifteenth Century

In the Atlantic Ocean some 559 miles southwest of Lisbon is the island of Madeira, which is called the Pearl of the Atlantic because of its mild climate, its luscious vegetation, its tropical flowers and garden-like terrain. This possession of Portugal has its capital city of Funchal on its southeastern shore. A few miles north of the city is a place known as Terreiro da Luta. It is here that the Blessed Virgin is said to have appeared in the fifteenth century to a young shepherd. After requesting that pilgrimages be observed in her honor, a statue of the Blessed Mother was miraculously discovered at the place of the apparition.

The statue eventually found its way a few miles south, closer to the capital city, to a place known as Monte. Here in a parklike setting is the eighteenth-century church which enshrines the statue known as Our Lady of the Mountain. The miraculous statue is found above the main altar, in a tabernacle worked in silver. As requested by the apparition, solemn pilgrimages take place every year on August 14 and 15.

The place of the apparition has not been forgotten. When Funchal was being bombarded in 1917 by German submarines, the Bishop of Funchal made a vow to erect a monument to the Virgin, provided that peace followed within a short space of time. The prompt answer to the Bishop's prayers is confirmed by the monument that was erected over the site where Our Lady of the Mountain is said to have appeared. Encircling the monument are anchor chains from torpedoed ships.

Our Lady of the Mountain has been designated the Patron Saint of Madeira.

— 68 —

OUR LADY OF MELLIEHA & MADONNA TAL-GHAR

Mellieha, Malta
First Century

Directly south of the island of Sicily in the Mediterranean Sea is the smaller island of Malta, which is graced by two miraculous images of the Blessed Virgin Mary. Here St. Paul and his companion St. Luke found safety after being shipwrecked at a place still known as St. Paul's Bay. The account of this adventure is given in Chapters 27 and 28 of the *Acts of the Apostles*, acknowledged to have been written by St. Luke. We read that while St. Paul was being taken to Rome as a prisoner on board ship, the following happened:

> And when we were fallen into a place where two seas met, they run the ship aground; and the forepart indeed, sticking fast, remained unmoveable; but the hinder part was broken with the violence of the sea. And the soldiers' counsel was, that they should kill the prisoners, lest any of them, swimming out, should escape. But the centurion, willing to save Paul, forbade it to be done; and he commanded that they who could swim, should cast themselves first into the sea, and save themselves, and get to land. And the rest, some they carried on boards, and some on those things that belonged to the ship. And so it came to pass, that every soul got safe to land.

For three months St. Paul and St. Luke remained on the island, doing what they could for the greater glory of God and the good of souls.

Since St. Paul's Bay is in close proximity to Mellieha, tradition has affirmed that the first Christian church on the island was founded in that city by St. Paul, who had settled there. This church consisted of a large cave which was dedicated and placed under the patronage of the Virgin Mother.

At the back of this cave, which is about 15 feet in depth, was a recess in the wall and it was here that St. Luke is believed to have painted the portrait of the Virgin Mother and Child which today is still venerated and held in the greatest esteem. Since the time of the Apostles it has been a favorite place of pilgrimage and the source of many miraculous favors.

The stone church that was later added to the original grotto was attached in such a way that the cave served as the sanctuary. The high altar was positioned in the rear of the cave area, which was left in its natural state.

The numerous ex-votos in this church attest to the favors received through the intercession of the Blessed Virgin Mary by virtue of petitions presented before the miraculous image. Numbered in the hundreds, the ex-votos take the form of miniature ships and boats and even coils of rope which tell of deliverance from shipwreck. Waxen arms, legs and other portions of the human body speak of other favors. The church also has a collection of paintings, most lacking artistic merit, which depict wonderful answers to prayer obtained at the shrine. In many cases the names and dates lend authenticity to the favors received.

This little church served as the parish church as far back as the time of St. Gregory the Great (d. 604). When Malta was invaded by the Turks, the people took refuge in the more southerly parts of the island. The infidels are said to have respected the grotto, even providing oil for the lamps in hopes of obtaining favorable voyages.

Because of Our Lady's protection, the sacred picture continued unharmed throughout the Turkish occupation. When peaceful times returned, the church, which had gradually fallen into a sorry state, was restored to its original condition and prestige.

Although the grotto is a favorite place of pilgrimage, it is visited by more people during periods of calamity. At such times pilgrims arrive in great numbers from Valletta, the capital. So it was in 1887 during a cholera epidemic when Bishop Buhaja led a procession to implore the intercession of the Mother of God. After Holy Mass, the people streamed through the grotto, where each person paused for a moment of prayer before the miraculous image. It was noticed with relief and gratitude that the epidemic abruptly ceased following the pilgrimage. In the years 1640, 1645 and 1814, widespread epidemics were arrested during similar pilgrimages to the shrine.

In 1740 a severe drought brought the people to the shrine for special services and a procession, and at that time a copy of St. Luke's picture was carried outside. A heavy rain fell as soon as the image re-entered the church.

The portrait of Mother and Child is undoubtedly of great age. A considerable portion has flaked away, but the Virgin is still quite visible. Faded golden stars adorn a blue veil that covers the Blessed Virgin's head and drapes over her shoulders. A golden halo surrounds her head, while a smaller one is seen about the head of her Child, who is on her right arm. A blue background and Greek words meaning "Mother of God" complete the picture.

Unfortunately, the portrait is marred by a large area of paint which apparently flaked away due to the natural conditions of the cave. This area begins at the Virgin's chest and carries downward, even to a bare space in the lower half of the Christ Child's body. For some inexplicable reason this area was smeared quite carelessly with a bright red color. This does not diminish the efficacy of the portrait, nor the admiration and devotion paid to it by the people. On the contrary, special graces and blessings continue to be awarded to the Virgin's faithful children who pray before this ancient image.

* * *

In addition to the miraculous portrait of the Blessed Mother in the grotto of Mellieha, there is also a miraculous statue in the same vicinity. This is kept in a vault excavated from rocks at a lower level than the church. The vault lies partly underneath the church, but is quite distinct from the church. The vault is entered by a flight of steps leading from the square adjoining the church.

The statue, known as the Madonna tal-Ghar, was hewn out of a hard white stone resembling granite and is larger than life-size. The Blessed Virgin stands majestically as she holds the Christ Child on her left. Her right hand is gracefully extended. The Virgin's crown is of the same stony material. The absence of a veil permits us to see her hair, which falls in graceful waves down her back. The Child is held higher than what seems a comfortable position, since He almost sits on the shoulder of His Mother. The Child has a charming and quite different aspect from most statues in that He holds both arms outward, as though inviting an embrace from His visitor.

The miracles connected with this statue have been extremely unusual, but have been observed by hundreds of visitors, many of whom have been known to possess respected and impeccable reputations. The miracles involved movements made by the statue.

Before hundreds of visitors, the stony right arm of the Virgin was seen to become flexible, like that of a living person. Our Lady was then seen to raise her hand and sign a cross of benediction over her clients. Some also saw the blessing being given by the Holy Child. Other movements also took place. One writer tells that, "...the occurrence is too well known in Malta to allow of contradiction; and from frequent repetition, during the last two centuries at least, is now a matter of common credence."

Writing in *The Month* for the November, 1893 issue, an English Jesuit, Rev. Father McHale, tells of a visit he made to the statue with 60 students from the Jesuit College in Malta. During this visit everyone present saw the statue's movements, which continued for a half hour. Rev. McHale paid two more visits and saw the wonder repeated. He thoroughly examined the statue and was able to assure himself that he was not deceived in what he had observed on three different occasions.

A different miracle was witnessed about a century ago when the authorities of the parish decided to move the Madonna to a shrine in the church above the grotto. This was undertaken with the bishop's permission. The following morning the statue, considerably heavy (being made of solid stone), was found to have been removed from the church. To the amazement of all, the statue was discovered in its customary place in the subterranean chapel. We can image the efforts made by the men who once again carried this heavy stone statue up the stairs and into the church above. But once again, the statue was found the next morning in its usual place. Finally, it was decided that no further displacement should be attempted.

Consider how fortunate the Maltese people are in their possession of two miraculous images of the Mother and Child: one image which might have been painted by St. Luke, and the other which has shown Our Lady's love for her devotees in extraordinary ways. But we need not be envious of the Maltese people since we, too, have the Mother's attention whenever we call upon her.

MADONNA TAL-GHAR. The miraculous statue on Malta pictured at left has produced unusual miracles, such as when hundreds of visitors saw the hard stone material move, the right arm signing a cross of benediction over the crowd and the image of the Holy Child also bestowing a blessing.

PAINTED BY ST. LUKE? The ravages of time have held no sway over the efficacy of the sacred portrait seen above, believed to be the work of the Apostle St. Luke. An unexplained splotch of red paint mars the surface of the painting, but the image is nonetheless cherished and venerated.

— 69 —

OUR LADY OF ZAPOPAN

Zapopan, Jalisco, Mexico
Sixteenth Century

For ten years this little image of Our Lady accompanied the Franciscan Fray Antonio de Segovia during his apostolic journeys among the Indians of Jalisco, Mexico. In fact, when the Indians of the area were warring against the Spaniards, Fray Antonio wore the little image about his neck while he attempted to negotiate a peaceful settlement. Having begun his missionary labors around the year 1530, he was having little success in converting the Indians and securing peace until he begged for Our Lady's help.

Our Lady gave her assistance in a most unusual manner. While Fray Antonio was preaching, luminous rays issued from the statue. This so impressed the Indians that they laid down their arms, agreed to peace and asked for Baptism. It is said that in one day more than 6,000 Indians converted to the Faith. Because of the large number of Indians who agreed to a peaceful settlement, Fray Antonio called the image *La Pacificadora,* that is, "She Who Makes Peace." On December 8, 1541, Fray Antonio gave the little image to the village of Zapopan.

The statue stands a mere 12 inches in height and represents Our Lady of the Immaculate Conception. It is made of *pasta de Michoacan,* which consists of corn and cornstalk mixed with glue. The hands are made of wood and are joined in prayer. When Fray Antonio donated the statue to the village of Zapopan, it consisted only of the upper half. The lower section was added at a later time and is somewhat out of proportion. Since the statue is normally clothed in beautiful vestments, the discrepancy is not noted. The statue of Our Lady has a wardrobe of many tunics and mantles adorned with precious stones, as well as various adornments including a gold-tasseled blue sash which she always wears. This denotes her military rank as "General of the Army of the State." Our Lady also holds a scepter, golden keys to the city and a golden stick called a baston, which also indicates her military rank.

The Virgin's gold, jeweled-encrusted crown rests atop her head and represents her Pontifical Coronation. A great halo adorned with gems surrounds Our Lady's head, and she stands upon a golden, star-tipped crescent moon. The statue is supported by a sculptured pedestal of silver which weighs over 120 pounds.

The statue was held in the greatest regard by the people of Zapopan and many were the miracles bestowed upon them by Our Lady. These favors were so numerous that Don Juan Ruiz Colmenero, the Bishop of Guadalajara, began a careful investigation in 1653. In the end, the Bishop issued a decretal declaring the image to be miraculous and appointed December 18 as Our Lady's feastday.

Our Lady of Zapopan bears three special titles, each with its own history.

She is regarded as the "Patroness of Guadalajara," the capital city of the state of Jalisco and the second largest city in Mexico. This title was earned toward the end of the seventeenth century when Our Lady tamed a terrible epidemic. The number of people suffering from the disease was so great that the Bishop of Guadalajara ordered the statue to be carried from Zapopan to his city five miles away. It is reported that the ecclesiastical archives contain a testimonial from members of the medical profession in Guadalajara, certifying that the plague disappeared in the presence of Our Lady. Once again in 1721 the image was brought to Guadalajara, where Our Lady once again dismissed the plague. Our Lady of Zapopan was also petitioned for protection against the fierce weather that assails Guadalajara during the rainy season. She has been declared awesome against storms, lightning and epidemics.

Beginning in the year 1734 to the present day, a great devotion to Our Lady of Zapopan is demonstrated each year when the statue leaves its sanctuary in Zapopan on June 13, the feastday of St. Anthony of Padua, and travels northwest to the capital city of Guadalajara. She visits every church in the city until October 4, the feastday of St. Francis of Assisi. On that day she is brought back to Zapopan in a procession with all the pomp and celebration worthy of a queen. With the image of Our Lady dressed in a medieval pilgrim costume consisting of a cloak and a broad-brimmed hat, she is borne along the way, protected by uniformed members of an honor society known as the "Guard of Our Lady of Zapopan." Taking part in the procession are dancers, mariachi bands, military bands, choirs, jugglers and Indian dancers from far away villages in traditional costumes. It is not unusual for airplanes to strew flowers along the route of the procession. At night the darkness is penetrated by fireworks, lights, music, dancing and more celebrations. One source estimates that a million people take part in these processions.

Our Lady of Zapopan also bears the title, "General of the Armies." In the year 1821, as she was entering Guadalajara on June 13 for her annual visitation of the churches, a "Year of Independence" was declared. Our Lady was then commissioned "General of the Army of the State" by civil authorities. She was honored by the Church and State on September 15 of the same year, when she was vested with the blue shoulder sash and the gold baston of a general.

When Guadalajara's water supply was cut off after the city had been seized in 1852, Our Lady was petitioned by General Blancarte to protect the city and was even given a 21-gun salute. It is said that Our Lady protected the city with admirable success.

Our Lady was once more honored when the Governor of Jalisco vested her image with a new sash and prayerfully requested that she always protect her children and the State of Jalisco.

Another title given to Our Lady is that of Queen of Jalisco. This was conferred on her in the year 1919, when the Vatican Chapter authorized the canonical coronation of Our Lady of Zapopan which took place with all solemnity in the cathedral of Guadalajara.

Our Lady of Zapopan was given yet another honor when Pope Pius XII raised the sanctuary in Zapopan to the rank of a minor basilica on January 10, 1940. Consecrated in 1730, the sanctuary is known throughout Mexico as the home of La Zapopanita, Our Lady of Zapopan, the source of graces and miracles.

LUMINOUS RAYS issued from the little image pictured above when it was being worn around the neck of a Franciscan missionary in sixteenth-century Mexico. The previously hostile natives were so impressed by the phenomenon that more than 6,000 were converted in one day. The wonder-working image, which measures a mere 12 inches high, represents Our Lady of the Immaculate Conception. The hands strike a prayerful pose. Our Lady of Zapopan holds a scepter, golden keys to the city of Zapopan and a golden stick which indicates her military rank as "General of the Armies."

— 70 —

OUR LADY OF GUADALUPE

Mexico City, Mexico
1531

The miraculous image of the Blessed Mother on a piece of 450-year-old fabric constantly intrigues its viewers, puzzles artists and baffles scientists. Its history began on September 9, 1531 when the Mother of God appeared to a 55-year-old Indian named Juan Diego. While hurrying on Tepeyac Hill to attend Mass at a Franciscan mission, Juan Diego heard a woman's voice calling him, not by his name, but by the affectionate diminutive, *''Juanito, Juan Dieguito.''* After a tender dialogue she requested that he visit the Bishop, tell his Excellency about the apparition and ask that a shrine be built in her honor.

The visions occurred five times, four to Juan Diego and once to his ailing uncle when the Lady effected his cure. The last apparition to Juan Diego occurred on Tuesday, December 12. To provide the Bishop with the sign he requested that would identify the apparition and confirm the supernatural aspect of what Juan had alleged, the Lady asked Juan to walk higher up the hill and to collect the roses found there—this in spite of the rocky nature of the place and its unsuitability for the growth of any type of vegetation. Nevertheless, Juan picked the roses that he found there. The lady arranged the flowers inside the scoop of the tilma, a cloak worn by the Indians, and cautioned him against disturbing or revealing his burden except in the presence of the Bishop.

When Juan opened his cloak for the prelate, he found not the rejection and skepticism he had received before, but the Bishop kneeling among the flowers, looking in reverential awe at a picture miraculously applied to the cloak—an exact likeness that Juan Diego identified as the Lady he had seen four times on Tepeyac Hill.

News of the miracle spread rapidly. Crowds continually gathered at the Bishop's house, forcing the ecclesiastic, who had kept the tilma in his private chapel, to remove the tilma to the cathedral of the city. There it was placed above the altar for all to see.

Juan Diego, the visionary of Guadalupe, lived 17 years following the apparition. During this time he was appointed as the official custodian of the tilma and was ever ready to relate the apparitions and to answer all questions concerning the image. He lived in a small room attached to the church and died at the age of 74, in the year 1548.

When the Spaniards and Indians completed the building of the church where the Lady had requested it, the image was transferred and was placed atop the altar, much to the satisfaction and rejoicing of the people.

The tilma itself is cactus cloth made from the maguey plant. It is a fabric similar to sacking that usually disintegrates within 20 years. Artists confirm that it is a fabric wholly unsuited to the application of paint. The garment is made of three strips, each one measuring 21 inches in width by 78 inches in length, with the image imprinted on two of the strips. In its golden frame the third panel, which hung on Juan's back, is folded behind the two front panels. Another source states that the tilma was made of only two straight pieces sewn together. Regardless, it is certain that two pieces are seen, and these measure 78 inches in length by 42 inches in width. They are joined with the original loose stitching that can be seen running the length of the panel along the left ear of the figure, down the left wrist to the knee and passing to the side of the angel's head. The figure of Our Lady measures four feet, eight inches in height.

The fabric has been examined often by experts in painting media, and they have declared that the fabric's loose weave and texture are unsuitable and unprepared for the application of paint. The fabric is so thin and of such a loose weave that if one stands behind it, the features of the basilica can be seen as clearly as through a trellis.

Artists have reported that the portrait was painted without brush strokes, but like a wash in four different media: oil, tempera, water color and fresco. The head and hands of the image were executed in oils; the rose-colored tunic, the angel and clouds were painted in tempera; the blue-green mantle in water color; the background in fresco. It is a successful combination unexpected on such a flimsy cloth. Moreover, the application was so permanent that, compared to man-made paintings dating from 1531, the image has required no restoration and remains to this day an artistic marvel.

In 1666, 135 years after the apparition, a Painters' Commission was formed to study the miraculous picture. Their conclusion was that:

> No other but God, Our Lord, could effect so beautiful a production; and that we hold without doubt and affirm without scruple that the imprinting of said picture of our Lady of Guadalupe on the tilma of said Juan Diego was, and must be understood and declared to have been, a supernatural work and a secret reserved to the Divine Majesty.

In the same year, 1666, the Scientific Board affirmed that:

> The continuance through so many years of the holy picture's freshness of form and color, in the presence of such opposing elements of time and decay, cannot have a natural cause. Its sole principle is He Who alone is able to produce miraculous effects above all the forces of nature.

Of more recent date a similar opinion was reached by Dr. Philip Callahan, a University of Florida Biophysicist who analyzed the painting in February of 1979. After studying infrared radiation photographs he found that the painting has no sketch underneath, a pre-requisite for almost all paintings, and that the original blue and pink pigments had not faded, although later touch-up work showed signs of age. Moreover, he discovered that the fabric had not been sized, a process that prevents rot, and that pollution from votive candles should normally have darkened and damaged the fabric during the 116 years it was left open to the elements. The scientist was especially impressed by the manner in which the rough cloth caused light diffraction, that is, an optical effect that causes the face of the image to appear white up close and olive at a distance. This same effect is found in nature when colors change under different angles, such as the smooth surface of bird feathers or butterfly scales. In his words, ". . .the original painting is miraculous."

For more than a century this self-portrait of the Blessed Virgin Mary remained uncovered atop the altar and was exposed to the enthusiasm of the people and to the effects of the atmosphere during several solemn processions. The devout and the sick were never prohibited from kissing or touching it with objects during these processions. Such repeated contacts would have damaged it had it not been miraculously guarded. Finally placed under glass in 1647, the pane was often removed for long periods of time at the request of the faithful who wished to have an unobstructed contact with it. One observer in 1753 counted more than 500 articles that were pressed to the image.

The picture painted by supernatural means was not exempt from human interference. Just as treasured statues and images are adorned with jewels and golden trinkets, so also the devotees of Our Lady of Guadalupe wished to express their love and gratitude by the application of various trimmings. Several additions were painted on the cloth, including angels in the clouds that soon faded and fell away; the rays of the sun were gilded, and these can be seen flaking away; the white moon, sheathed in silver, turned black and is still chipping off; and a crown painted on the head is now scarcely noticeable. It is believed by custodians of the shrine that other embellishments were added, including the gold border of the Virgin's mantle, the stars, and the embroidery design on the gown. These are thought to have been added during the sixteenth century. This theory is questioned, however, since all man-made additions have faded while others are still in the process of flaking away. These three embellishments: the gold border, the stars, and the embroidery, show no sign of fading or flaking. Hence, many consider them to be part of the original portrait.

The image escaped serious injury and possible destruction on two occasions: once, when a goldsmith who was cleaning the frame accidentally spilled nitric acid that ran along the left side of the tilma, miraculously leaving only a faint streak; and a second time, on November 14, 1921, when a powerful bomb, hidden in a bouquet of flowers, was placed on the altar during the Calles persecution. The metal altar crucifix directly beneath the image was twisted in the blast and marble decorations and stained-glass windows were shattered, yet the tilma and its protective glass remained miraculously unharmed. The curved crucifix that attests to the strength of the explosion is kept in a glass-fronted case for all to see.

Certain contradictions intrigue the thousands who view the image each day. While a century of touching and devout kissing wore away some of the paint, especially of the hands, yet when seen from a distance or when photographed, all are perfectly colored and formed. Moreover, the details are sharpest when viewed from a distance, unlike those of other paintings in which details are sharper when one draws nearer. The intensity of the coloring is likewise of interest since it pales when one is close to it and darkens at a distance. Another reversal exists in the shrinking and expanding of the image, that is, the painting seems large in its position, but appears reduced in size when one draws near.

Many who have closely examined the face of the portrait have reported seeing the image of a man reflected in the Lady's eyes. A bearded face is seen, a shoulder, and part of a halo in a three-quarter image. This likeness matches exactly the contemporary portraits of Juan Diego. This phenomenon was first discovered in 1929 by Alfonso Marcue Gonzales while he was examining photographic negatives. Carlos Salinas made a similar discovery in 1951, although the findings were not immediately made known. Only after the conclusions of a commission were presented to him did the Archbishop give permission for the discovery to be made public by a radio broadcast on December 11, 1955, the eve of the Feast of Our Lady of Guadalupe. Confirmations of this discovery were made in 1956 by Doctor Javier Torroello Bueno, an oculist, and by Dr. Rafael Torija Lavoignet. Optometrists who examined the eyes more recently have observed that, in addition to the image of the man, the eyes reflect light rays, just as human eyes do when examined optometrically.

The natives who first studied the image read messages that were not apparent to others. Since the Lady stood in front of the sun, they understood that she was greater than their sun god Huitzilopochtli. Their moon god, Tezcatlipoca, likewise lost stature, since the Lady stood upon the moon's crescent. The broach at her throat with its small black cross reminded the Indians of the crucifixes of the Spanish friars and the symbol on the banner of Captain Hernando Cortes. They understood by this cross that the Lady was bringing the true religion to the Mexicans. That she was held aloft by a child with wings singled her as a heavenly being, yet her hands joined in prayer meant that there was one who was greater than she. The white fur at the neck and sleeves was taken as a mark of royalty, as were the 46 golden stars and the border of gold. The bluish-green of the mantle was taken as a color reserved to divinity. It was the reading of the picture that converted whole tribes to the Faith.

The origin of the name Guadalupe has always been a matter of conjecture. While many strongly believe that the portrait was named for the statue of Our Lady of Guadalupe in Spain, it is, nevertheless, also believed that the name came about because of the interpretation of the words used by the Blessed Virgin during the apparition to the ailing uncle of Juan Diego. An account of the apparition written by Don Antonio Valeriano three years after it occurred is translated:

> Here is told how he, Juan Bernardino, had seen his nephew and he said to him how she, the Blessed Virgin, had asked him to explain to the bishop, to set before him and to relate what he had seen and the manner in which marvelously she cured him and will thus be known, or named, or called, Entirely Perfect Virgin Holy Mary of Guadalupe, her precious image. . .

Since Guadalupe is Spanish, and the Lady spoke in the Indian dialect, the word was taken to be the Aztec Nahuatl word *"coatalocpia,"* which is translated: *"coatl"* for serpent, *"tlaloc"* for goddess, and *"tlalpia"* for watching over. Another version is the Aztec, the word *"te coatlaxopeuh,"* which is pronounced *"te quatlasupe"*: *"te"* meaning stone, *"coa"* meaning serpent, *"tla"* being the noun ending which can be interpreted as "the," while *"xopeuh"* means to crush or stamp out. Both words when pronounced rapidly sound remarkably like Guadalupe. Whichever is the valid Aztec word, both words refer to the feathered serpent god Quetzalcoatl, whose images are found on many Aztec ruins. To this fierce serpent god the Indians annually offered 20,000 men, women and children in bloody sacrifice. The significance of the name Guadalupe was understood by the Indians to mean that the Virgin would crush their fearsome serpent god. This went far in converting eight million Indians in the seven years following the apparitions.

The stone serpent, taken to represent Satan, reminds us of the biblical passage in *Genesis*:

> And the Lord God said to the serpent: Because thou hast done this thing, thou art cursed among all the cattle, and beasts of the earth: upon thy breast shalt thou go, "and earth shalt thou eat all the days of thy life.

> I will put enmities between thee and the woman, and thy seed and her seed: she shall crush thy head, and thou shalt lie in wait for her heel. (*Gen.* 3:14-15)

Bishop Zumarraga, to whom the portrait was first revealed, emphatically sealed the confusion regarding the name when he understood the Indian word to mean Guadalupe, since he and his staff were familiar with the shrine of Our Lady of Guadalupe in Spain. Many believe, however, that the Bishop's understanding of the name and his pronouncement in the matter were made in error.

Of the 45 Popes who have reigned since the creation of the miraculous portrait, 25 have issued decrees concerning it. The earliest recorded decree is that of Pope Gregory XIII, dated 1575, that extended the indulgences granted by his predecessors. This implies that indulgences were granted shortly after the apparitions of 1531. Our Lady of Guadalupe was appointed National Patroness by Pope Benedict XIV in 1754. December 12 was set aside as a Day of Obligation, with an octave which could be celebrated with a special Mass and Office. The same pontiff wrote:

> In the image everything is miraculous, an image emanating from flowers gathered on completely barren soil on which only prickly shrubs can grow. . .an image in no manner deteriorated, neither in her supreme loveliness nor in its sparkling color. . .God has not done likewise to any other nation.

Pope Pius VII permanently attached the sanctuary to the Basilica of St. John Lateran, and Pope St. Pius X granted the unusual privilege of permitting Mexican priests to offer the special Mass of Our Lady of Guadalupe on the twelfth day of every month.

Three Popes have ordered the crowning of the image: Benedict XIV, Leo XIII and Pius XII. Pope Paul VI reintroduced an ancient custom by sending a golden rose to the shrine. Pope John Paul II, on a visit to Mexico in January of 1979, visited the image in its new basilica adjacent to the old church and paid homage to the 450-year-old relic.

JUAN DIEGO was favored in 1531 with five apparitions of the Blessed Mother. Little did the humble servant of Our Lady imagine that more than 450 years later he would be known by Catholics everywhere as the wearer of the miraculous tilma, or cloak, on display in Mexico City which bears the marvelous image of Our Lady of Guadalupe.

THE BLESSED VIRGIN as Our Lady of Guadalupe as she appeared to Juan Diego in 1536. It has been established scientifically that the image on the fabric of Juan's tilma could not have been rendered by human means. This self-portrait of Our Lady was exposed for more than 100 years to devout visitors who showered their kisses upon it and touched objects to it. Such repeated contacts would certainly have damaged the image had it not been miraculously guarded. (Photo is used with permission from Queen of the Americas Guild, Inc., P.O. Box 851, St. Charles, IL 60174.)

— 71 —

OUR LADY OF THE REMEDIES

(Nuestra Señora de los Remedios)
San Bartolo Naucalpan, Mexico City, D.F.
1540

Witnessing the triumphant entry of Hernando Cortez into the Aztec capital in 1519 was this image of the Blessed Virgin which had been brought from Spain with the Conquistadors. When the Indians rose against the Spanish on July 8, 1520, the Spaniards fled for their lives across the Puente de la Mariscala. The image at this time was in the care of a soldier, Juan Rodriguez de Villafuerte, who found that he was unable to carry it further because of the confusion taking place. Hiding the statue and its case under some maguey plants, he fully intended to retrieve it, but never did. One report claims that the soldier was cut down by an Aztec arrow and died at the foot of the plant.

During the next 20 years the broad leaves of the plant grew around the statue and its case, hiding it from view. Finally, in 1540, an Indian chief, Juan Cuautli, a recent convert to the Faith, heard a sweet voice calling him while he was hunting. Thinking it was his imagination he paid little heed, but a few days later, he again heard the voice and was led to the discovery of the case and the statue. Juan brought the image to his home, where he enshrined it and kept it supplied with flowers and candles.

Gradually people started gathering at the humble shrine, until it became so popular that they were visiting all day and part of the night—which, needless to say, proved to be a great inconvenience to Juan's family.

Finally, at the suggestion of the local schoolteacher, Juan built a little chapel for the statue. When on two occasions the statue was missing from the chapel—only to be found at the Maguey plant, and particularly since the sweet voice had requested a chapel at the place—Juan built a small shrine where he had found the image.

Some years later, in 1574, when the Spanish governor heard

the story of the statue's discovery and saw the chapel which was now in serious need of repair, he ordered the building of a beautiful church to house the image. The statue is now venerated above the main altar in the sanctuary of Los Remedios, only yards from its place of discovery.

Our Lady of the Remedies soon became famous for her success in solving problems of great scope and severity. During difficult times she was carried in procession from her sanctuary along an eight-and-a-half mile route to the cathedral in Mexico City. It is reported that between the years 1576 and 1922 the image traveled to the cathedral a total of 75 times. Three of these processions were occasioned by great public calamities.

During the pestilence of 1576, physicians at the Hospital Real tried in vain to identify the scourge and discover a cure. When over 2,000 people died during that year and the year following, Archbishop Don Pedro Moya de Contreras and Viceroy Don Martin Enriquez ordered the removal of Los Remedios to the cathedral. After a nine-day novena, during which Our Lady was invoked under her title "Health of the Sick," the image was returned to her sanctuary. Only then did the heavy rains begin which continued for several months, purifying the air and ending the pestilence.

Another novena was ordered when a great drought devastated the region in 1597. When farm fields became parched and starvation threatened, the Viceroy, Don Gaspar de Zuniga y Acevedo, requested that the miraculous statue be taken to the cathedral. As soon as the procession left the sanctuary with the image, rain began to fall. During each day of the novena the rain continued, effectively breaking the drought.

Our Lady of Los Remedios once again came to the assistance of her stricken children when she ended the drought of 1616. The drought not only damaged crops, but brought insupportable heat which was attended by an epidemic that devastated Mexico City. In addition to the drought and the epidemic, the lack of provisions also doomed many to starvation. Once again the people turned to Our Lady of Los Remedios. Accompanied by a large procession, the image left the sanctuary for the cathedral and arrived on June 11. The rain came soon thereafter, the drought ended, the epidemic was dismissed and the land became so fertile that the year developed into one of the most fertile in the history of the region.

In addition to being the remedy of various afflictions, Our Lady also holds a high military rank. The titles conferred upon her began when French troops invaded Spain in 1809. Because of the statue's ties with Spain, the image was brought to Mexico City and was loaned to the convents of various religious orders which were somehow affiliated with Spain. When it visited the Convent of St. Jerome, it was dressed with the insignia of a captain general of the Army of Mexico, which was then known as New Spain. The regalia became so popular that the image remained vested in this manner for many years. From that time on Our Lady of the Remedies became something of a patroness and member of the military.

When the insurgent Hidalgo and his troops were marching on Mexico City in October 1810, the Viceroy, Venegas, arranged for a bodyguard of 30 lancers to protect the shrine of Los Remedios. Worried that the image might fall into the hands of the enemy, who had already committed all manner of evil deeds, the Viceroy eventually had the image conveyed to the cathedral, for there it would be better protected. The next day the Viceroy visited the miraculous statue. Falling on his knees before Our Lady, he placed in her hands his own staff of office, begging her to defend the city from devastation. Commissioned as the chief officer of the troops, Our Lady did not disappoint the confidence the Viceroy and the people placed in her. The advance of the enemy was soon halted, some say at the very gates of the city.

As a demonstration of gratitude for this victory, a procession took place in Mexico City four months later, on February 21, 1811. Assembled in ranks along the main thoroughfare were the militia of the city and the Battalions of Noblemen of Ferdinand VII. This procession of the military was arranged "so that, by command, they might render to the sacred image the military honors corresponding to the rank of captain general."

Our Lady of the Remedies is a wood sculpture of the Madonna and Child. Measuring about 11 inches in height, Our Lady stands upon a crescent moon and holds the Child on her left, while her right hand holds a baton. The features of both figures are badly disfigured due to the ravages of time and the caresses of the Mexican people during the statue's early history. Our Lady and her Child wear beautiful garments as well as valuable ornaments and strings of pearls donated by her grateful children. At one time the image possessed 16 complete changes of vestments, all of which were heavily embroidered and decorated with costly jewels.

The feast of Our Lady of Los Remedios is celebrated on September 8 with an annual fiesta, but pilgrims begin arriving as early as September 1, many remaining during the next eight days. Hundreds of Mexican Indian families travel from all parts of the country. They sleep in the courtyards at night, and in the morning they attend one of the many Masses offered in honor of Our Lady. The finale is the great fiesta on the feastday.

Although Los Remedios and her Child are badly disfigured, the statue is beautiful in the sight of her devotees. They turn to Our Lady in all their difficulties, placing their confidence in her for the relief of their ailments and, since she is a member of the military, they rely on her for the protection of their property and their country.

OUR LADY OF THE REMEDIES is a wood sculpture standing 11 inches high. It is apparent from the photo above that time has taken its toll on the statue, as have countless caresses from the people who have visited the miraculous image.

(Left) A more recent rendition of Our Lady of the Remedies.

BEAUTIFUL GARMENTS adorn Our Lady of the Remedies and the Christ Child. Devotees of Our Lady of Los Remedios place their confidence in her for protection and relief from ailments. Each year, hundreds of families travel to Mexico City in September for the annual fiesta celebrated there.

— 72 —

OUR LADY OF OCOTLAN

Tlaxcala, Mexico
1541

Called the Land of Grace, the state of Tlaxcala is located in the highlands on the slopes of the Sierra Madre Oriental mountains and is regarded by many as being the most beautiful area in Mexico. At one time Tlaxcala was considered the most populous and largest city in the country, until it suffered a catastrophic loss of population during an epidemic of smallpox beginning in 1541—a loss from which it has never recovered. It has been estimated that nine out of ten Indians died as the result of the epidemic.

Just ten years after the spectacular apparitions of the Blessed Mother to Juan Diego, during which he received the heaven-sent picture known as Our Lady of Guadalupe, another Juan Diego was thrust into history.

His last name was Bernardino, and he worked for the friars of the Franciscan monastery in Tlaxcala. Because his relatives in Xiloxostla were stricken with smallpox, the friars gave Juan Diego Bernardino permission to travel to the River Zahuapan to gather water which the Indians thought contained medicinal properties that would relieve their fevers. After filling his water jar he continued on his journey toward Xiloxostla and began to make his way through a thick grove of ocote trees, when he abruptly halted at the sight of a beautiful woman of regal bearing standing among the trees. Her reassuring smile drew him closer. She then greeted him with a heavenly voice, "May God preserve you, my son! Where are you going?"

Overcome by the woman's beauty and surprised at seeing her among the trees, Juan Diego hesitated before he was able to reply, "I am taking water from the river to my sick ones who are dying."

"Come with me," the lady said, "and I will give you water to cure the disease. It will cure not only your family, but all who drink of it. My heart is ever ready to help those who are ill, for

I cannot bear to see their misfortune."

With the prospect of obtaining miraculous water that would certainly cure his relatives, Juan Diego followed the lady with happy anticipation. When they came to a depression in the ground the lady indicated a spring of fresh water.

"Take as much as you wish of this water," she told Juan Diego, "and know that those who are touched by even the smallest drop will obtain, not merely relief from their illness, but perfect health."

Juan Diego quickly emptied his jar and filled it with the clear water of the spring. When he turned toward the lady to express his gratitude, the lady entrusted him with a message for the Franciscans at the Monastery of San Lorenzo. "Tell the religious for me that in this place they will find my image. It will not only manifest my perfections, but through it I shall generously bestow favors and kindness. When they find the image, they are to place it in the chapel of San Lorenzo."

When the lady disappeared among the trees, Juan Diego continued on his way to Xiloxostla with the jar of precious water. Reaching the bedside of his afflicted relatives he told them about the apparition of Zoapiltzin, the lady-woman, and gave each of them a few drops of the water. Juan Diego watched in amazement as they quickly regained their health. News of the healings traveled swiftly, bringing many who wanted to learn the details of the apparition and to beg for a few drops of the miraculous water. The Lady kept her word. Everyone who drank the water instantly recovered their health.

Since it was already late in the day, Juan Diego waited until the next day to journey to the Monastery of San Lorenzo. When he told the friars about the apparition and the miraculous spring, the Franciscans reserved judgment. But after questioning the humble Indian on three occasions during the day, they decided that his story had some merit. They made plans to follow him to the miraculous spring at night, to avoid the curiosity of the natives. Nevertheless, the friars were seen leaving the monastery. Since no one traveled in Tlaxcala at night, the Indians were highly suspicious and decided to follow them.

As they traveled along they watched as a reddish glow brightened the trees in the distance. Then, after the group rounded the eastern slope of the Cerro de San Lorenzo, they discovered the cause of the glow. The grove of ocote trees was afire. The largest tree in the grove, and this one tree alone, was burning along its entire length. After watching for a few moments, they decided to leave since it was very late at night and nothing could be done until daybreak.

After Holy Mass the next day, the Franciscans and a large number of Indians returned to the grove. What they saw was puzzling. The fire was extinguished, but only the lower branches of the trees were burned. This seemed extraordinary since it was then the dry season and the ocote tree, a type of pine tree, was one that would burn fiercely if torched. The tallest tree that had been engulfed in flames along its entire length, was indeed blackened. Why the other trees were not completely consumed in a similar manner remained a mystery.

One of the friars, who had brought an ax with him, was instructed by the superior to chop down the trunk of the large tree. A Mexican chronicler of the time reports:

> A new marvel met their eyes: Within the trunk of the fallen tree was visible the image of the Holy Mother of God, representing the mystery of her Immaculate Conception—which can be seen today in the temple lovingly erected later by her children. . . In this manner the tale of Juan Diego was fully verified in the presence of many witnesses. The apparition of the Virgin Mary to her servant Juan Diego was a happy reality, on the day she showed him the medicinal water and sent him to advise the religious where they would find her sacred image.

The superior, after discovering the statue, arranged an orderly procession to the chapel of San Lorenzo. Hymns were sung and prayers were recited while branches from the ocote trees were waved in jubilation. Arriving at the chapel, the superior removed the statue of San Lorenzo and placed the figure of the Virgin Mary in its niche. Prayers of thanksgiving were then offered.

It is reported that the Indian sacristan of the chapel resented the removal of the statue of San Lorenzo and its relegation to a side table and decided to remedy the situation. On three successive nights he removed the statue of the Blessed Virgin and restored the statue of San Lorenzo to its former position of honor. Each night he hid the statue of the Blessed Mother in a different place and locked the church for the night, but each morning the statue of the Blessed Virgin was found in the niche, with the statue of San Lorenzo on the side table. Finally convinced of the supernatural character of the events, he confessed to one of the religious all that had taken place.

From the earliest times the statue was called *Nuestra Señora de Ocotlatia,* which means, "Our Lady of the Burning Ocote." It is now simply called Our Lady of Ocotlan, Ocotlan being the Nahuatl word for "place of the pine tree."

The statue of Our Lady is about 58 inches tall. It represents the Immaculate Conception with hands joined in prayer. It is usually dressed in costly vestments and wears a golden crown surrounded by a halo of stars. The crown represents Our Lady's pontifical coronation of 1906.

Our Lady of Ocotlan is a place of pilgrimage not only for the people of Tlaxcala, but also for those from throughout Mexico and especially from Mexico City which is a relatively short distance away. In addition to the miraculous statue, which is the primary source of interest, there are a number of places which the pilgrim may visit. A chapel stands in the ancient ocote grove where Our Lady appeared to Juan Diego. The place of the miraculous spring is still indicated, and in Xiloxostle, the birthplace of Juan Diego, holds some interest. Unlike the tomb of the first Juan Diego, which has been lost to memory, the tomb of Juan Diego Bernardino is found near the altar of the oratory in the Temple de Santa Isabel.

The Basilica of the Virgin of Ocotlan is regarded as one of the finest in Mexico. Started in the middle of the eighteenth century by an Indian architect, Francisco Miguel, the building was completed in the mid-nineteenth century. Of particular interest is the niche, or Camarin, above and behind the high altar which contains the miraculous statue of Our Lady. The wall behind the altar fairly dazzles the viewer with its numerous sculptures, all surrounded and covered with gold. It has been estimated that the basilica contains more than 200 pieces of sculpture.

OUR LADY OF OCOTLAN (right) is represented by a statue 58 inches tall which portrays the Immaculate Conception.

IMAGE IN A TREE. The marvel of Our Lady of Ocotlan began in 1541 when Juan Diego Bernardino was graced by an apparition of the Blessed Mother, who provided him with some water that speedily restored the health of his relatives suffering from smallpox. Our Lady told Juan that her image would be found at the location of the miraculous spring from which the water had been taken, as proved to be true; the statue of Our Lady of Ocotlan was miraculously discovered within the trunk of a fire-damaged tree.

A CROWN OF GOLD and a halo of stars adorn the statue of Our Lady of Ocotlan. The crown represents Our Lady's pontifical coronation in 1906.

— 73 —

OUR LADY OF THE ANGELS

Mexico City, D.F.
1595

Crops were ruined, disease threatened and the simple huts of the poor were swept away when heavy rains in 1580 caused lakes to pour their excess into Mexico City. Among the debris carried by the waters was a painting on canvas of the Blessed Virgin which came to rest in the barrio of Coatlan. It was rescued by an Indian named Isayoque, who descended from Aztec nobility.

Isayoque was so struck by the beauty of the image that he built a small adobe chapel for its enshrinement. Unfortunately, the effects of the flood caused the paint to flake off and the canvas to deteriorate. Since the portrait could not be restored, he commissioned an artist to paint an exact copy on the adobe wall of the chapel. In 1595, probably after Isayoque's death, church authorities authorized public worship in the little chapel. For a time the portrait was known as The Assumption of Isayoque, but later it came to be called Our Lady of the Angels.

The portrait is one of great beauty. With her eyes lowered and her head inclined, Our Lady gracefully folds her hands in prayer. Her dress is decorated with artistic tracings, and her mantle sweeps around her to be caught up under her left arm. Rays project from around her body and are star-tipped around her head. Standing upon a crescent moon, she is surrounded by little angels whose heads rest upon outstretched wings. It is a truly beautiful rendition of our heavenly Mother.

When devotion languished, the chapel began to disintegrate until it was completely ruined, all except one wall that was left standing—the wall that contained the painting of the Madonna. The place was almost forgotten until the flood of 1607, when Coatlan was again visited by high waters. In their distress the people remembered the holy painting and rebuilt the chapel as soon as the waters receded.

Some years later, after yet another flood, that of 1629, the chapel again fell into ruins and once again only the wall containing the portrait was left standing. The unusual aspect of this occurrence is that the flood waters reached up to the face and hands of the image and remained at that height for a period of five years. When the water finally receded the image was left exposed to the rain and heat of the sun. Despite this miraculous preservation the ruined chapel was again forgotten, except for a shepherd who used it as a corral for his flock.

Attempts were made in 1737 and in 1744 to rebuild the chapel. But when these plans were abandoned, Church authorities forbade veneration of the image and in 1746 sealed it behind grass mats and boards. It would reasonably be expected that the painting would have been ruined by its contact with the mats that absorbed water from periodic rains, but when the coverings were removed the following year the painting was found to be completely unharmed and its beauty preserved.

Once again the portrait was exposed to the elements until 1776 when a tailor, Jose de Haro, was passing by on February 28. Stopping his coach, he inspected the ruins and saw, in a beam of light, the beautiful features of Our Lady of the Angels. Ashamed at the pitiful surroundings to which Our Lady was subjected, he received the permission of Church authorities to restore the shrine. Using his own funds and those collected from his friends, Jose de Haro rebuilt the chapel into a magnificent church and served as its custodian until 1790, when he resigned because of poor health.

Due to its great popularity and the celebrity of Our Lady's miracles, the shrine came to the attention of Pope Pius VI. In 1793 he affiliated the church with the basilica of St. John Lateran in Rome and granted generous indulgences. Pope Gregory XVI gave permission for a special Office in the Roman Breviary to the cultus of Our Lady of the Angels. Pope Pius IX likewise recognized the shrine by granting it the Jubilee of the Portiuncula with all its indulgences. It was this Pope who was given a copy of the portrait, which he framed and kept beside his bed. It was one of the few possessions he took with him when he hastily left the Vatican in 1848 for the security of Gaeta during the tumult that developed over his refusal to join the war against Austria.

The image was finally honored when Pope Pius XI authorized the pontifical coronation of Our Lady which took place on October

28, 1923, with Archbishop Don Jose Mora y del Rio performing the ceremony.

The miracles of healing attributed to Our Lady of the Angels are numerous. There is an account dated November, 1852 of a Spanish soldier, attached to the Spanish Legation in Rome, who was mortally wounded, but who was cured almost immediately after being touched with a copy of the holy image.

That the portrait is regarded as miraculous is well deserved, not only for Our Lady's miracles of healing and the awarding of countless spiritual graces, but also because of its very preservation. In the various destructions of the sanctuary only the wall of the painting was preserved and neither floodwaters, nor the elements, nor the wet mats with which it was covered, nor the pelting rains or glaring sun, nor the corrosive action of the saltpeter found in the soil caused the slightest damage.

It is reported that the hands and the beautiful face of the Madonna have never been retouched and the wall has never been rebuilt. It stands today in the Church of Our Lady of the Angels in Mexico City, on the exact site of Isayoque's first chapel.

— 74 —

OUR LADY OF COMPASSION

(Nuestra Señora de la Piedad)
Mexico City, D.F.
1595

Shortly after the Monastery of Our Lady of La Piedad was given to the Dominican Order on March 12, 1595 by Don Luis de Velasco II, the Viceroy of New Spain, a Dominican priest and a lay brother were sent to Rome on business for the Order. One of their assignments was to obtain a painting of Our Lady of Compassion for their chapel.

Upon their arrival in Rome, they selected an artist of great reputation and paid in advance for his work. Some difficulty arose later when the artist would not set a date for the completion of the painting. The Dominicans settled their other business and were forced to extend their visit due to the failure of the artist to proceed with the commission. For reasons they could not explain, the artist repeatedly promised the painting, yet was indifferent to the assignment and only had a preliminary sketch on canvas when the Dominicans visited the studio for the last time.

Since they had already over-extended their stay in Rome, they accepted the sketch with great misgivings, realizing that their superiors in Mexico would be greatly disappointed with both the time they had spent in Rome and the large amount of money they had paid for a canvas with only a black charcoal sketch. With heavy hearts they boarded a ship for Mexico with the sketch carefully packed and crated.

While crossing the Atlantic the travelers feared for their lives when they encountered a fierce storm that raged around them for days. Advised by the Dominican priest that they should entrust their safety to Our Lady Star of the Sea, the passengers and crew did so and promised to erect a chapel in Mexico should they arrive safely. The storm abated almost immediately, much to their relief. As they had promised, they collected a large sum of money, which they entrusted to the Dominican priest.

Arriving at Vera Cruz, the Dominicans made their way overland to their monastery in Mexico City. After telling their confreres about the sketch on canvas, they were confronted with the expected disappointment. Some of the Dominicans quietly accepted the situation; others expressed their complaints. Still others agreed that they could have obtained an acceptable painting in Mexico for less than was paid for a canvas with black markings. However, as the carton was opened and the covering was being drawn back they saw color, and then more color, until a great painting was revealed—one depicting a pieta of extraordinary beauty.

This pieta, however, was different from most they had seen. With the body of the Crucified Christ sitting upon a low brickwork, the Sorrowful Mother stands behind her Son, supporting Him in an upright position by holding Him under both arms.

Greatly relieved and delighted with what they saw, the Dominicans immediately thought the travelers had meant to surprise them. The travelers, for their part, were standing in absolute amazement. Knowing for a fact that they had obtained a canvas with a charcoal sketch, they related the details of their visit to Rome: the difficult artist and their frequent visits to his studio, their reluctant acceptance of the charcoal sketch, the storm at sea, their prayer to Our Lady, and the calming of the storm. After hearing their story, all agreed that the painting was a supernatural gift of Our Lady.

The painting, now under the protection of glass, is displayed to the veneration of the faithful in the Sanctuary of Nuestra Señora of La Piedad. It is a large painting measuring almost nine feet in height and eight and a half feet in width. The colors are still bright and clear after almost 400 years.

Many miracles have been worked through the intercession of Our Compassionate Mother. A good number of these have been formally certified by an ecclesiastical tribunal.

A BEAUTIFUL PIETA. A colorful painting that has worked many miracles, Our Lady of Compassion is considered a supernatural gift of Our Lady.

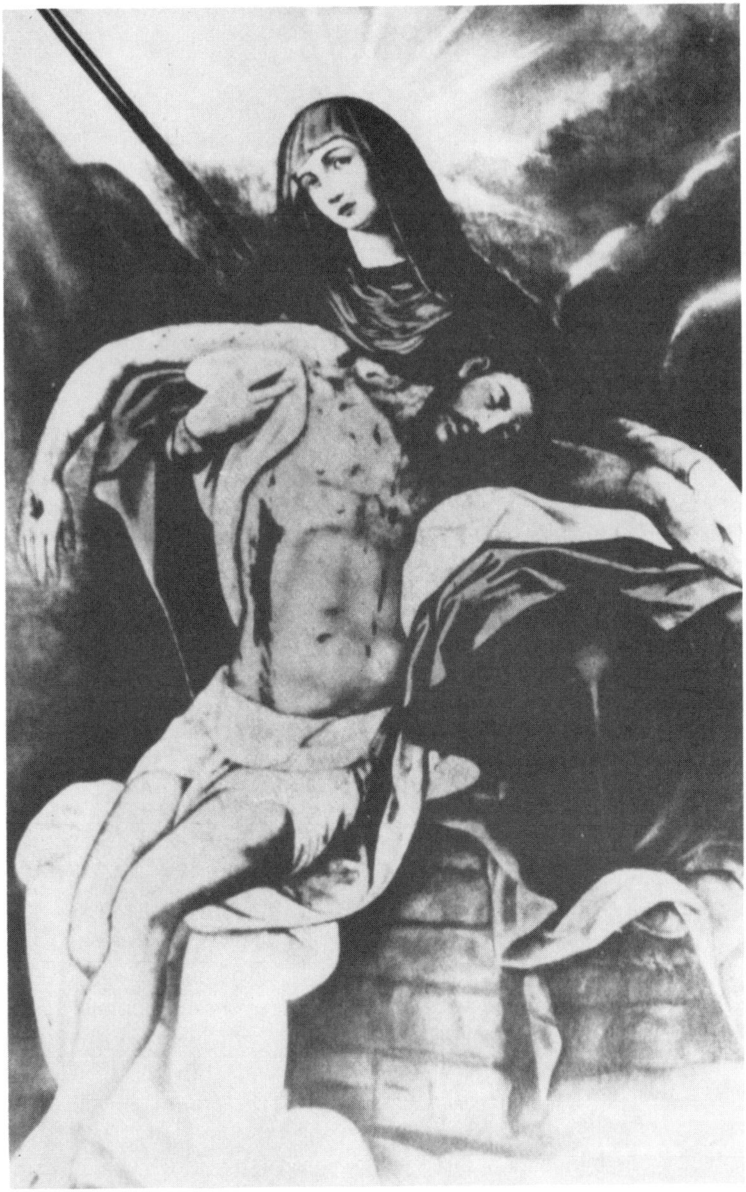

— 75 —

OUR LADY HEALTH OF THE SICK

(Nuestra Señora de la Salud)
Patzcuaro, Michoacan, Mexico
Sixteenth Century

When Bishop Don Vasco de Quiroga wanted a statue of the Blessed Virgin for the Christian community of Patzcuaro, he persuaded a member of the Tarascan tribe to sculpt it for him. Accustomed to fashioning idols, the Indian's statue was well received and is the one that is now venerated as the miraculous image of Our Lady Health of the Sick.

That particular title was affixed to the statue because of the apostolic labors of the Bishop who had founded a hospital for the Indians in the pueblo of Santa Fe in Mexico, and another in Patzcuaro, which was dedicated to St. Martha. The statue was first placed in the hospital chapel, where the Bishop entrusted the sick and the Tarascans to the care of the heavenly Mother.

When stories of cures and outstanding favors began circulating, both the Tarascans and the lofty Spaniards began to visit the hospital chapel to present their needs before the image of Nuestra Señora. As a result of the Bishop's labors, Our Lady Health of the Sick was known throughout Mexico as a wonder-working statue when Bishop Don Vasco de Quiroga died in 1565 at the age of 96.

The next cleric who enters the history of the miraculous statue is the Reverend Juan Melendez Carreno, who was named Pastor of Patzcuaro toward the end of the seventeenth century. Having received a great favor from Our Lady of Patzcuaro, he meant to show his gratitude by promoting devotion to Our Lady. He accomplished this by inaugurating a weekly procession in which the image was carried through the streets of the city while the Fifteen Mysteries of the Rosary were recited.

The clothing of statues had been in vogue for many years when Reverend Melendez decided to vest Our Lady, but to accomplish this, certain alterations had to be made. His plan was opposed on all sides since neither the Indians nor the Spaniards wanted the statue changed. Nevertheless, Reverend Melendez arranged for the project to be accomplished in secret. Legend tells us that the statue was taken one night to the sacristy, where the sculptors were ready to make the required modifications. When hammer and chisel were picked up and brought near the statue, the Virgin assumed an expression of great sorrow while a fluid, like perspiration, began to pour from her face. Everyone present was terror-sticken. Since no one dared to approach the statue, the plan was temporarily abandoned.

When the Jesuit priest, Bernard Rolandegui (who was a distinguished theologian) was asked for his recommendation, he suggested that while prayers were being offered before the image, the clergy should ask Our Lady's permission to make her statue more beautiful. When this was done, the sad expression disappeared. Work commenced without difficulty except that Our Lady refused to permit the sculptors to touch her head or hands. When they attempted to repair a scarred eyebrow, Our Lady refused their efforts. Varnish repeatedly applied to the area would not adhere and continually dropped off. The slight defect is still noted.

After the modifications were made and the statue was dressed in regal vestments, it was returned to the chapel. Seeing Our Lady clothed so magnificently, the people were delighted and all agreed that the statue had been greatly improved. The chapel, however, looked drab by comparison. So, funds were next collected from throughout Mexico for a new chapel; it was dedicated on December 8, 1717.

The wonder-working powers of Our Lady Health of the Sick became so well known that a solemn coronation of the image was decreed in a Pontifical Brief of Pope Leo XIII dated April 5, 1898. The actual coronation took place the following year on the feast of the Immaculate Conception.

Favors abounded at the shrine, so many, in fact, that a list of the miracles performed through the intercession of Our Lady was compiled by the Jesuit Father Pedro Sarmiento. The recipients of these favors, as well as those who witnessed the miracles, gave sworn testimony as to the accuracy of the reports, they being people of character and integrity.

One of the most unusual miracles was the appearance of a star on the forehead of the statue. Its first appearance occurred during the epidemic of 1692, when many fell victim to the disease. The Reverend Melendez decided to appeal to Our Lady Health of the Sick by performing a nine-day novena of prayer and by carrying her image in a procession through the streets of the city. The morning following the procession, the priest entered the church to offer Mass on the first day of prayer when he saw the star upon the forehead of the statue. Unable to find an explanation for its appearance he approached Don Francisco Lerin, a devout Spaniard who had dedicated himself to the care of Our Lady's sanctuary. Don Francisco, however, was just as curious about the star's appearance as were the people who entered the church for Holy Mass, all of whom clearly saw the star and its lovely brightness.

It is recorded that the epidemic began to diminish from that time on, the star losing its brightness in proportion to the number of victims who were recovering their health. On the last day of the novena, the star disappeared entirely.

Trustworthy witnesses have testified that the star has re-appeared at various times in its history as a prelude to some important event or the granting of an important miracle.

Our Lady Health of the Sick is well known for another miracle, this being the alleviation of droughts, the most notable being that of 1692. With streams drying up, fish, cattle and sheep dying and crops shrivelling from lack of water, the people asked for the statue to be taken through the streets of the city. When all was arranged and the bearers of the statue and the clergy were standing in readiness as the statue was being removed from its niche, the sky darkened and rain fell in torrents, successfully breaking the drought. The Lady has performed similar wonders during other droughts.

In addition to ending droughts, Our Lady has also been known to revive dried or abandoned wells and springs. The most memorable of these miracles took place in 1714 at the Rancho Huitzo in Pinzandaro when the spring that watered the cattle dried up. Help was requested of Don Fernando Vaca, Colonel in the armies of the Crown and Lieutenant General of Pinzandaro. He arranged for Our Lady's statue to be taken to the Rancho Huitzo in procession and for a Holy Mass to be offered, praying that through the intercession of Our Lady the spring would be restored.

While the altar was being arranged for Holy Mass, Juan Manuel Cantor tested the spring bed, but found only dryness. When the Mass was completed, such a volume of water rose to the surface that it gushed from its source. As though to demonstrate her generosity, Our Lady caused other springs to appear which provided water in excess of what was needed. Sworn testimonials were gathered from all the witnesses to this miracle.

For three centuries the little statue of Our Lady has been dearly loved and venerated by the Indians and the people of Patzcuaro. Known for restoring peace, giving needed rain during droughts, restoring wells and springs, it has even dismissed epidemics. But most of all, the Blessed Virgin is known as *Nuestra Señora de la Salud,* Our Lady Health of the Sick, the worker of miracles and a guiding star for her faithful children.

OUR LADY HEALTH OF THE SICK was already known throughout Mexico in 1565 as a wonder-working statue. When repairmen attempted to alter the sculpture according to directions from the local priest and contrary to the wishes of the people, the image is said to have assumed a sorrowful expression and seemed to perspire from the face.

— 76 —

OUR LADY OF SAN JUAN DE LOS LAGOS

(Our Lady of St. John of the Lakes)
San Juan de los Lagos, Jalisco, Mexico
1623

The second most popular image of Mary in Mexico, second only to Our Lady of Guadalupe, is the statue of Our Lady of St. John of the Lakes. In the early years of the seventeenth century, the holy Franciscan missionary Fray Miguel de Bolonia brought the statue to the village, then known as San Juan Bautista Mezquititlan, which was inhabited by the Nochiztleca tribe. Depicting the Immaculate Conception, it soon became a favorite of the Indians and was the center of their devotion. It became known beyond the village during the year 1623 when, according to an early legend, a spectacular miracle occurred.

A certain aerial acrobat was traveling along the Camino Real, the King's Highway, from San Luis Potosi to Guadalajara, performing in the towns along the way. His act included his wife and two daughters. His stunts included swinging from one high point to another by means of ropes, in somewhat the same fashion as trapeze artists of today. To add excitement and an element of danger, the artists had to fly over swords and knives which were stuck in the ground with their points positioned upward.

While performing in the village, the younger daughter, a child of six or seven, slipped, fell upon the knives and was mortally wounded. After preparing the body and wrapping it in burial cloths, the grieving parents brought the child's body to the chapel of Our Lady of San Juan for burial.

Meeting them at the door of the chapel was the 78-year-old Ana Lucia, the wife of Pedro Antes (the caretaker and custodian of the beloved statue). Feeling pity for the grieving family, she exhorted them to have confidence in La Virgencita, who could restore the child to them. Taking the statue from its altar in the sacristy where it had been consigned because of its poor condition, Ana Lucia laid it on the child's dead body. In a few moments they detected a slight movement under the shroud. The parents quickly unwrapped the cloth to discover the child well and unharmed. This first miracle of Our Lady of San Juan de Los Lagos became known in neighboring villages and towns. Numerous other miracles and favors followed, until now Our Lady is venerated by pilgrims from throughout Mexico and the United States.

The statue was in poor condition at the time of the first miracle because of its composition. Made of *pasta de Michoacan,* a combination of cornstalks and glue, it was brittle and considerably damaged by the elements. Because of its sad state, the grateful father asked if he might take the statue to Guadalajara to have it restored. The pastor, Don Diego Camarena, gave his permission and sent two Indians of the village to accompany him so that they could return the statue to the chapel while the acrobat went on his way.

As soon as they arrived in Guadalajara they were approached by a man who asked if they were in need of someone to repair a statue. Since he was an artist, he offered his services. After settling on a price, the artist was entrusted with the statue. In a few days the image was returned beautifully restored, with the face and hands of exceptional beauty. The artist however had vanished, and no one could tell the acrobat anything about him. The circumstances surrounding the artist have always remained a mystery.

The spread of devotion to the miraculous image required a larger sanctuary, so one was built in 1631. The popularity of the chapel was such that on July 14, 1678, Don Juan Santiago de Garabito, the Bishop of Guadalajara, ordered an accounting of all the miracles worked through the intercession of Our Lady of San Juan during the preceding ten years, as well as other information regarding the sanctuary. The detailed reply presented by Nicolas de Arevalo provides the researcher with all the facts regarding the early history of the image and its sanctuary.

By the year 1732 the sanctuary was unable to accommodate the multitudes who pilgrimaged from all parts of Mexico to observe the feasts of Our Lady. The first stone for a magnificent temple was laid in November of the same year.

A great distinction was awarded the shrine on August 15, 1904 when the statue was liturgically crowned by Don Jose Jesus Ortiz, the Archbishop of Guadalajara. Pope Saint Pius X authorized the crowning because of the great devotion to Our Lady of San Juan de Los Lagos, the antiquity of the statue, and the abundance of miracles attributed to Our Lady's intercession through the miraculous image.

The crown used for the ceremony is of gold measuring some seven inches high and weighing six pounds. It is adorned with 197 precious stones including diamonds, emeralds and sapphires.

Although the statue is made of a substance composed of cornstalks and glue which has a tendency to crumble in a relatively short time, the image has remained in excellent condition for over 350 years. Measuring about a foot in height, the face is well-proportioned and slightly dark in color; the hands are gracefully joined in prayer. The statue is clothed in beautiful garments and stands atop a crescent moon. Above the image are two angels of silver who support between them a silver ribbon with the words in blue enamel: *Mater Immaculata, ora pro nobis.*

The main feast days are February 2, which is Candlemas Day and December 8, the feast of the Immaculate Conception. The wonder-working statue is found in the parish church named for the Immaculate Conception, where it draws thousands of pilgrims from all over Mexico. The feasts are times of great joyfulness and are observed with fiestas, dancing, bullfights, cockfights and various amusements.

However, inside the church great solemnity is observed as local pilgrims demonstrate the urgency of their needs by traveling on their knees from the back of the church to the main altar.

RESTORER OF LIFE. The first miracle performed by Our Lady of San Juan de los Lagos occurred in 1623; a dead child was restored to life when the statue pictured above was applied to the youngster's body. Numerous other miracles and favors followed, and today thousands of pilgrims travel each year to the parish church in Jalisco, Mexico, named for the Immaculate Conception. There the miraculous statue is housed, and local pilgrims demonstrate the urgency of their petitions by traveling on their knees from the back of the church to the main altar.

— 77 —

OUR LADY OF THE ROUND

(Nuestra Señora de la Redonda)
Mexico City, D. F.
1670

The sixteenth century church which houses this miraculous statue has somewhat of a rounded configuration, due to the shape of its apse and camarin. It is for this reason that the statue became known as Our Lady of the Round.

When it became the custom to clothe statues in fabric, it seemed practical, when a statue was needed, for only beautifully sculptured face and hands to be supplied. These were then used by a less skilled craftsman who would attach them to a rudely sculptured torso which would then be covered with costly garments.

During the early seventeenth century, when a statue was needed for the Monastery of La Redonda, the General of the Franciscans, Fray Rodrigo de Zequera, who was then in Spain, sent to his confreres in Mexico the face and hands for a statue to be completed by a Mexican artist. When the superior of the monastery received the parts for the statue he was so pleased with the beauty of the face that he showed it to a number of people, one of whom, an old Indian woman, offered to have the rest of the statue constructed for him.

When she arrived at her home with the face and hands, she was met by three men who introduced themselves as craftsmen of monuments and statues. When they offered to complete the statue for her, she accepted their offer and provided them with a workroom. They stayed for three days and then left without a word. The Indian woman discovered—to her amazement—not a roughly hewned torso that would be hidden under fabric, but a statue beautifully sculptured in its entirety. All the villagers who gazed on it were overcome with wonder and regarded the visit of the workmen and their finished product as something of a miracle. When the statue was carried to the Monastery of La Redonda, the superior and his community marveled at the completed product and enshrined the statue in their chapel with great pleasure and satisfaction.

Many miracles were attributed to Our Lady by her faithful children, one of which took place in the year 1670 when the village was deprived of rainfall for six months. Owing to the flimsy nature of the Indian dwellings and the ever-present prospect of a disastrous fire, as well as the threat of disease, the people of La Redonda petitioned the Dean of the cathedral, Don Juan de Poblete, for a license to conduct a procession with the statue of Our Lady of the Round with the intention of imploring Our Lady for a heavy rainfall.

Permission was granted, but with one restriction: They were not to process out of the parish, but only up to the neighboring parish of Santa Catalina and then along the street of San Lorenzo.

On July 9, while the procession was in progress, rain began to fall in such torrents that the bearers were forced to protect the statue by hurriedly seeking shelter in the Monastery of San Lorenzo. Whereas the whole district was in dire need of rainfall, Our Lady demonstrated the reality of her extraordinary power since rain fell only in the area taken by the procession.

Another miracle took place on December 11, 1676, when the old church of San Augustin was engulfed in flames. The statue of La Redonda was hurriedly brought to the scene. All the witnesses were struck with wonder when the flames immediately died down in the presence of Our Lady. La Redonda was triumphantly returned to her church by the more than 3,000 people who participated in a spontaneous procession.

The third miracle is another instance of Our Lady providing rain. This took place in 1696, when rain was absent during most of the month of June. The situation was so desperate that the statue of La Redonda was brought to the cathedral where the Viceroy and the Canons began a solemn novena of prayer. At the conclusion of the novena the statue was returned to her sanctuary. As soon as the statue was in its place, rain fell in such abundance that the reservoirs were filled to overflowing, crops were saved and enough water was collected to meet the needs of the people.

The posture of La Redonda is unique among the miraculous images of the Blessed Mother. Standing with the left foot supported by a cloud, Our Lady seems to have taken a step higher as her right foot, also upon a cloud, is slightly elevated. With her garments caught, as it were, in a breeze, Our Lady looks heavenward with her open right hand raised higher than her shoulder. The left hand, also open, is extended, but falls downward at hip level. Although the statue is regarded as a representation of Our Lady's Assumption, the whole attitude of the statue seems to be one of pleading expectation. Our Lady seems to be stepping upward to the throne of God, reaching for a favor which she intends to transfer to her earthbound children, a function she has lovingly performed at the Church of La Redonda for over 300 years.

RAIN FELL during times of drought when Our Lady of the Round in Mexico City was petitioned for divine assistance. In 1676 the statue was rushed to the scene of a church fire, and the flames immediately died down. The very posture of the statue seems to indicate Our Lady's desire to beseech God for favors for her devotees.

— 78 —

OUR LADY OF THE LIGHT

(Nuestra Señora de la Luz)
Salvatierra, Guanajuato, Mexico
1676

According to popular legend, during the early part of the seventeenth century a mysterious light appeared on various nights in one of the rooms of an abandoned hut located in an Indian village named Guatzindeo. Since the village was part of the Hacienda San Buenaventura, the proprietor, Don Antonio Martin Tamayo, felt it his duty to determine the cause. At first he sent servants, but since they always returned without an explanation, saying there was neither light nor fire, he went himself to investigate in the company of a Franciscan religious. In the hut they found a great deal of trash, but then, under some discarded items, they discovered a badly damaged statue of Our Lady.

Don Antonio carried the statue to the hacienda and later sent it to Patzcuaro for repair. When it was returned, the extraordinary beauty of the statue was such that the Tamayo family built a chapel where the statue could be available for public veneration. Because of the mysterious brightness which prompted its discovery, the statue was given the name, Our Lady of the Light.

It is said that after its enshrinement, many people witnessed the image giving forth rays of light on a number of occasions. When it was taken on pilgrimage to the churches of nearby Salvatierra, the image occasionally repeated its luminous display. This phenomenon, of course, alerted the attention of people from the surrounding areas and a great number from faraway places, many of whom reported outstanding favors received through the intercession of Our Lady of the Light.

During the rainy season each year the miraculous statue was taken from its chapel in the Indian village of Guatzindeo to Salvatierra, where the people pleaded for enough rain to insure a bountiful harvest. Our Lady of the Light was also petitioned during epidemics, when prompt relief was always obtained.

When the Bishop of Valladolid, Spain, Don Juan de Ortega Montanes, was journeying to Mexico City, he became seriously ill while passing through Salvatierra. Since he was a great devotee of Our Lady, the Bishop offered Holy Mass at her altar in the Church of Our Lady of Carmen, where the miraculous statue was then being venerated. During the Mass the Bishop struggled against illness and weakness, but at the completion of the Mass, he felt a sudden surge of health and vitality. The Bishop marveled at his swift restoration to health and attributed his recovery to the motherly concern of Our Lady of the Light.

A sworn document dated 1676 made by someone who is now unknown relates the following:

> Many are the wonders which this sacred image has worked. For instance, when it began to be venerated in its first chapel, the undersigned witness knows that one night a thief entered to rob her of her crown and jewels. The thief confessed later that when he tried to take the crown, the sacred image turned away her sovereign countenance without letting him despoil her of her crown. And that neither was he able to leave the chapel until, on the following day, the story was told to one of the Alcaldes Ordinary, a certain Aguirre. This latter had him strangled to death, and his body set as an example and warning at the entrance of the bridge.
>
> Other wonders are so common and so frequent through the favor of Her Majesty, for the succor, patronage, and benefit of this city, that everyone can testify to them, as is evident. For all know that when they need rain, as soon as they take their case to the Lady for prosecution, she obtains rain for them. The same thing happens when any disease, plague, or epidemic begins. Relief comes quickly, as soon as it is asked for.

The statue was one time seriously injured when it was brought to Salvatierra for a nine-day novena. As the statue on its platform was being carried through a door, its head struck the top of the door frame and sustained a deep gash to the face. After studying the injury, many expressed the sad opinion that the injury was beyond repair. Almost at once a man in the crowd stepped forward and offered to repair the statue, saying that he was a sculptor of some experience. Since the people wanted the statue repaired as quickly as possible for its display during the novena, they relinquished the statue to his care.

The artist arrived early the next morning and immediately set about his work. At mid-morning he was offered food and drink, but he refused. At noon he was again offered a meal, which he also refused. During the afternoon he announced that he had completed the work, but that the statue should not be touched until the paint dried. He then left without being paid and never returned. Despite many inquiries his identity was never established. Since the statue showed not the least trace of its injury, the identity of the mysterious stranger was the subject of much speculation.

The municipal government of Salvatierra petitioned the Crown in 1743 for permission to build a sanctuary for Our Lady of the Light. When the venture was approved by the Viceroy, Conde de Fuenclara, work on the structure was started immediately. Since 1808 the miraculous statue has been venerated in this sanctuary.

The statue of Our Lady is one of great beauty. Holding the Child Jesus on her left arm, she holds a feathery branch and a baton in her right hand. Her head leans slightly toward the Child, a condition caused, they say, when she recoiled from the thief who attempted to steal her crown. She and her Child are dressed in beautifully embroidered garments. Standing upon a star-tipped half moon, with hair flowing over both shoulders, she wears a lace veil and the crown of her queenship. The Child Jesus is likewise beautiful as He holds an orb and wears a crown somewhat similar to that of His Mother.

In a Papal Brief dated September 16, 1938, Pope Pius XI granted the honor of a Pontifical Coronation for the image of Our Lady of the Light. The miraculous statue was crowned with a golden diadem in the name of the Supreme Pontiff by Dr. Don Leopoldo Ruiz y Flores on May 24, 1939.

MYSTERIOUS BRIGHT LIGHT prompted the discovery in 1676 of a badly damaged statue under a pile of trash. A luminous display continued to issue from the statue after it was repaired, and many favors were received by people who asked for the intercession of "Our Lady of Light." The beautiful statue was crowned with a golden diadem in 1939.

— 79 —

OUR LADY OF THE ANGELS

(Our Lady of the Assumption)
Tecaxic (Toluca), Mexico State, Mexico
1684

The image of Our Lady which has been venerated in Tecaxic for over 300 years is painted on a tilma, a cloak of cotton. It somewhat resembles the image of Our Lady of Guadalupe since Our Lady of the Angels assumes the same posture, with hands joined in prayer while golden rays burst behind her. Her mantle, however, is held by small angels who lift her toward billowing clouds. A detail that is very interesting is the left ear, which is prominent against her dark hair, as though Our Lady wishes to demonstrate her willingness to listen to the sorrows and joys of her children.

In addition to the figure of Our Lady, the bottom of the portrait depicts two apostles who look sadly into an empty sepulcher with its casket of jasper. While the apostles look downward, two holy women are gazing upward as angels carry the Virgin to the glory of Heaven. In the top portion of the painting the Heavenly Father, amid banks of clouds, is awaiting the arrival of the Queen of Heaven.

The name of the town, Tecaxic (tecaxitl), means place of rocks in the Nahuatl language. In the early history of the painting, Tecaxic was a thriving pueblo which had received the Faith through the preaching of the Franciscans who journeyed there from their monastery in Toluca. When the plague of 1640 caused the death of most of the population, the pueblo was abandoned. Also deserted were the huts and a tiny hermitage wherein was hung the painting depicting Our Lady of the Angels.

In time the hermitage became a complete ruin. The fierce wind and storms of the rainy season broke the roof and the doors. Huge holes appeared in the walls until the painting was left completely unsheltered and at the mercy of the elements. It was pummeled by rains and dust and scorched by a glaring sun.

As an example of the conditions endured by the painting, the story is told of Fr. Antonio de Samano y Ledesma, who one day was caught in a sudden rainstorm near the hut. He decided to take shelter in it but when he was unable to find a dry spot, nor a corner where he could escape the rain, he decided to continue on his way. The hut was incapable of providing even a semblance of protection for the priest or the painting.

Despite the weather, the painting remained unharmed; in fact, the colors are fresh and vivid in the entire painting. The preservation of the cloth is truly remarkable when one considers that it was painted on cotton of a loose, coarse weave that would normally rot under the conditions it was subjected to for so many years. Even more curious is the fact that it was painted in a medium known as distemper, a simple painting substance in which the pigment is mixed, or tempered, with an emulsion of egg yolk or sometimes with both the white and the yolk of the egg. It is an unstable medium that can ordinarily be smeared by rubbing.

After its placement in a new shrine, the miraculous nature of the painting was well established and officially recorded in the year 1684 by Fray Baltazara de Medina, Censor for the Holy Office of the Inquisition.

Reliable witnesses testified to the remarkable cure of a woman from the pueblo of Sinacantepec who journeyed on foot to visit the Virgin of Tecaxic. Crying in pain because of a cancerous arm that was to be amputated the next day, she recommended herself to the Holy Virgin, begging for her help and compassion. Since medications had failed her, she thought to obtain a healing poultice from the shrine itself. Scraping dust and earth which clung to the frame of the painting, she mixed it with saliva and applied it to her diseased arm. She then returned home. The next day, when the surgeon, Cristobal Mejia, arrived to amputate the arm, he discovered it to be completely cured without any mark or lesion. They could do no less than attribute the miracle to Our Lady of the Angels.

On another occasion an Indian woman from the pueblo of Calimaya arrived at the shrine totally blind, only to regain her sight on her way home. She returned to the shrine to give thanks to Our Lady and to report the cure to Francisco de Fuentes, who recorded it.

Still another time four men came to the shrine from the pueblo of Comalco, carrying between them a woman on a grass mat. The poor woman, crippled in her hands and feet, was completely unable to care for herself. Carried inside the church on a Thursday morning, she walked out well and strong two days later. The miracle was witnessed by many, who marveled at the power of Our Lady.

The report of these and many other miracles prompted Fray Jose Gutierrez, the Guardian of the Convent of San Francisco in Toluca, to begin the building of a new sanctuary in 1650. Miracles continued to be awarded by Our Lady in the new church, but one of the most charming involves the mysterious singing and the display of lights that emanated from the shrine.

It is told that Pedro Hidalgo, a highly respected citizen of Almoyola, was accustomed to doing business in Toluca. The road that stretched between these two pueblos passed through Tecaxic. Pedro Hidalgo's journey took him past the chapel of Our Lady of the Angels. There he often heard music of remarkable beauty, especially on Wednesdays and Saturdays. Sometimes he felt compelled to investigate the identity of the singers, but each time he entered the shrine he discovered only silence and solitude.

Sometimes when he passed the shrine at night he saw lights flickering through the windows. Thinking that services were being conducted and that the light was coming from numerous candles, he decided one night to take part in the service, only to find a darkened church when he opened the doors. On other occasions he saw the same lights, but as before, he found only a darkened church when he opened the doors. One night, thinking that the Indians had extinguished the candles in fear of him, he entered the church, called out and walked around only to find that he alone was there.

Pedro Hidalgo related these unusual incidents to his friends. Because of his unblemished character and the great respect with which he was regarded, they believed all he told them. Some out of curiosity, and others out of devotion, went at night to the shrine. Some heard the singing and saw the lights; others did not.

The miracles that occurred at the shrine, as well as the reports of the mysterious singing and display of lights, spread through the region and beyond, initiating a great devotion to Our Lady of the Angels.

RESEMBLING OUR LADY OF GUADALUPE, the 300-year-old image of Our Lady of the Angels in Tecaxio, Mexico is painted on a tilma, or cotton cloak. Some of the miraculous events associated with the image include the cure of a cancerous arm that was to be amputated, restoration of vision to the blind, and the healing of a crippled woman.

— 80 —

OUR LADY OF SANTA ANITA

Santa Anita, Jalisco, Mexico
Seventeenth Century

Many unusual and mysterious events have surrounded this small wooden sculpture known as Our Lady of Santa Anita. Measuring only a foot and a half high, it dates from before the year 1700 when an elderly hermit, who came from Europe, carried it with him as he traveled through Mexico. Upon reaching the little Indian village then known as Atlixtac, but which now is called Santa Anita, the holy man became seriously ill. A Christian Indian woman named Augustina, who was regarded by the villagers as their *curandera,* or native doctor, took the hermit to her humble dwelling and cared for him. In spite of her efforts, it became increasingly evident that her patient would die. Realizing the gravity of his illness, the hermit entrusted his treasured statue of Our Lady to Augustina, as she held it in great veneration. Following the hermit's death, Augustina hid the statue, fearing that the authorities might take it from her. It was then that the Blessed Virgin began to grant special favors on behalf of Augustina's patients.

As a devotee of the Blessed Mother, Augustina would encourage her patients to have devotion and confidence in the Mother of God. After each visit to the sick, she would routinely light a candle before Our Lady's image and would carefully observe the features. If the face became bright and glowing, Augustina knew that the patient would recover. If the face of the image became dark, she knew that her patient would soon die. She would then notify a local priest and prepare her patient for the reception of the Sacraments.

When the Franciscans at Tlajomulco learned of the prophetic image they questioned Augustina. She told how the face of the image changed in color, and by this method she was able to prognosticate health or death. Understandably skeptical, the friars decided to test the alleged marvel and carried the statue to their friary.

On their arrival, they placed the image in the cell of a friar who was ill. The ailing religious looked intently at the image and exclaimed, "You are beautiful, O Lady, but very dark." Soon thereafter, he died a holy death.

The image was returned to the Indian woman, but when she died it was placed in a local chapel. Soon devotion to Our Lady's image diminished until it was almost completely neglected.

In the middle of the seventeenth century, a Franciscan friar, Ignacio Tellez, was traveling through the village and visited the chapel. He was astonished to see an image of the Blessed Mother in a dirty and ragged condition. After learning of its unusual history and the many marvels that had attended it in the past, he resolved to restore the image to its former prestige. He had the statue vested in new garments and began to build another sanctuary directly opposite the chapel. The first stone of this new sanctuary was laid on the feast of the Assumption in the year 1700.

During the consecration ceremony, Friar Nicholas de Ornelas Mendoze, the chronicler of the Franciscan Province of Jalisco, told of new miracles of healing attributed to the miraculous statue—in particular the case of Friar Jose Nunez, the Superior of the monastery of Tlajomulco. The friar had been suffering for a lengthy time with a sickness that was accompanied by a high fever. After the Sign of the Cross was made upon his chest with oil from the lamp that burned before the image of Our Lady, the friar was immediately cured.

When a terrible epidemic of influenza swept through Mexico in 1918, it was promptly arrested when the holy image was carried in procession through the streets of the village.

A new and different marvel attended the image sometime later when the Franciscans of the monastery became aware that they were being forewarned by three knocks of the approaching death of one of their members. Known as golpes, these rappings are instinctively recognized as warnings, and have been associated with the relics and pictures of various Saints including St. Paschal Baylon and Bl. Anthony of Stroncone.

The little image of Our Lady of Santa Anita, holding the Child Jesus on her left arm, is now held in the greatest veneration. Of Spanish origin, it is made of wood and was painted over gilt by the process known as estofo. The tunic is of opaque vermillion, while the mantle is green enamel. Restored about the year 1918, the image's wardrobe consists of several garments, all beautifully embroidered in elaborate designs and bordered in golden fringes and tassels. Jeweled crowns adorn the heads of both figures, and a golden halo of rays and stars is positioned behind the head of the Holy Mother.

The miraculous statue welcomes her devotees who regularly visit from outlying villages. Each year solemn novenas are made and a grand fiesta is celebrated in her honor with great rejoicing.

A HERMIT FROM EUROPE carried this small wooden sculpture with him to Mexico in the seventeenth century, where it gained a reputation for miraculous healing powers. Later in the statue's history, it was given credit for forewarning residents of a Franciscan monastery when one of their members was about to die. To this day, devotees regularly visit Our Lady of Santa Anita in Jalisco, Mexico and celebrate a grand fiesta in her honor.

— 81 —

OUR LADY OF THE MIRACLES

(Nuestra Señora de los Milagros)
Tlaltenango, Morelos, Mexico
1720

The statue of Our Lady of the Miracles is enshrined in the church of San Jose, which was built in 1523 by Hernando Cortez, the Spanish conqueror of Mexico.

The image was first presented in the year 1720 toward the end of May when two young men, both handsome and cultured, traveled from Acapulco to Tlaltenango. After their arrival, they secured lodging for the night in the inn operated by Dona Agustina Andrade. They left the next morning, after entrusting their hostess with a decorated box they intended to reclaim on their return journey. However, the young men never returned.

The box remained in the room where it had originally been placed and was somewhat overlooked by the family of Dona Agustina until the night two months later when heavenly music was heard coming from the room. The whole family was roused. With music wafting about them, the family approached the doors, opened them and to their amazement discovered rays of light pulsing from the box and a heavenly fragrance filling the room.

Fearful that the civil authorities might confiscate the box, they planned at first on keeping the miraculous happenings a secret. But soon afterward they felt themselves bound to reveal the miracle to the clergy and their devout friends.

The first cleric to learn of the miracle was Fray Pedro de Arana, the pastor of the Church of the Assumption in Cuernavaca. The civil authorities were also alerted in the person of the mayor at the Palacio. He, together with Fray Pedro and other ecclesiastical and civil authorities, journeyed to Tlaltenango to investigate the unusual occurrence.

Arriving at the door to the room, the authorities ordered all lights to be extinguished before they entered. After crossing the threshold they too saw rays streaming from the box, and also perceived the perfume that sweetened the air. After recovering from the initial surprise, Fray Pedro was appointed to open the box. After prying off the lid, all present were amazed to discover a statue of the Blessed Mother clothed in an exquisite rose tunic and blue cloak.

All agreed that the miraculous statue should be entrusted to Fray Pedro, who carried it to the Church of San Jose, with the ecclesiastical and civil authorities in attendance. A novena was started the next day and ended on September 8, the birthday of the Blessed Mother. Since 1720 a fiesta has taken place every year on September 8 in commemoration of the phenomenal events that occurred before the statue was revealed to the devotion and admiration of the people of Tlaltenango.

After numerous miracles were distributed by the Holy Virgin, the title conferred upon her was Our Lady of the Miracles. The title is most appropriate, judging from the countless ex-votos covering the walls of Our Lady's shrine.

The Bishop of Cuernavaca, the Most Reverend Sergio Mendez Arceo, placed a golden crown on the head of the miraculous image on December 8, 1954, and designated it Our Lady, Queen and Patroness of the City and the Diocese of Cuernavaca.

HEAVENLY FRAGRANCE and music emanated from a box streaming with light which had been left by two young men at an inn in Mexico in 1720. When the box was opened, the statue of the Blessed Mother pictured above was discovered. The owners of the box never returned to reclaim it, as they had said they would. In 1954 the statue, known as Our Lady of the Miracles, was crowned and designated Our Lady, Queen and Patroness of the City and Diocese of Cuernavaca, Mexico.

— 82 —

OUR LADY OF THE THUNDERBOLT

(Nuestra Señora del Rayo)
Guadalajara, Jalisco, Mexico
1807

When the Dominican nuns of Guadalajara settled in their convent in 1792, a statue had already been installed which represented Our Lady's Assumption into Heaven. The nuns added a pearl rosary and converted it into an image of Our Lady of the Rosary, a devotion promoted by the Dominican Order. The statue was situated in a dormitory and was the object of quiet devotion until an extraordinary event took place on August 13, 1807.

At 2:30 a.m. a violent storm shook the very foundation of the convent. Lightning flashed while thunder boomed over the countryside. The nuns were already having difficulty sleeping when a bolt of lightning flashed right through the dormitory, knocking over a night lamp and filling the place with smoke. In total darkness, the terrified nuns screamed and groped about for safety. In the flickering light of a candle they discovered, to their relief, that all the sisters were unharmed. What they next saw filled them with wonder.

The statue of Our Lady had been struck by the lightning. Its clothing and hair were scorched and its eyes of crystal were shattered. The bolt of lightning had made a direct strike. Amazingly, the Child Jesus in His Mother's arms, nor the religious pictures on either side of the statue, nor the sisters sleeping within a few feet of the statue, were hurt.

In thanksgiving for their miraculous escape from harm, the sisters carried the statue to the church adjoining their convent, and there a Mass of Thanksgiving was offered the next morning. The statue was then placed in the convent chapel. Five days later another strange event took place.

At 3:30 p.m. on August 18, Sister Maria Teresa de San Joaquin enlisted the help of two workmen to carry the statue from the chapel to the cell of a nun who was desperately ill. While the workmen were preparing to lift the statue, the chapel grew dim as rain clouds gathered for another storm. As the chapel grew even darker, the statue of Our Lady became illuminated from the head to the breast. The workmen were both astonished and fearful, as were the sisters who watched while the statue pulsed with a soft, unearthly glow.

Since it was time for Vespers, Prioress Sister Maria Francesca de la Conception gathered all the sisters in the chapel for the recitation of the Psalms. They prayed peacefully while the statue glowed in its heavenly light. Suddenly, the peace of the chapel was shattered, and the nuns struck with terror, when thunder shook the chapel and lightning exploded in intense brightness. When they recovered, a wonder presented itself. Our Lady's image, which had been blackened and scorched from the earlier lightning strike in the dormitory, was now restored to its original colors. Even the pearl rosary had recovered its luster; and the crystal eyes, shattered for the past five days, were now clear.

The events were so unusual that an official investigation was conducted. The facts were later verified by the chaplain of the Church of Jesus Maria, Don Manuel Cervino and by the Governor of the Episcopal Chancery, Don Jose Maria Gomez y Villasenor.

Many are the miracles attributed to Our Lady of the Thunderbolt. Among them is the cure of Sister Maria de Jesus Cecilia de San Cajetano, who was instantly and completely cured from spinal paralysis after suffering from the affliction for many years.

Another case of spinal paralysis was instantly cured when Dona Micaela Gomez de Contreras was being carried to the Church of Jesus Maria, where she was to attend a Solemn High Mass being offered in her honor. Dona Micaela had been enduring the paralysis for a period of 32 years, from 1824 until 1856, when she was completely restored to health.

The statue of Our Lady of the Thunderbolt is 41 inches in height. She is clothed in rich robes and stands upon a half moon of silver. The Child on her left arm is also clothed in costly vestments. Both hold golden scepters and rosaries and both wear golden crowns which were placed upon their heads during the Pontifical Coronation that took place on August 18, 1940. Conducting the ceremony was the Archbishop of Guadalajara, Don Jose Garibi Rivera, who served as the Pontifical Delegate of His Holiness.

The principal feastday of Our Lady of the Thunderbolt is observed each year on August 18, the anniversary of the miraculous restoration of the statue. On this day great crowds from throughout the state of Jalisco gather in the Church of Jesus Maria to visit and to wonder at the statue which experienced two extraordinary manifestations of nature and the healing power of God.

LIGHTNING STRUCK the beautiful statue pictured above in 1807, located in a Dominican convent at Guadalajara, Mexico. Damage to the image was miraculously undone a few days later, when lightning struck again.

— 83 —

OUR LADY OF SCHIEDAM

Schiedam, The Netherlands
1379

A biographer of St. Lydwine of Schiedam (1380-1433) gives us some details concerning the miraculous statue which was often visited by the Saint during her childhood. We are told that a sculptor arrived in Schiedam with a wooden statue of Mother and Child which he intended to sell at a fair in Antwerp. Although the statue seemed to require two persons to lift it, it was nevertheless light enough for one. The sculptor was only pausing in Schiedam long enough to book passage on a ship bound for Antwerp. After passage was arranged, the sculptor carried the statue aboard the ship, but as soon as it was on board, the statue became enormously heavy.

For an inexplicable reason, it became impossible for the vessel to leave its mooring. More than 20 sailors struggled to set the ship free, but without suçcess. Their efforts soon attracted a crowd, which found great amusement at their difficulty. Embarrassed and exhausted, the sailors admitted their inability to perform a task that had always been routine. The unusual situation required an investigation and, as a result, attention was drawn to the statue and its sudden increase in weight. The order was given for the statue to be taken ashore. When the sculptor refused, the threat was made that if he would not leave voluntarily, both he and the statue would be thrown overboard.

The statue that had become heavy as soon as it was on board ship suddenly became light when the sculptor agreed to take it ashore. As the sculptor disembarked among the acclamation of the people, the boat sailed away without the slightest difficulty. It was everywhere declared that the mysterious event indicated that the Blessed Virgin was intent on having her statue remain in Schiedam.

When the parish priest was informed of what had taken place at the dock, he also agreed that the statue must remain in their city. After meeting with the members of the trade guilds, the priest acquired the statue and placed it in the church.

The statue was entirely of wood, exquisitely carved and beautiful in every detail. The Virgin Mother was depicted standing, holding the Child Jesus on her left arm and a scepter in her right. Her garments fell in graceful folds, while lenghts of hair trailed on her shoulders. She was crowned and her face was beautiful, but she appeared sad as she looked downward.

The city of Schiedam is well known for the miraculous statue, but its fame seems to rest more on its famous resident, St. Lydwine of Schiedam. One of the Saint's biographers declares that little is known of the early life of this Saint, but that he is certain of two particular facts: that the miraculous statue was made a little before her birth, and that during her childhood she delighted in visiting it. At the age of seven years, when she was charged with bringing lunch to her brothers at school, she fulfilled this task as quickly as possible so that she could visit the church to pray before the miraculous statue. Once when she was very late in returning home, she answered her mother's questions by stating, "I went to salute Our Lady the Virgin, and she returned my greeting with a smile."

Later, of course, St. Lydwine became a victim soul afflicted with various illnesses that made a journey to the church impossible.

During the Reformation the original statue was destroyed, but a replica was made which has proved to be enormously popular.

ST. LYDWINE OF SCHEIDAM (1380-1433) often visited this wooden statue, which demonstrated in 1379 that it did not want to be removed to another city.

— 84 —

THE SWEET MOTHER OF 'sHERTOGENBOSCH

'sHertogenbosch, The Netherlands
1380

At first the statue was despised, mocked, ridiculed, insulted and smeared with paint. In the end it was honored by an Emperor, two Popes and countless members of the faithful.

During an enlargement of the Church of St. John in 1380, an apprentice mason was examining a pile of stones in the builders' shed when he came upon a mutilated wooden statue of Our Lady. He was about to chop it for firewood when he was stopped by the architect. Since it was Holy Thursday, and because it was then the custom to place all movable statues around the Easter Sepulcher, the mason carried it inside the church and placed it among the other statues. It is uncertain if he did this in atonement, or for amusement. When the parishioners saw the contrast between the dirty statue of the rock pile and the beautiful statues of the church they were horrified and criticized the statue with words that were both mocking and insulting. When they called for the statue's immediate removal, the young mason retaliated with words that were equally insulting: "You are just as old and ugly yourselves!" The voices quieted, and the statue remained in its place.

After the Easter celebrations, when the other statues were returned to their niches, Brother Wouter, a lay brother, decided to place the statue in the side chapel dedicated to St. Michael.

When the sacristan, Dierik van Loet, realized that not one person liked the mutilated statue, he gave permission for Brother Wouter to do whatever he wanted with it. When Brother Wouter went into the chapel to remove the statue, he found it too heavy to move. After a time, some painters who were working close by jokingly smeared the figure with yellow paint. Later a piece of embroidered linen was placed around the shoulders of the Madonna. Brother Wouter, in the meantime, went in search of the statue of the Holy

Child that was obviously missing. Brother Wouter found the small image the following year, 1381, when he saw children on Orthen Street playing with a wooden doll. This proved to be the missing figure, since it fitted perfectly and was made of the same wood and craftsmanship.

Standing 3′ 3″ in height, both Mother and Child are made of oak. The Madonna's mantle falls in folds to below the knee, while the robe reaches to the floor where the slipper of the right foot is visible. Both hands of the Madonna are extended. In her right hand the Madonna holds an apple. The Holy Child is seated on His Mother's left hand in what seems a curious position, completely away from the body of His Mother. The Mother, seems to hold the Child away from her with one hand in an effortless, but unnatural, manner. Mother and Child are portrayed with pleasant expressions, making them both very appealing.

During the same year, 1381, the year during which the figure of the Child was returned to His Mother, we are told that a noble lady named Oda had the statue moved from St. Michael's chapel to that of St. Martin. The parishioners still mocked and ridiculed the statue, especially when a workman drew charcoal eyes on the face. A visitor to the chapel saw this and exclaimed, "What a deformed, yellow statue it is!" It would seem that Our Lady had sustained enough abuse, since she appeared to the woman that night in a dream and sweetly reproved her. "Why do you call me ugly who am beautiful, and dwell in eternal Heaven. I tell you to have recourse to me so that you may overcome your sufferings and gain Heaven also." The woman is said to have stirred from the dream fully repentant. To make amends, she agreed to pay for repairs to the statue which included the correction of the broken arm and the services of an artist to repaint the facial features.

During the same year another woman declared with amusement that it looked as if the Madonna had jaundice. The woman is said to have fainted on the spot. She was subsequently confined to her bed for a fortnight until she promised to make amends.

Still another unusual event occurred in the same year, 1381. Hadewych van Vichten, a housewife who had been lame for three years, reportedly had a vision in which Our Lord promised a cure if she would visit the rejected Virgin in St. John's Church and place there an ex-voto in the form of a miniature leg. She did as Our Lord suggested—and was instantly cured.

After this miracle, the noblewoman, Oda, had the statue repaired by a gifted artist whose work seemed to please the parishioners. When a fire ravaged the church and threatened to harm the statue, a spark of love seemed to stir in the people. While the crowd watched the fire, a voice sounded over the roar of the flames: "Save yourself, Sweet Mother!" Immediately some of the people rushed in, grabbed the statue and carried it to safety. After the shrine was repaired, the parishioners happily enshrined the statue in its usual place. From then on the statue was known as Sweet Mother, even to the present day, 600 years later.

Graces, favors and cures began at once to reward those who had devotion to the Sweet Mother. During times of religious and political stress, the Sweet Mother gave encouragement to the people and rewarded the confidence placed in her. Due to these countless favors, the statue of the Sweet Mother became widely known, attracting people from near and far, and even members of royalty including Emperor Maximilian. In the year 1841, when a Chapter of the Golden Fleece was held at 'sHertogenbosch to honor Our Lady, among the nobles who attended were Ferdinand of Castile, Ferdinand of Naples, Edward IV of England, Philip I of Spain and others.

In preparation for the royal visitors, the statue's flaws were corrected and the garments polychromed in colors which we see today. The Virgin is in scarlet and her Holy Child in green, while gold enhances borders and strands of the Madonna's hair. Gothic roses were added to the tunic and precious crowns were placed upon the heads of both figures. Fully restored and in regal attire, the Virgin and Child welcomed their royal visitors.

A procession around the town became an annual event which, from 1511, has taken place on the Sunday after the feast of the Visitation. Although the town has grown, the procession still wends its way along the streets of its original route which is known as the *Omgang,* "The Going Round."

During the time when iconoclasm prevailed, the statue was removed from the church and remained in exile for 262 years. While the statue was absent, the chapel of the Virgin was visited as before—but the annual procession was suspended, since these were strictly forbidden. Undaunted, the people still made the *Omgang* by walking nonchalantly, at night or during the day, in twos and threes as though they were simply taking a stroll. The authorities were aware that all were going in the same direction, but since their going was not organized, no action was taken against them.

The statue of the Sweet Mother was finally restored to its chapel in 1828. Fifty years later, in observance of the anniversary of its return, Pope Leo XIII ordered the coronation of the statue. Later, St. Pius X granted the privilege of an Office for the feast, which is held on the same day as the annual procession, the Sunday following the feast of the Visitation.

The statue of the Sweet Mother is located in the chapel at the west end of the basilica. Everything is so arranged that the chapel is accessible even though the main doors of the basilica might be closed. The chapel is crowded with ex-votos and is always ablaze with candles. As in countless shrines around the world, some of these ex-votos are in the form of miniature body parts of wax or metal which signify the areas healed in answer to prayers. Among these ex-votos in the chapel are miniature legs placed there in 1381 by Hadewych van Vichten, who was mentioned previously, after she was cured by the Sweet Mother.

— 85 —

OUR LADY STAR OF THE SEA

Maastricht, The Netherlands
1400

Located in the area where a fragment of southeast Holland dips sharply southward, the city of Maastricht is completely landlocked by Belgium and Germany, yet it honors an ancient statue of the Virgin known as Our Lady Star of the Sea. Since the city is bisected by the Meuse River, the statue no doubt obtained its name because of the many bargemen and sailors who availed themselves of the city's docks. Since the early fifteenth century, when the statue was brought to the Franciscan church, countless sailors have visited the Madonna to petition for safe voyages. Not only have sailors honored the Blessed Mother, but also the people of Maastricht and countless others from various nations who have displayed a thriving devotion throughout the centuries and who have sometimes guarded the statue with heroic efforts.

The traditional claim which local historians regard as reliable is that a chapel of Our Lady was founded in Maastricht in the early Christian days. During the tenth century a church of cathedral proportions was built near the river bank. It is this church that still enshrines the miraculous statue which was given to the church in the year 1400 by Nicholas van Harlaer when he joined the Franciscan Order at Maastricht.

The statue is of wood, about four feet tall, a beautiful example of late thirteenth-century sculpture. The Virgin Mother's head is inclined to her left as she holds the Holy Child on her left arm. The right hand of the Virgin Mother holds a small, round vase which was intended originally as an inkwell, but its quill pen was replaced long ago with a lily. This is reminiscent of a devotion once popular in Flanders known as Our Lady of the Inkpot. While the Blessed Virgin was sculptured with a veil, dress and mantle, all of which hangs in graceful folds, the figure of the Infant Jesus is completely unclothed. It is usually outfitted, however, in one of its many brocaded dresses, while the Virgin Mother is adorned in a matching mantle. Both figures wear costly crowns. Regarded as one of the most beautiful of all the medieval statues of Our Lady, it is the face of this one which invites study since the expression is difficult to define.

There are reports of miracles occurring early in the statue's history, but records of these have either been lost or poorly kept. Early in the seventeenth century, however, one of the Franciscan friars, Rev. Henry Sedulius, proved to be a conscientious recorder and researcher who compiled information concerning the miracles that had occurred since 1556, most notably the miracle involving Agnes Schryvers, which had taken place that year. Rev. Sedulius' compilation of miracles was published in 1609.

Rev. Sedulius knew Agnes Schryvers when she was already an adult, but the miracle actually occurred when Agnes was a child. Born dumb and lame with asthma and other bronchial afflictions, the child was taken by her mother to visit the miraculous statue on Easter Monday, when both took part in the annual procession. While Holy Mass was in progress the mother left Agnes in the Lady Chapel while she went into the main church for the Consecration. During the mother's absence, Agnes, for the first time in her life, stood up and started to walk toward the church door. Her first words were those for her own encouragement which she repeated with each step, "Go on! Go on!" She refused her father's attentions and continued walking while swinging her arms and repeating, "Go on! Go on!" Agnes was completely cured from that moment and enjoyed robust health for the rest of her life.

Every year after this spectacular cure, the registry of miracles was supplemented with more miracles and outstanding favors which flowed from the generous hand of Our Lady.

Few statues have had the adventures and clandestine travels as has this statue. These journeys began in 1570 when the dreaded Protestants took the city. When danger threatened, a miller, Jan van Ceulen, took the statue home and entrusted its safety to several neighbors in succession.

One day, while the statue was hidden in the loft of a local convent, a Calvinist soldier found it and tried to slash it with his sword. His arm was instantly paralyzed as he prepared to strike. Another soldier, seeing the difficulty, ridiculed his companion and prepared to succeed in harming the statue where his friend had failed—but with the same result. Complaining to the nuns that they had apparently bewitched the statue, it was smuggled over the garden wall that night for safekeeping in the home of Maria Luckers, a pious widow.

After a few years of peace, the city was captured by Frederik Hendrik, who soon instigated an anti-Catholic persecution. When the Franciscan protectors of the statue were expelled, the statue was taken across the river to the city of Wyck. From Wyck the statue was smuggled to Lichtenberg, and then to Tongres. During the French Revolution it was once more smuggled from house to house. During its various returns to Maastricht, while its original shrine was in disrepair, it was also kept for various lengths of time at various churches in or near Maastricht.

During the statue's exile in Lichtenberg an unusual event took place. Between November 9 and December 8, for one whole month, a lark was seen to visit the temporary shrine of the statue. Many observed that the lark would pause for a time to sing a sweet song to the Virgin Mother. On December 8, when the friars carried the statue down to the boat to take it to the city of Vise, the lark joined them. It circled around the box in which the statue was hidden and then flew away. This is reminiscent of the white doves in our own time, when in the year 1946 they nestled under the statue of Our Lady of Fatima for almost two weeks, neither eating nor drinking. Beginning at the city of Bombazral in Portugal, the doves remained with the statue as it was brought from city to city, eventually arriving at Lisbon for the celebrations commemorating the third centennial of the country's dedication to the Immaculate Conception. During the journey the three doves remained, despite the playing of bands, the noise of the crowds and the buffeting of flowers which were tossed at Our Lady's image. Photographs of the doves were published in newspapers throughout the world.

When the statue of Our Lady Star of the Sea was returned to Maastricht for the last time, it was kept in what was called the Portiuncula Chapel. Since formal processions were then forbidden, the usual Easter Monday function was held in the garden, but many of the people continued to walk what they thought was the old route of the procession. Since the processions had been suspended during the statue's many travels, the former route of the procession was uncertain. Finally a dispute arose concerning the exact route, which was known as "The Way." A story is told that one Easter

Monday night, an old woman, Mother Anna, who was deep in prayer before the miraculous statue, was surprised to see it suddenly surrounded by rays of light. When the statue became animated, Our Lady descended from the altar of the shrine and walked from the chapel through the street to Our Lady's Church. There the Blessed Mother seemed to kneel for a few moments at the door before returning to the shrine in the Portiuncula Chapel.

When Mother Anna reported that the Blessed Mother had retraced the route of the original procession, no one believed her until they visited the shrine. There they found the skirts of Our Lady's robes stiff with mud. From then on, even to our own time, those who want a special favor make a pilgrimage along "The Way" while reciting the Holy Rosary. They end their private devotion with a prayer at the feet of the Madonna. Today, wayside shrines line the path indicated by the vision.

During the years, custodians have been aware that the statue never collects dust or cobwebs. The same curious situation has also been noticed at Oropa, Italy with regard to its statue of Our Lady. Although protected behind glass, dust nevertheless seeps through crevices in the framing and accumulates around the figure, but never has a particle of dust fallen on the faces of Mother or Child.

The miraculous statue is now venerated in a special chapel in the ancient church of Our Lady, which has been raised to the rank of a basilica. The chapel is near the door where Mother Anna saw Our Lady kneeling.

PERSECUTORS were prevented from slashing the statue known as Our Lady Star of the Sea (at right) in 1570 when two soldiers raised their swords, only to find that each man's arm was instantly paralyzed. Among the other amazing characteristics of the statue, it has been noted by custodians that the faces depicting Our Lady and the Infant Jesus never collect any dust.

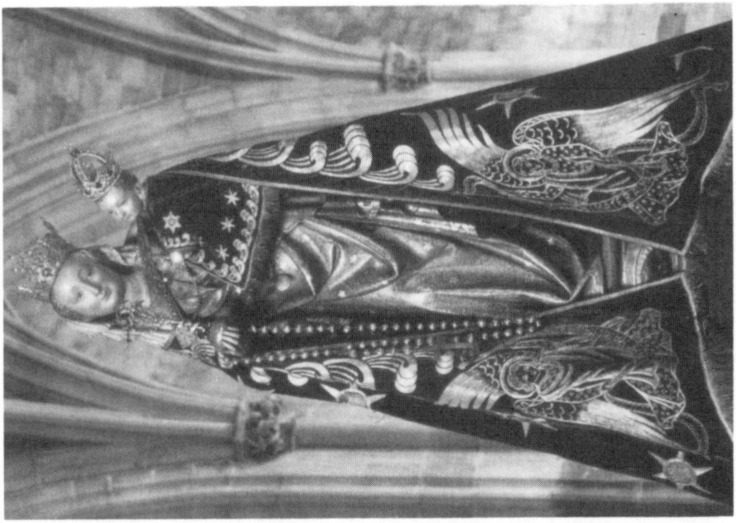

AGNES SCHRYVERS was cured of lameness and other physical afflictions when she visited this statue as a child, in the year 1556. Many cures and favors have since been credited to Our Lady Star of the Sea.

— 86 —

OUR LADY IN THE SAND

Roermond, The Netherlands
1418

A small wooden chapel dedicated to Our Lady in the Sand *(Onze Lieve Vrouw in 't Zand)* once stood on the sandy flats outside the city of Roermond. It was much frequented by pilgrims during the early fifteenth century and was well known for its statue and the many miracles that were granted through the influence of Our Lady.

The existence of the chapel is confirmed as early as June 24, 1418, when the Mayor and Council of Roermond wrote a letter in which they instructed Matheus Peuten (the parish priest of the Kerspels church) that he should assume "the care and management of the Lady Chapel in the Sand outside the Zwartbrueck Gate, recently built at the instance of the Carthusian Prior and Sir Gerard Van Vlodrop." Other writings of the time also tell of the chapel and the wonderful miracles granted there. Unfortunately, the fires of 1554 and 1665 destroyed most of the city's archives, as well as much of the documentation regarding these early cures and favors.

Our attention now turns to an apparently unbroken local tradition which relates that Wendelinus, the son of a Polish knight, while looking for work, came upon the farm of Gerard Muggengebroeck. Unable to find more elegant work, and because of his extreme need, he agreed to work for the farmer as a shepherd. The year was 1435. One day, while the sheep grazed on the flatlands, Wendelinus became enormously thirsty and went in search of water. Coming upon a well that was known to have run dry, he nevertheless tried to obtain some water and found not only a quantity of fresh water, but also a small statue of Our Lady. It was soon learned that the statue had been enshrined near the well in a tiny, primitive chapel.

When a blind girl was cured after a novena in honor of Our Lady of the Sand, the parish priest ordered that the statue be taken to the large parish church. In accordance with his wishes, the statue was carried there in a solemn procession, but the next day, when the statue was missing from the church, it was found once more by the well. It was then decided that a special chapel would be built at the place for its enshrinement.

The popularity of the shrine spread rapidly, as indicated by Fr. Luncenius, who gave the City Council a list of the offerings made by the pilgrims from 1467 to 1495.

All was not peaceful for the shrine. It had to contend with Protestant iconoclasts and certain Spanish governors. One of these governors, Blasius van Vegersheim, ordered the destruction of the chapel in 1578. The people protested, but the shrine was destroyed nonetheless. The statue, however, was rescued and found refuge in St. Christopher's Church.

Having witnessed and experienced the special protection of Our Lady in the Sand, the Dean of the Cathedral, Heer Petrus Pollius, was inspired in 1610 to erect a new chapel for Our Lady. Three years later it proved necessary to enlarge it. For this endeavor Archduke Albert and Archduchess Isabella contributed 100 guilders.

Miraculous cures continued as before. In a declaration of Theodore John Kremers dated April 28, 1610, he tells of his miraculous cure and his promise to make a pilgrimage to Our Lady's Chapel *"in het Zand."* Early records tell that James a Castro, the Bishop of Roermond, verified in 1613 that a woman from Heinsberg was suddenly cured at the shrine. Fr. James Wijns, a Jesuit, sent documents to Fr. Heribert Rosweide in 1623 in which he stated that the Mayor and Council vouched for seven miracles received from Our Lady in the Sand.

In addition to wonderful cures, a miracle of another kind took place in 1624 when a conflict developed between Spain and the Protestant north. When it seemed that the Protestants would prevail, the Marian Brotherhood made an urgent pilgrimage to the chapel. Almost immediately the water of the Ysel River froze to permit the crossing of a Catholic army that soon defeated the Dutch Calvinists.

The well that had figured so prominently in the recovery of the statue was enclosed within the chapel during an enlargement made in 1684. The well can still be found at the side of the altar. Measuring 26 feet deep, the top is covered with glass as a safety precaution. Because of its inconvenient location inside the chapel, a pump carries water along pipes to faucets on the outside of the chapel for the convenience of pilgrims who collect the water. The well has never been known to run dry, even in the driest season, and many are the recorded cures gained from use of its water.

When Holland was occupied by French Revolutionary troops, the chapel was closed. The statue was taken to the pastor's house for safekeeping and then to a secret location. Finally on February 26, 1800, the chapel was reopened. The statue, however, was not returned until September 8, 1802.

Measuring a mere 13½ inches, Our Lady in the Sand is said to resemble the beautiful figures of the Delft school and is thought to have been made about the year 1400. Our Lady stands while holding the Holy Child on her right arm. Her left hand supports His feet. The Holy Child, for His part, holds an apple in His left hand while His right arm hangs by His side. The back of the figure is rough, indicating that it was meant to stand permanently against a wall. In 1866 the statue was carefully renovated by the Dutch architect, Cuypers.

The miraculous statue was awarded two distinctions in the year 1877: It was recognized as an historical monument by the Dutch Government, and it was given a papal coronation on the command of Pope Pius IX. During this ceremony Bishop de Paradis officiated, together with the Papal Nuncio. After witnessing the devotion of the huge crowd that attended the ceremony, the Papal Nuncio reported that he found in Roermond a devotion as great as any in Rome.

When the great Jubilee was observed in 1935, the 500th anniversary of the finding of the statue in the well, the whole city participated with the thousands of pilgrims who came from every village around. The celebration was considered of such importance that even the city streets were gaily decorated.

During World War II a bomb fell just outside the church causing severe damage, but the chapel of Our Lady was unharmed. The city suffered greatly not only from air raids, but the hostile deportation of men and boys to work in German factories. Those who refused to go were executed. Finally, in January of 1945, when a total evacuation was enforced, the rector of the shrine placed the miraculous statue of Our Lady in a satin bag and took it with him. Upon reaching Germany, the statue was enshrined in the Catholic church of Leeuwarden, where devotion to Our Lady in the Sand grew to be as intense as it had been in Roermond. The following June, when the people were permitted to return to Roermond, they found the city devastated. The church was badly damaged, but usable, and the Chapel of Our Lady was preserved. Without delay the holy statue was returned to its niche. In thanksgiving for their return, and in appreciation for the hospitality given the miraculous statue in Germany, the Bishop of Roermond returned to Leeuwarden on August 3, 1947 to enthrone in the church of refuge an exact replica of Our Lady in the Sand.

Many are the cures that are still reported at the shrine and by use of the water from the well. Processions are still held on the feasts of Our Lady, and on these occasions the little statue is taken from her shrine and placed above the high altar in an elaborate shrine.

— 87 —

OUR LADY OF THE ROSARY

("La Naval")
Quezon City, The Philippines
1593

Sculpted by a non-Catholic Chinese artist who was later converted through the intercession of the Blessed Mother, the image of Our Lady of the Rosary was commissioned in 1593 by the Spanish Governor of the Philippines, Luis Perez Dasmarinas, who wanted the statue to memorialize both his deceased father and his own regime. The statue was entrusted to the Dominicans in Manila and was enshrined in Santo Domingo Church, where it received an outpouring of love and devotion.

Fifty-three years later, in March, 1646, while Spanish invaders were still governing the islands and were outright enemies of the Dutch, the people were shocked to learn that a fleet of five Dutch war ships was bearing down on Manila. Carrying the triple threat of conquest, pillage and Dutch Protestantism, the enemy had chosen a time when Spanish warships were unavailable for defense.

Two commercial galleons, "The Rosary" and "The Incarnation," were donated by their owners and were quickly outfitted in preparation for battle. While sailing into position for the confrontation, the men prayed the Rosary and dedicated themselves to *La Naval,* Our Lady of the Holy Rosary.

The five Dutch ships were well-equipped with canons, firearms and trained seamen; the two Spanish-Filipino cargo ships were poorly fitted with a few guns. At the end of the day it seemed unbelievable that the Dutch fled the area while the defenders of the city returned home in glory, praising Our Lady for her protection.

For the next four months the two cargo ships patrolled the waters; then, in July, they discovered they had been trapped in a narrow strait by not five, but seven Dutch ships. Since their position did not afford a proper angle for battle, they prayed and waited. Fearful that they would be attacked, they vowed that if they were victorious they would pilgrimage barefoot to the Church of Santo Domingo to thank Our Lady of the Rosary. Through the intercession of *La Naval,* the two cargo ships were apparently unseen in the fading sunset since the Dutch ships turned toward Manila without firing on them. The two cargo ships then gave chase and closed in. At sunrise the next day the Dutch retreated in disgrace. As soon as the victors arrived home, they gratefully fulfilled their vow.

After the next battle the people of Manila began to call the cargo ships "the galleons of the miracle." After the fourth confrontation and victory the name was confirmed. Yet a fifth time the Dutch fleet appeared for battle. Anxious to defend their honor and restore their pride, the Dutch resolved to win at any cost. The advantage was definitely theirs when they found the two cargo ships anchored with the wind against them. Unable to move, the two cargo ships fought where they were and defeated the enemy so badly that they limped away, never to return.

Our Lady of the Rosary and the men of her two cargo ships defeated 15 well-equipped warships.

This victory at Manila is similar in many respects to the great naval victory at Lepanto, which was also credited to the intervention of Our Lady and the power of her Holy Rosary. In both instances Our Lady miraculously defended and granted victory to the seamen who placed their trust in her.

Sixteen years after the successful defense of Manila, an Ecclesiastical Council was convened in Cavite to study the unusual aspects of the five naval victories. The Council consisted of theologians, canonists, and prominent religious. On April 9, 1662, after studying all the written and oral testimonies of the participants and eyewitnesses, the Council declared that the victories were:

> granted by the Sovereign Lord through the intercession of the Most Holy Virgin and devotion to her Rosary, that the miracles be celebrated, preached and held in festivities and to be recounted among the miracles wrought by the Lady of the Rosary for the greater devotion of the faithful to Our Most Blessed Virgin Mary and Her Holy Rosary.

This decree was signed by all eight members of the Ecclesiastical Council.

Before the victories, but more especially since then, the people of the Philippines have lavished *La Naval* with their most loving devotion and reverence. The greatest tribute was paid Our Lady when the statue was canonically crowned on October 5, 1907 by the Apostolic Delegate to the Philippines, Msgr. Ambrose Agius.

When the church of Santo Domingo was bombed in 1941, the statue was hidden for its protection and was later transferred to the chapel of the University of Santo Tomas. It was here that thousands of Our Lady's devotees visited the miraculous statue in observance of the third centennial in 1946. When the shrine at the new Santo Domingo church in Quezon City was completed in 1954, *La Naval* was carried there in a boat-shaped carriage during a solemn procession attended by the Philippine hierarchy, public officials, priests, nuns and thousands of *La Naval's* faithful children. During the Marian year of 1954, the Philippine bishops declared the Church of Santo Domingo in Quezon City to be the National Shrine of Our Lady of the Rosary. Yet another honor was conferred on Our Lady when she was acknowledged as the patroness of the capital city of the Philippines.

The statue that is so dearly loved by the Filipino people stands 4′8″ tall and is made of hardwood, but ivory covers the faces and the hands of Mother and Child. The statue is perhaps the most resplendent of the statues mentioned in this volume. With the Christ Child on her left side, gently supported by the Virgin's left hand, Our Lady's right hand holds a scepter and a 15-decade gold rosary that is draped in such a fashion that it wraps around the hands of Mother and Child. Both figures are clothed in exquisite golden dresses and mantles that are heavily embroidered with golden thread.

An unusual ornament adorns the figure of the Mother of God. Against the lace that encircles the head is a golden, gem-studded circle. The bottom of this circle rests against the chest of the Madonna. Resembling a golden aura, both small and large rays, richly enhanced with jewels, extend from the circle. Atop the head of the Madonna rests a magnificent crown that matches the one worn by her Child. To further display the love that the Filipinos have for the Mother of God, they have encircled the golden aura and the crown of the Madonna with an even larger halo of gold, with jewels sparkling at the tips of 24 large rays and 24 small rays.

The Blessed Mother has slightly Oriental features and is quite lovely. The Christ Child is exceptionally appealing with a beautiful face, fat cheeks and a plump little hand raised in blessing. The statue with its costly robes, halos and crowns is one of the most beautiful of the miraculous images mentioned in this volume.

The Church of Santo Domingo was damaged several times by fire and earthquakes and was finally destroyed in 1941 by bombs, yet the statue has never been damaged. *La Naval* is presently treasured by the Filipino people in the new Santo Domingo Church in Quezon City, a few miles from Manila. During the Marian year of 1954 the church was designated as the national shrine of Our Lady of the Rosary.

The anniversary of the vow made by the defenders of Manila during the second naval battle is still observed each year by the people of the Philippines who pilgrimage to the miraculous statue to demonstrate their love for Our Lady of the Rosary and their gratitude for the miracles of protection that took place almost 350 years ago.

OUR LADY OF THE ROSARY, sculpted in 1593, was beseeched for divine intervention in the year 1646 by sailors who were being attacked by warships. The result of the naval battle that followed was recognized by an ecclesiastical council in 1662 as "among the miracles wrought by the Lady of the Rosary for the greater devotion of the faithful . . ."

ORNATE GARMENTS adorn the figures of Mother and Child known as Our Lady of the Rosary at Quezon City, Philippines. Magnificent crowns and a glorious halo testify to the love that Filipino devotees have for the Mother of God and her Son. The statue is housed in the shrine in Quezon City, the Philippines.

— 88 —

OUR LADY OF ANTIPOLO

(Our Lady of Peace and Good Voyage)
Antipolo, The Philippines
1626

Bells rang and canons fired when the galleon, El Almirante, arrived in Manila Bay from a trading voyage with Acapulco, Mexico. On board was Don Juan Nino de Tabora, Governor-General of the Philippines: however, it was not only for him that the bells rang, but also for the arrival of a statue of the Blessed Virgin that had been sculptured and blessed in Mexico. It was March 25, 1626, only 55 years after the founding of Manila by Legaspi.

Carved from a dark hardwood, the statue was taken in solemn procession from the galleon to the Jesuit church of San Ignacio in Intramuros. A solemn Mass was sung in Our Lady's honor, and here the statue remained until Fr. Pedro Chirino, S.J. was chosen parish priest of Antipolo and its neighboring towns. When he left, the precious statue went with him. Since the mission church of his new assignment was located at that time not at Antipolo, but in a neighboring region called Santa Cruz, the statue was installed with simple ceremonies at Santa Cruz.

It was shortly afterwards that the unusual occurred. According to the traditional account, the blessed image disappeared from the church at Santa Cruz on two occasions. Each time it was discovered near Antipolo, in the branches of a tree called tipulo, a word from which Antipolo derived its name. To prevent future mysterious transfers, the tree was cut and its trunk made into a pedestal for the statue. Since the Lady had apparently indicated her liking for that particular location, a church was soon erected on the site and the statue enshrined within.

The statue of Our Lady of Antipolo reigned in peace and benevolence until the year 1639, when the Chinese of the town rose in revolt and killed many of the inhabitants. Even though the church was burned, the statue of Our Lady of Antipolo refused to submit to the flames. Frustrated, the Chinese desecrated the image by piercing it with lances. Although the statue retains some of the wounds that were inflicted at that time, it was spared serious disfigurement.

When the disturbances continued, Governor-General Don Sebastian Hurtado de Corcuera had the Virgin rescued and transferred to Manila. It was later taken to the town of Cavite, where it was venerated for the next 14 years.

During the year 1646, while the statue was still at Cavite, 12 Dutch ships entered the port with the intention of conquering the town. Their efforts were unsuccessful. It was widely believed then, as it has been ever since, that the town was saved because of the protection given it by the presence of Our Lady of Antipolo.

With the Dutch warring against Spain in the Pacific Ocean and with the added threat of mutinies, pirates and incompetent navigation, the Filipinos encountered enormous difficulties in continuing their trade with Mexico. It was finally decided to sail under the protection of the miraculous statue. Their confidence in the Blessed Virgin was well placed, since 10 successful crossings were made with the miraculous statue between the years 1648 and 1748.

Since the voyages of the ships were both peaceful and successful, Governor-General Manrique, by a public decree of September 8, 1653, named the statue "Our Lady of Peace and Good Voyage."

After each voyage the statue of the Blessed Virgin was received at the Manilla harbor by the two highest officials of the country, the Captain-General and the Archbishop, the occasion being observed as a religious holiday. Each arrival was greeted with the joyful pealing of bells and the singing of hymns, since the success of each voyage was attributed solely to the protection and guidance of Our Lady. Following the initial greeting, the people followed in procession along the Pasig River, where triumphal arches spanned the waterway. Benedictions were given at altars along the river bank, and choirs sang hymns. Sometimes poems were recited dedicated to the Virgin's miraculous powers. When the procession arrived at the church in Antipolo, the statue was restored to its place of honor until it was needed for the next voyage.

When Governor-General Juan de Arrechedera wanted to honor the Blessed Virgin, he decided in 1746 to place in her hands the cane which was a sign of his authority. After almost 250 years, the statue still holds this long cane which also came to symbolize Our Lady's loving authority over the hearts of the Filipino people.

The miraculous statue was especially honored on November 27, 1926, when it was brought to Manila for its canonical coronation. With the greater part of Catholic Manila assembled, the Lady of Antipolo was crowned with a coronet of diamonds while the prayers of the multitude rose in homage and love.

But once again the safety of the miraculous statue was jeopardized when the Japanese threatened the Philippines in 1944. The priests at Antipolo were warned by a Japanese army chaplain, Ikeda. He told them of the bitter fighting expected to take place in their town and suggested that the head and arms of the beloved statue be removed and hidden for safekeeping against the time when the Japanese would eventually meet the Americans. The sacristan, Copio Angeles, refused to mutilate the statue, but agreed to disguise and hide it. The place he chose to conceal the miraculous statue was the area under the convent kitchen. When the Japanese invaded Antipolo in 1944, the church became their arsenal, and when the United States confronted them in battle, the Japanese burned whole blocks of the town. During the conflict, the parish priest and his assistant were killed, as were two sisters of the church school.

To save the miraculous statue from destruction, more than 500 people gathered to accompany it over rough and steep mountain trails to safety. At night artillery fire from both sides brightened the dark woods and whistled a grim accompaniment to the people's prayers. The refugees visited numerous villages with their precious statue until, eventually, the statue was placed in the safety of the church at Quiapo. It remained there until October 15, 1945 when, with solemn ceremonies and accompanied by thousands of devotees, the statue of Our Lady was returned to her home in Antipolo.

When the United States granted independence to the Philippines in 1947, the people turned to Our Lady to protect the country and lead it safely on its course as an independent nation.

Since Antipolo was severely damaged during the war, a national fund campaign was started for the reconstruction of the church. The people responded generously and the shrine was soon completed and blessed. It is now regarded as a National Shrine and the center of Marian devotion in the Philippines.

The statue of Our Lady of Antipolo is greatly revered and dearly loved. With a solemn expression, and while staring straight ahead, the arms of the statue are held waist high and are in such an unusual stance that one supposes the Blessed Mother had previously held a figure of the Christ Child. A rosary is now entwined on both hands. The people have demonstrated their devotion by providing Our Lady of Antipolo with a wardrobe of various crowns, coronets, earrings and garments. The statue is unique in that Our Lady does not wear a veil. Instead, long locks of hair fall from beneath her crown and gracefully surround her shoulders.

The love which the Filipino people have for this miraculous statue is expressed beyond the seas to Rome, where Our Lady of Antipolo has been chosen patroness of the Pontifico Collegio Filipino chapel in the seminary, where students from the Philippines are prepared for the priesthood.

His Holiness Pope John Paul II announced the erection of the new Diocese of Antipolo on January 24, 1983. This district was formerly part of the Archdiocese of Manila. His Holiness designated Our Lady of Antipolo as the titular of the new diocese.

There are many traditional practices observed in honor of Our Lady of Peace and Good Voyage. What is known as the Antipolo Season starts on the first Tuesday of May and ends on the first Tuesday of July. The most important of the traditional practices has its origin more than 200 years ago, when an epidemic raged through Antipolo. The parish priest then advised the people to look for the highest location in the area where the image could be brought in procession. Mass was offered at the top of the hill and God was implored, through Our Lady's intercession, to dismiss the epidemic. Within a few days the epidemic was halted. Since 1947, on the first Tuesday following the third of May, the image of Our Lady is brought to the top of the hill in a procession attended by hundreds of people.

Another tradition is the procession of the Virgin around the town of Antipolo after the completion of every novena and on every first Sunday of the month throughout the year, just before the Angelus in the evening. It is called the Procession of Peace, and prayers are offered for peace in the Philippines and in the world. For this procession Our Lady is carried in a structure made like a galleon. On her return to the shrine she is incensed, blessed with holy water and showered with rose petals.

Since Our Lady is regarded as Our Lady of Good Voyage, it is still the custom to bring one's vehicle, new or old, to the shrine for a blessing. The vehicles range from a simple bicycle to a tourist bus or truck. It is also the custom to visit the shrine before leaving on a voyage to ask for Our Lady's protection. Another visit of thanksgiving is made after returning from abroad.

The statue which is so highly regarded and loved by the Filipino people is found above the main altar of the National Shrine of Our Lady of Peace and Good Voyage at Antipolo, Rizal.

DARK HARDWOOD was carved into the statue of Our Lady of Antipolo, the Philippines, in 1626. When the parish priest of Antipolo was assigned to a neighboring region called Santa Cruz, he took the statue with him. However, the blessed image twice disappeared from the church at Santa Cruz and was discovered in the branches of a tipulo tree near Antipolo.

THE UNUSUAL STANCE of Our Lady of Antipolo suggests that the image of the Blessed Mother previously may have held a sculpture of the Christ Child. The highly revered image has survived many perils, including fires, lance attack, danger at sea and artillery fire. Known as Our Lady of Good Voyage, the image of Our Lady is visited by many who bring bicycles, trucks and other vehicles to the shrine at Antipolo for a blessing.

— 89 —

OUR LADY OF CZESTOCHOWA

Czestochowa, Poland
Date Unknown

The origin of this miraculous image is unknown, but a charming legend has prevailed through the ages. It reveals that after the Crucifixion, when Our Lady moved to the home of St. John, she took with her a few personal belongings—among which was a table built by the Redeemer in the workshop of St. Joseph. When pious virgins of Jerusalem prevailed upon St. Luke to paint a portrait of the Mother of God, it was the top of this table that was used to memorialize her image. While applying his brush and paints, St. Luke listened carefully as the Mother of Jesus spoke of the life of her Son, facts which the Evangelist later recorded in his Gospel.

Legend also tells us that the painting remained in and around Jerusalem until it was discovered by St. Helena in the fourth century. Together with other sacred relics, the painting was transported to Constantinople where her son, Emperor Constantine the Great, erected a church for its enthronement.

The portrait of Mother and Child was revered by the people, but not so by the Saracen tribes who besieged the city. History records that during the seige the senators and citizens carried the precious image in procession through the streets and around the dikes. The Saracens are said to have been frightened by what they saw and fled in dismay.

Later, during the dreadful reign of Emperor Izauryn, who was embittered against holy objects and destroyed many by fire, the image was saved by his wife, the Empress Irene. She displayed remarkable cunning by hiding it in the palace of the Emperor—the very place where Our Lady's enemies would never think of searching for it.

The portrait remained in Constantinople for 500 years, until it became part of several dowries and eventually found its way to Russia and the region of Russia that later became Poland.

After the portrait came into the possession of Polish prince St. Ladislaus in the fifteenth century, it was installed in a special chamber of his castle at Belz. Soon afterward, when the castle was besieged by the Tartars, an enemy arrow entered the chapel through a window and struck the painting, inflicting a scar on the throat of the Blessed Virgin. The injury remains to this day, despite several attempts through the years to repair it.

Chroniclers tell us that St. Ladislaus determined to save the image from the repeated invasions of the Tartars by taking it to the more secure city of Opala, his birthplace. This journey took him through Czestochowa, where he decided to rest for the night. During this brief pause in their journey, the image was taken to Jasna Gora (meaning "bright hill"). There it was placed in a small wooden church named for the Assumption. The following morning, after the portrait was carefully replaced in its wagon, the horses refused to move. Accepting this as a heavenly sign that the portrait was to remain in Czestochowa, St. Ladislaus had the image solemnly returned to the Church of the Assumption. This occurred on August 26, 1382, a day still observed as the feast day of the painting. Since it was St. Ladislaus' wish to have the portrait guarded by the holiest of men, he ordered the building of a church and monastery for the Pauline Fathers, who have devoutly ensured the security of their charge for the last six centuries.

Having escaped the rampage of Emperor Izauryn, and damaged by a Tartar's arrow in the area of the Blessed Virgin's throat, the portrait was next placed in peril by the Hussites who embraced extravagant heresies. They invaded the monastery of the Pauline Fathers in 1430 and plundered the richly decorated sanctuary. Among the items stolen was the portrait of Our Lady. After placing it in a wagon, the Hussites proceeded only a short distance before the horses refused to move. Recalling that a similar incident had occurred to Prince Ladislaus some 50 years before—and realizing that the portrait was the cause—the heretics threw it to the ground. It broke into three pieces. One of the robbers drew his sword, struck the image and inflicted two deep gashes. While preparing to inflict a third gash, he fell to the ground and writhed in agony until his death.

The two slashes on the cheek of the Blessed Virgin, together with the previous injury to the throat, have always reappeared—despite repeated attempts to repair them.

The portrait again faced danger in the year 1655. At that time 12,000 Swedes confronted the 300 men who were guarding the sanctuary. Though vastly outnumbered, Our Lady's defenders were successful in bitterly defeating the enemy. The following year, the Holy Virgin was acclaimed Queen of Poland.

Closer to our own time, on September 14, 1920, when the Russian army assembled at the River Vistula and prepared to invade Warsaw, the people had recourse to Our Lady. It is recorded that the following day, the feast of Our Lady of Sorrows, the Russian army quickly withdrew after the image of Our Lady appeared in the clouds over the city. In Polish history this victory is known as the Miracle at the Vistula.

Unlike the Russian army, which failed to take the city, the Germans proved more successful in invading and capturing Poland. After they had claimed the city of Warsaw, one of Hitler's orders was the suspension of all pilgrimages. In a demonstration of love for Our Lady and their confidence in her protection, a half million Poles secretly journeyed to the sanctuary in defiance of Hitler's orders. Following the liberation of the nation in 1945, a million and a half people expressed their gratitude to the Madonna by praying before the miraculous image.

Twenty-eight years after the Russians' first attempt at capturing the city, they successfully took control of the entire nation in 1948. During that year more than 800,000 brave people pilgrimaged to the sanctuary on the feast of the Assumption, one of the three feastdays of the portrait, even though they passed under the gaze of Communist soldiers who routinely patrolled the streets. Today, the people continue to honor their beloved portrait of the Madonna and Child, especially on August 26, the day that has been reserved for its celebration since the time of Prince Ladislaus.

Because of the dark coloration of the Madonna's face and hands, the image has been affectionately called the Black Madonna, a phrase reminiscent of the *Canticle of Canticles,* "I am black but beautiful." The darkness is ascribed to various conditions, of which its age is primary. During its existence it was hidden for safekeeping in many places which were far from ideal for the storage of works of art; furthermore, countless candles were burned before it, causing it to be almost constantly embraced by smoke. Additionally, it was handled innumerable times, resulting in unintentional abuse.

Without the frame, the painting is approximately 19 inches high by about 13 inches wide and is almost a half inch thick. A cloth stretched across the back depicts scenes and designs representing the history of the painting and some of the miracles performed through the intercession of the Madonna.

The miracles attributed to Our Lady of Czestochowa are numerous and spectacular. The original accounts of these cures and miracles are preserved in the archives of the Pauline Fathers at Jasna Gora.

Papal recognition of the miraculous image was made by Pope Clement XI in 1717. The crown given to the image by the Pope was used in the first official coronation of the painting, but this symbol of Our Lady's queenship, unfortunately, was stolen in 1909. The crown was replaced by one of gold encrusted with jewels, a gift of Pope Pius X.

Among the most distinguished visitors to the shrine can be counted Jan Casimir, King of Poland, who journeyed there in 1656. After placing his crown at the foot of the Virgin's altar he vowed, "I, Jan Casimir, King of Poland, take thee as Queen and Patroness of my kingdom; I put my people and my army under your protection. . ." May 3, the day on which this vow was made, was designated by Pope Pius XI as the feast of Mary under the title "Queen of Poland."

In modern times, Pope John Paul II, a native son of Poland, prayed before the Madonna during his historic visit in 1979, several months after his election to the Chair of Peter. The Pope made another visit to Our Lady of Czestochowa in 1983 and again in 1991.

THE ORIGIN of Our Lady of Czestochowa is said to date back to the early days of Christianity. The famous portrait may have been painted by St. Luke on the top of a table built by Our Lord in the workshop of St. Joseph. In modern times, Pope John Paul II returned to his native country, Poland, in 1979, 1983 and 1991 to pray before the miraculous image.

ST. HELENA discovered the miraculous painting in the fourth century and took it to Constantinople. There her son, Emperor Constantine the Great, erected a church for the image's enthronement. History records that hostile Saracen soldiers were frightened away when the precious image was carried in a public procession. In the fifteenth century, when the portrait was kept at the castle of St. Ladislaus, a Tartar arrow entered the chapel window and struck the painting. Fifty years later Hussite heretics attempted to make off with the portrait, but found that their horses refused to move. (St. Ladislaus also had been unable to move the image earlier, when his horses refused to pull the wagon in which the image had been placed.) The Hussite robbers became angry and threw the precious painting to the ground. Two deep gashes were inflicted, but the sword-bearer fell to the ground when he attempted to inflict a third wound.

— 90 —

OUR LADY OF FETAL

Reguengo do Fetal, Portugal
Twelfth Century

Three shrines in Portugal are only a few miles from each other and all three indicate a location where Our Blessed Mother appeared to shepherd children. We are all aware of the great basilica dedicated to Our Lady of Fatima. The other two shrines, only a few miles from the Fatima basilica, but in opposite directions, are those dedicated to Our Lady of Fetal and Our Lady of Ortiga.

The sanctuary of Our Lady of Fetal ("fetal" meaning "fern cluster"), stands upon a little hill. The village of Reguengo is located below, where the Stations of the Cross begin as one starts the one-mile climb to the Sanctuary of Fatima.

Many centuries before Our Lady appeared at Fatima to three shepherd children, she appeared to a single little shepherdess at Reguengo do Fetal at a time when the villagers were enduring the hardships of a severe drought. Not only were the people suffering, but the sheep were suffering as well, since their once-rounded bodies were now gaunt and almost wasted. Accustomed to the lush greenery of the meadows, the sheep now had to search hard for a few blades of grass. It was the conditon of a certain small herd, and her own sad state, that made the little shepherdess cry when she was pasturing her sheep outside the village of Reguengo on the slope of a hill.

Suddenly the little shepherdess felt a presence. Looking up with tear-filled eyes she saw to her surprise, in the midst of a cluster of ferns, a Lady who spoke gently.

"Why are you crying, my child?"

"I am hungry."

"You must go and ask your mother for some bread."

"I did ask her already, but she hasn't any."

"Go home," the Lady insisted, "and ask your mother again to give you some bread. Tell her that a Lady ordered you to tell her that there is bread in the chest."

The shepherdess ran home to tell of the vision and convey the message of the Lady. The child's vision of the mysterious Lady was believed without a single doubt when, true to the Lady's word, bread was found in the chest. Indeed, a great deal of bread was found—this of such texture and sweetness that it seemed as if it had been baked by angels.

After eating as much as she wanted, the little girl ran back to the hill. There she again saw the Lady, who gave her the following message: "Tell the people of your village that I am the Mother of God, and that I wish them to build a shrine for me on this spot of the ferns, a shrine wherein I may be praised and honored."

After the villagers were told of the apparitions and the mysterious supply of delicious bread, they hurried to the place of the ferns and found there a small statue of Our Lady. Nearby they discovered a spring where no spring had been before. It seemed that Our Lady had consecrated the place when miracles were effected by means of this water's application to the bodies of the sick.

After the rains came to end the drought, the building of a shrine was immediately begun. It was here, probably at the beginning of the twelfth century, that the miraculous image was exposed for the veneration of the faithful.

Unfortunately, it is not known in what year the apparitions took place, when the primitive shrine of Our Lady of Fetal was erected, nor do we know the name of the little shepherdess.

We do know that in 1585 a larger and more elegant church was built. It was to this shrine that countless pilgrims made their way, as they still do today (especially during Lent) for the recitation of the Rosary and, during the month of May, to offer flowers. Also popular are the days between the end of September until the first Sunday of October. During this time a solemn novena of preparation is held for the traditional feast of Our Lady of Fetal. This festivity is noted for a most unusual attraction known as "the illumination of the snails," when shells of snails are used as little lamps.

Many persons of distinction have recognized the shrine. King Edward confirmed an ancient privilege of the sanctuary's Brotherhood whereby the members were given the right to collect alms for the maintenance of the shrine. Don John III provided a largess to the members and steward of the Brotherhood. Donna Maria I, by a provision of 1791, authorized a Free Fair on the first Sunday of October. Don Manuel de Aguiar, a former Bishop of Leiria, sent two artistic altars with retables of carved wood and twisted pillars.

During a national drought in May, 1896, Don Joseph II, the Cardinal Patriarch of Lisbon, asked for public prayers to be recited to Our Lady of Fetal for an abundant rainfall. In gratitude for Our Lady's prompt answer to their prayers, and as a memorial, the Cardinal Patriarch granted indulgences to those who recited a *Salve Regina* before the image of Our Lady of Fetal. The shrine became better known throughout Portugal as a result of this appeal for prayers, but more so because of the almost immediate answer to the appeal.

The miraculous statue, which is kept in a niche above the main altar, depicts the Blessed Mother in a seated position with the Child Jesus on her left knee. As a reminder of the miracle that took place the day of the apparition so many years earlier when bread was miraculously provided in a chest, the Child Jesus holds in each hand a rounded loaf of bread, one of which He places into the hand of His Mother, who smiles pleasantly.

OUR LADY OF FETAL (right) is a small statue that was found by villagers who went to view the spot at which a little twelfth-century shepherdess had been graced by an apparition of Our Lady. The girl had been instructed to "tell the people of your village that I am the Mother of God, and that I wish them to build a shrine for me on this spot. . ."

THE SANCTUARY or shrine of Our Lady of Fetal, Portugal from the rear of the chapel. (Pictures on this page, Page 391 and Page 392 are reprinted with specific permission from SOUL Magazine, Washington NJ 07882; Copyright 1988).

ADORNED WITH FLOWERS, the altar of Our Lady of Fetal is here viewed close up. During May of each year, countless pilgrims show their devotion to Our Lady by bringing flowers. The apparition of the Blessed Mother at Fetal took place more than 400 years before her appearances at nearby Fatima, Portugal.

THE ANCIENT STATUE of Our Lady of Fetal, which is normally kept in the niche over the altar.

— 91 —

OUR LADY OF ORTIGA

Casal Santa Maria (Fatima) Portugal
Date Unknown

Located in the central portion of Portugal are three shrines dedicated to the Blessed Mother. With the great basilica of Fatima separating them, the shrine of Our Lady of Fetal is a short distance away in one direction, while the Shrine of Our Lady of Ortiga is in the other. While the great basilica of Our Lady of the Rosary is a shrine of worldwide interest, the two smaller ones are cherished as centers of prayer for local residents. All three shrines are sites where the Blessed Virgin appeared to shepherd children, and all three have obtained the approval of the Church.

The history of the Shrine of Our Lady of Fetal is mentioned in the previous chapter. The history of the Shrine of Our Lady of Ortiga involves, in the same way, a poor shepherdess—but unlike the shepherdess at Fetal who was enduring the hardships instigated by a drought, the little shepherdess of Ortiga had to endure other difficulties since she was both deaf and dumb.

One day, while the child was tending her sheep outside Casal Santa Maria, a hamlet in the parish of Fatima, a beautiful Lady suddenly appeared over a group of ortiga bushes. Smiling pleasantly, the Lady asked the little girl if she might have one of her lambs. Unable to speak a moment before, and not knowing the sound of words because of her deafness, the child nevertheless spoke as though she had always had the ability to do so. Her first words, which the Virgin alone heard, were: "I would have to have permission of my father."

The Lady continued to smile as the child ran off to get the necessary permission to fulfill the Lady's request.

The child's father was overcome with emotion as the child related the details of the vision and the Lady's request for a lamb. Grateful that his child could now hear and speak, he told her to give the beautiful Lady whatever she desired. News of the miraculous cure was spread quickly through Casal Santa Maria. Many came to see for themselves that the mute child had indeed been favored with a heavenly cure. After hearing from the child's own lips the great wonder that had taken place, the villagers followed the little shepherdess to the site of the apparition. There, to their amazement, they found, in the midst of the ortiga bushes, a wooden statue of Our Lady holding the Child Jesus. Filled with devotion and admiration, they carried the statue to the village.

But that night another miracle occurred. The statue disappeared, only to be found the next morning in the ortiga bushes at the place of the apparition.

There was no doubting that the Blessed Mother was indicating her preference for the site and her desire to have a chapel erected there. The Lady's silent request could not be ignored, and a small chapel was soon built to enshrine the miraculous statue. This chapel was eventually replaced by the one that now stands. In 1801 Pope Pius VII granted a Plenary Indulgence to those who visited the shrine on July 1, the feast of Our Lady of Ortiga.

The miraculous statue is obviously of a venerable age and depicts a full-faced, crowned Madonna holding the Child Jesus on her right arm. Her left hand holds a book which the Child touches with His right hand. With rosy cheeks and a straightforward stare, the Virgin wears a light rose-colored robe and a light blue mantle. The Child wears a yellow-orange dress and leans close to His Mother.

* * *

There are a number of similarities between the apparition at Fetal and that at Ortiga. Our Lady appeared both times to poor shepherd girls as they were tending their flocks. The Virgin appeared over vegetation to girls who were afflicted in different ways—one from long-term hunger, the other from two bodily impairments. We do not know the names of either visionary, and we do not know the exact date of Our Lady's visitations—except that they occurred centuries before the great appearances of Our Lady of Fatima.

The apparitions at Fetal and Ortiga seem to be a preparation for the apparitions to the three shepherd children at Fatima, since this poses another similarity. The visionaries were, once again, shepherds to whom the Blessed Virgin appeared over vegetation while they tended their flocks. But unlike the visions at Fetal and Ortiga, Our Lady appeared at Fatima six times to warn the world of future dangers and to request the consecration of Russia and the recitation of the Rosary as a means of gaining world peace.

Whereas the great basilica at Fatima is a spectacular, worldwide shrine that attracts millions of pilgrims each year, the two little chapels of Ortiga and Fetal are quiet and humble. But they have been blessed in a special way, with heaven-sent statues of the Virgin and Child which have been cherished by the people for centuries.

CENTRAL PORTUGAL is home to three shrines dedicated to the Blessed Mother: Fatima, Fetal and Ortiga. The lovely statue above depicts Our Lady of Ortiga.

BEAUTIFULLY CLOAKED, Our Lady of Ortiga has a history similar to Our Lady of Fetal in that the Blessed Virgin also appeared to a shepherd girl.

— 92 —

OUR LADY OF KAZAN

Fatima, Portugal
Thirteenth Century

Among the Russian people, the icon of Our Lady of Kazan is one of the most beloved and venerated images of the Blessed Mother.

According to expert opinion, the icon dates from the thirteenth century and was painted on wood in the typical Greek Byzantine style. The image depicts the head and shoulders of the Blessed Virgin Mary with the Infant Jesus standing upon her knee. Although the work is almost entirely covered with a rizza of precious gold, the image beneath it is completely painted with pigments that extensive X-ray examinations have indicated are perfectly preserved. The faces of Our Lady and the Infant Jesus are visible, as is the right hand of the Child, which is superimposed on the neck of His Mother in a posture of benediction. The golden rizza dates from the seventeenth century and is encrusted with more than 1,000 diamonds, emeralds, oriental rubies, sapphires and pearls. While the greater part of the stones have been on the icon for centuries, a few donated stones have been added in recent years.

The icon is thought to have been painted in Constantinople. Historians believe it was brought to Russia by way of the Black Sea and the Don River and then to the city of Kazan, where it was enshrined in a monastery.

The image was lost in 1209 when the Tartars sacked the city, destroyed the monastery and killed its inhabitants. It was recovered more than 350 years later, in the year 1579, when the city was being rebuilt following a disastrous fire.

A child is credited with discovering the image among the rubble of her house, which her father was then restoring. Named Matrona, the child of nine told of a heavenly Lady who indicated a place where she should dig to recover an icon. Two appearances of the Lady were ignored by the parents and neighbors, but when a third vision threatened punishment, they promptly began to sift through the ruins. It was Matrona who unearthed the image, which was wrapped in old rags. Although it had been buried for over three centuries, the image was undamaged.

News of the miraculous discovery spread throughout the city, bringing thousands to the place of the apparitions. With the Archbishop carrying the icon, a solemn procession was formed to escort the icon to nearby St. Nicholas Church. Later it was enshrined in the Cathedral of the Annunciation in Kazan. Still later, when a copy of the icon was made and sent to Czar Ivan the Great, he issued orders that the original icon should be enshrined in the chapel of the convent that he wanted built over the place of the discovery. It was in this convent some years later that Matrona and her mother were to become members and take monastic vows.

When Russia was besieged from within and without by enemies, and several laid claim to the Russian throne, Bishop Germogen called upon the patriotic Russians to fight the impostors and resist the foreign invaders, assuring them that they would be supported and protected by the Mother of God. He was himself imprisoned by Polish troops in 1612 and suffered a martyr's death by starvation. In retaliation, the Russian people organized behind the Greek Bishop, Arsenius, who was visiting Russia at the time. In a vision, St. Serge, founder of the Holy Trinity Monastery in Zagorsk, appeared to the Bishop and assured him of a victory under the protection of Our Lady. Hearing this, the Russians took the holy icon as a victory banner and stormed the walls of the Kremlin, liberating Moscow on November 27, 1612. The Russian troops hailed Our Lady of Kazan as the liberator of Russia. To commemorate the victory, the Church proclaimed October 22 as the feast day.

The icon was again used as a victory banner by Czar Peter the Great in his battle against the forces of Charles XII of Sweden in 1790.

The image experienced a number of transfers to places of honor, each new place seemingly attempting to overwhelm the icon with splendor and expressions of reverence. On the famous Red Square in Moscow, Prince Pozharsky, commander-in-chief of the people's militia, built a basilica dedicated to the Lady of Kazan. The icon was transferred there, but when the capital was moved from Moscow to St. Petersburg, Czar Peter built a special shrine for the image and had it removed to this new place of honor.

Following Napoleon's defeat, which was attributed to the intercession of Our Lady, the Kazan Basilica was constructed to house the holy icon. It was finally consecrated during the reign of Alexander II. The czar offered all the war trophies and battle flags of the Napoleonic invasion to the shrine as tokens of Our Lady's victory. The icon remained there until the Russian Revolution of 1917. In 1929 the Kazan Cathedral in St. Petersburg was desecrated and converted into a museum, which it remains to this day.

Although it is uncertain how the image was removed from Russia, it is speculated by some that it was sold after the Revolution, together with other icons, church vessels, religious and national treasures, at a time when the new government was hard-pressed for funds. It eventually appeared in private hands in Poland, and then in England in 1935.

In 1960 the icon was loaned to a pious group who brought it in pilgrimage to Russian Orthodox churches throughout the United States in the hope of raising enough funds to reclaim it. Solemn celebrations and sacred liturgies were observed during each of its visits. It was also displayed with reverence in the Russian Orthodox Pavilion at the New York World's Fair of 1964-1965. The icon was eventually redeemed by the Apostolate of Our Lady of Fatima and was enshrined on July 26, 1970 in the Byzantine chapel of the Icon of Kazan in Domus Pacis, Fatima, Portugal.

After more than 50 years of wandering among private owners, the icon is now housed in a holy setting. It is hoped that one day it can be returned to its former sanctuary on Russian soil.

OUR LADY OF KAZAN dates back to ancient times. The painting is almost entirely covered with gold and precious gems.

— 93 —

OUR LADY OF THE PILLAR

Zaragoza, Spain
40 A.D.

Tradition tells us that St. James the Apostle journeyed to Spain to spread the Gospel and was already there in the year 40 A.D. when he paused to pray beside the River Ebro with seven of his disciples. Our Lady, who was still living in Jerusalem, was at the same time praying for the success of his missionary endeavors when she appeared to St. James. He and his disciples all shared in the beautiful vision that was accompanied by celestial music and a radiant light. After words of encouragement and a request for a chapel, the Blessed Mother gave him the small jasper column on which she stood as evidence of her appearance.

Supported by the vision and the tangible evidence of its authenticity, St. James spread the Faith throughout Spain which is now under his patronage. After dying a martyr's death he was buried at Santiago de Compostello, where his shrine attracted more pilgrimages by far than did those of the other Apostles.

The chapel that the Virgin requested was soon built over the place of the apparition but was eventually destroyed, as were several succeeding replacements. The pillar survived, as did the ancient statue that had been placed upon it. In fact, the statue survived the invasions of various conquerors: the Romans, Goths, Moors, Muslims and Vandals. It likewise witnessed the invasion of more peaceful throngs including prayerful pilgrims, all the kings of Spain, Queen Blanca de Navarra in 1433, and numerous Saints including St. Teresa of Avila, St. John of the Cross and St. Ignatius of Loyola.

The present church dates from the seventeenth century. In its chapel amid a splendid setting stands the statue, which seems quite diminutive by contrast. Measuring about 15 inches in height, it stands upon its jasper pillar that rises about six feet. The column is now covered with silver and bronze, but a small portion of the jasper has been left exposed. This section of the pillar is framed by a golden oval and, according to the custodians of the shrine, it is "worn out due to millions of kisses."

The wall directly behind the statue is of green marble and is studded with 148 stars, 80 of which are jeweled.

The wooden statue is a simple one of the Blessed Virgin, smiling pleasantly. The Christ Child, who holds a small bird, is supported by the Virgin's left hand; her right hand holds the mantle that drapes all about them. On certain days of the month the statue is dressed with a cape heavy with jewels and gold embroidery that partially conceals the pillar. Jeweled crowns are worn by both Virgin and Child, and a golden burst of an aureole is added to the jeweled halo that is affixed to the marble directly behind the head of the statue.

The Church of the Virgin of the Pillar, built over the place where St. James the Apostle prostrated before the Virgin's miraculous visit, was declared a national museum on May 22, 1904. An impressive crowning of the Virgin took place on May 20, 1905.

Persistent reports since ancient times have it that the pillar is occasionally surrounded by a fragrance of roses which is readily perceived. A spokesman for the shrine recently attributed the fragrance to the disinfectant that is used daily on the column to discourage the transmittal of disease due to the number of people who touch and kiss it. However, one might consider that the reports of the perfume were made consistently from ancient times when disinfectants were unknown—and perfumed samples awaited invention only in recent years.

The people of Zaragoza regard the statue as a legacy from their forefathers and demonstrate a tender devotion and a fierce loyalty to it. Since the original church of the Virgin of the Pillar was the first one raised in honor of the Blessed Mother, it is believed the present church will last as long as the Faith.

During his historic tour of Spain in November 1982, Pope John Paul II visited this ancient shrine of the Blessed Mother and later the same day recited the Rosary there during a worldwide radio broadcast.

A SIMPLE WOODEN STATUE of the Blessed Virgin only 15 inches tall, Our Lady of the Pillar stands upon a jasper column covered with silver and bronze that is about six feet in height.

CENTURIES OLD, the drawing above demonstrates the prayerfulness of the faithful toward Our Lady of the Pillar.

THE MAGNIFICENT ALTAR (right) of Our Lady of the Pillar dwarfs the miraculous ancient statue. The Church of the Virgin of the Pillar is said to be built upon the place in Spain where St. James the Apostle and his disciples shared in a beautiful vision of Our Lady, who at the time was living in Jerusalem.

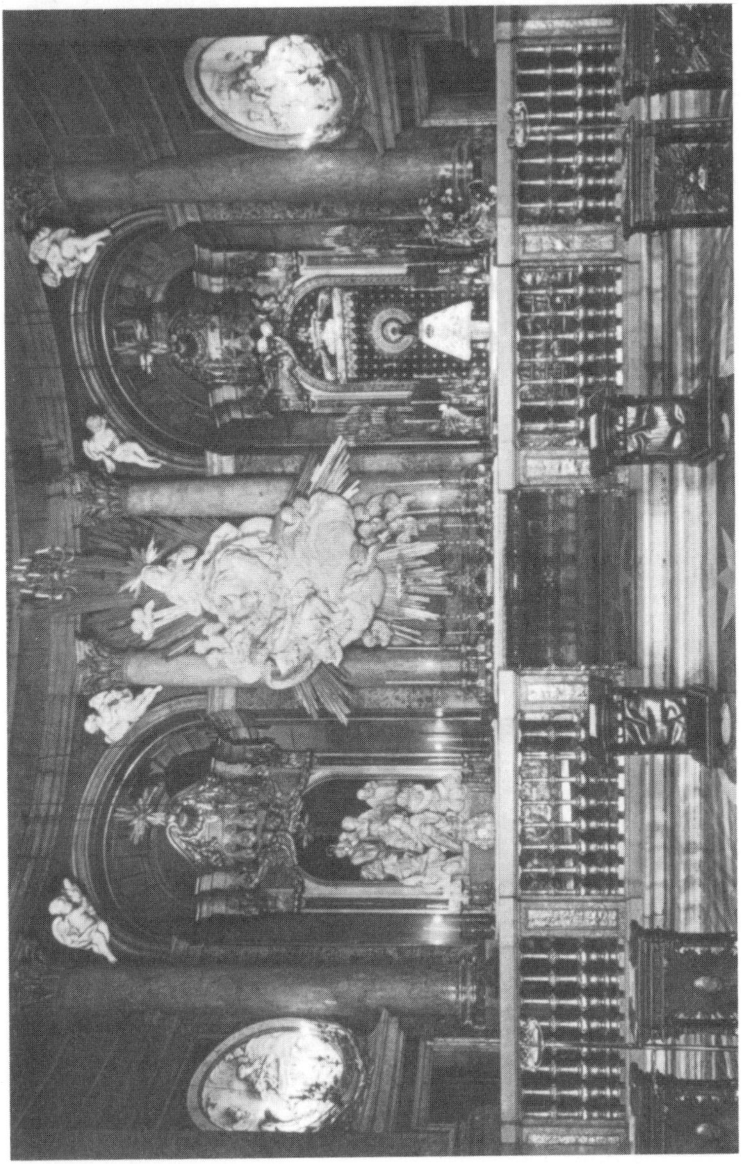

THE BLESSED VIRGIN represented as Our Lady of the Pillar has been visited by St. Teresa of Avila, St. John of the Cross and St. Ignatius Loyola.

— 94 —

OUR LADY OF GUADALUPE

Guadalupe, Caceres, Spain
580

The statue of Our Lady of Guadalupe which was given by Pope Gregory the Great to the noted churchman, Bishop Leander of Seville, was lost to the soil of Spain for 600 years, to be restored not by persons high in ecclesiastical ranks, but by a humble cowherd who acted under a heavenly influence.

Treasured by the people of Spain since its presentation in the year 580, it was during the frightful time of the Moorish invasion of 711 that the statue was hidden for safekeeping. One report tells that it was hidden in a cave under a churchbell; another that it was buried in an iron casket. Whichever the case, it was hidden in the province of Caceres with pertinent papers that documented its history. Those who had secured the statue eventually died during the conquest, and it was thus lost for centuries.

Christianity suffered hardships during the many years of the Moorish occupation, but devotion to the Mother of God was maintained in secret, only to flourish once again after the liberation.

Great emotion was experienced by the people in 1326, when a cowherd named Gil Cordero related that while he was searching for a lost cow a radiant Lady emerged from a nearby forest. After indicating a place where he should dig to unearth a treasure, she requested that a chapel be built there.

When ecclesiastical authorities were summoned to the place, they found the entrance to an underground cave and the statue with its documents. Although it had been hidden for 600 years, the statue of Oriental, unstained wood was examined and pronounced to be in perfect condition. The chapel that was later built by order of King Alfonso XI, and the statue enthroned therein, were named "Guadalupe," for the village located near the place of discovery.

With great pomp and majesty, the King of Spain visited the chapel in 1340, 14 years after the statue's discovery. Many noblewomen through the years have also visited the statue of Our Lady. They have always maintained that the image was a symbol of the Virgin's royal maternity, since the statue holds in its left hand the Child Jesus while the right hand clasps a scepter.

Women of nobility have provided many elaborate garments which have adorned the miraculous statue. These jeweled robes and mantles, all decorated with golden embroidery, constitute a costly and extensive wardrobe. The most luxurious item in this collection is a headdress containing 30,000 precious stones that is worn only on special occasions.

The popularity of the shrine was at its height during the time of the great discoveries of Columbus, who reportedly carried a replica of the statue with him, as did the Conquistadors. Furthermore, it is said that Christopher Columbus prayed at the shrine of Guadalupe before making his historic voyage, and that upon discovering the West Indies Island of Karukera on November 4, 1493, he renamed it Guadalupe in honor of the Blessed Mother.

The shrine of Our Lady of Guadalupe is located in the church of the fortress-like Monastery of Guadalupe. The statue is found behind the main altar in a room called the Camarin, which is richly decorated. The decor befits the queen of the shrine, who sits on a modern enamelwork throne fashioned in 1953. The priceless garments of Our Lady can be viewed in the Reliquary Cabinet, a room adjoining the shrine-room.

HIDDEN FOR 600 YEARS, the unstained wooden statue of Our Lady of Guadalupe (Spain) was discovered after a radiant Lady appeared to a peasant who was looking for a lost cow. The image is thought by some to be a symbol of the Blessed Virgin's royal maternity. Christopher Columbus is said to have prayed at the shrine.

— 95 —

SANTA MARIA OF EL PUIG

El Puig, Valencia, Spain
622

This holy image of the Blessed Mother holding the Child Jesus is a Byzantine work of art that takes the form of an alto-relief or low-relief—that is, the figures extend outward from its background. The marble image dates from before the year 622, when it was hidden to protect it from the mischief of the Moors, who threatened to attack. The place of its concealment was lost to memory for six centuries, but the miraculous was exerted in the year 1223 when the image of Holy Mary of El Puig was found and brought to light.

The discovery occurred in this manner: When James I the Conquistador was captured and imprisoned at Carcassonne, he made a vow that, if released, he would help other prisoners by founding a religious order for the ransoming of Christian captives from the hands of the infidels. The king was released, and he lost little time in fulfilling his promise. On August 1, 1223 he was favored with a vision of the Blessed Mother. In the vision, she approved the founding of the Order and asked that it be named the Order of Mercy for the Redemption of Captives. A similar vision was granted to the King's confessor, St. Raymond of Pennafort, who was told by the heavenly visitor that he should assist the king and St. Peter Nolasco in establishing the order.

Since it was undecided where the first house of the Order should be located, Heaven once more intervened by the appearance of seven brilliant stars that were seen hovering over a tiny hillock in El Puig called Castillo ("the castle"). Not only did the King witness the twinkling of the seven stars, but the townspeople did, as well.

Realizing at once that the hillock was the place favored by Heaven, work was immediately started on the foundation. When a workman thrust his pickaxe into the ground and struck a metal object, a large bell was discovered. Under the bell was found an image of the Blessed Mother. No questions had to be asked concerning its origin, since its history was discovered etched in Gothic characters on the side of the bell. A priest from Daroca named Zimenes, who was an eye-witness to the discovery, recorded the inscription found on the bell and the reason for its concealment underground.

The stars that appeared on the hillock to indicate the site of the monastery once more appeared, this time over the steeple of the completed monastery church. It is said that the appearance of the stars occurred at intervals during the next several years. This was not the only phenomenon that took place at El Puig. Another heavenly favor was granted when angelic voices were heard during the chanting of the monks. Especially on Sundays, the invisible singers joined their voices to those of the congregation during the singing of the *Salve Regina.* Eventually the sanctuary became known as the Angels' Room.

In addition to the people of El Puig who saw the stars and heard the angelic voices, the people of Valencia were likewise favored. This took place when the image was temporarily enshrined there in the year 1588, during a 16-day celebration planned by King Philip II. During this visit the angelic voices were heard each day while the seven stars were visible each night traveling mysteriously along the route taken by the statue from the Angels' Room at El Puig to the Cathedral of Valencia.

Our Lady of El Puig has shown her powerful protection in favor of many kings of Spain. These and many other crowned heads have visited her image, including James I, Alfonso el Sabio, Peter III, Felipe II, Juan Carlos I and Dona Sofia. Even Peter the Cruel visited the shrine in thanksgiving for his victory over the Moors who violently attacked El Puig. Although Peter's army was vastly outnumbered, they were nevertheless armed with prayer and Our Lady's protection. They won the day with only three casualties, whereas the battlefield was strewn with Moorish dead.

The image of the miraculous Mother and Child is enshrined over the main altar of the monastery known as Real Monasterio de Santa Maria de El Puig, which was rebuilt between the sixteenth and eighteenth centuries. The miraculous image has been consistently guarded by the Order of Mercy.

A BYZANTINE MARBLE CARVING, Santa Maria of El Puig originated prior to the year 622, when it was hidden from attacking Moors and was lost for 600 years. Miraculous circumstances surround the image's re-emergence, including unexplainable angelic voices and seven mysterious stars visible in the night sky.

— 96 —

OUR LADY OF MONTSERRAT

Montserrat, Spain
718

The mountain named Montserrat is located approximately 20 miles northwest of Barcelona, in the geographical center of that part of Spain known as Catalonia. Its name is Catalan for "sawn mountain," which seems appropriate since its numerous rock formations from a distance appear somewhat like the teeth of a saw. Unlike any other mountains in the world, the cone-shaped formations rise almost perpendicularly to amazing heights and are smooth and convoluted. The highest cone rises to a height of nearly 4,000 feet, while the circumference around the entire base of the mountain is measured at about 12 miles. The church which contains the miracle-working statue of the Madonna and Child is situated almost halfway up this unusual mountain.

Legend relates that the miraculous image was first known as *La Jerosolimitana* (the native of Jerusalem), since it is believed to have been carved in that city during the early days of the church. The statue was eventually given to St. Etereo, Bishop of Barcelona, who conveyed it to his country.

Legend also reveals that in the seventh century, when Saracen infidels invaded Spain, the Christians of Barcelona bravely defended their city for three years until defeat seemed imminent. Realizing that they could no longer resist, they decided to remove their treasured image of Our Lady to a secure hiding place. Under full secrecy, but with the knowledge of the Bishop and the Governor of the city, a group of Christians carried the statue to Montserrat. There they placed it in a small cave. This translation took place on April 22, 718. A full account of the origin of the miraculous image, the cause of its removal and the place of its exile were recorded and carefully deposited in the archives of the city.

Even though the location of the statue was eventually erased from memory, the people of Barcelona never forgot the holy image during the 200 years of its exile. But in the year of Our Lord 890, on a Saturday evening, shepherd boys from Monistrol, a village at the foot of Montserrat, were destined to bring about the discovery of the treasure.

While tending their flocks that night the shepherds were amazed to see lights and to hear singing coming from the mountain. When this was repeated, the shepherds reported the situation to their priest, who investigated. When the priest also heard the singing and saw the mysterious lights, he informed the Bishop, and he also witnessed the phenomenon. The statue of Our Lady was discovered in a cave and was brought out and placed in a small church that was soon erected. This humble church eventually developed into the present church that was completed in 1592.

While the shrine does not dispute the preceding legendary accounts, caretakers there prefer to stress that hermitages existed on the mountain in the seventh century. There is also historical evidence that in 888 there existed on Montserrat a chapel which was dedicated to the Mother of God. This is regarded as the origin of the present sanctuary. Eventually a little monastery was added, and this grew rapidly, thanks to the fame of the miracles wrought there by the Blessed Virgin. According to material provided by caretakers of the shrine, the statue that still presides over the monastery was introduced in the twelfth or thirteenth century. This statue might have replaced an earlier one, which could have been destroyed during one of the various political upheavals which will be considered later.

Carved in wood, the statue is in a sitting position and measures slightly over three feet in height (95 centimeters). In accordance with the Romanesque style, the figure is slender, with an elongated face and a delicate expression. The dress of the Virgin consists of a tunic and cloak both gilded and plain in design which is draped in a stylized manner. Beneath the crown is a veil enhanced with geometric designs of stars, squares and stripes that are accented in subtle shades of color. The right hand of the Virgin holds a sphere, while the other is extended in a graceful gesture. The Child Jesus sits on His Mother's lap and also wears a crown and stylized garments. His right hand is raised in blessing; His left hand holds an object described as a pine cone. A cushion serves as the Madonna's footstool, and she is seated upon a chair that has substantial legs and whose back is topped by smooth, cone-shaped finials. The statue is highly esteemed not only as a religious treasure, but also because of its artistic value.

The statue is almost entirely gilded except for the face and hands of Mary, and the face, hands and feet of the Infant. These parts have a brownish-black tint. Unlike many ancient statues that are black due to the nature of the wood or the effects of the original paint, the dark color of Our Lady of Montserrat is attributed to the innumerable candles and lamps that have burned day and night before the image. With the passage of time the smoke seeped into the figure, causing it to blacken in a gradual manner. Because of this darkness it is affectionately called *La Moreneta,* The Dark Little One. By virtue of this coloration the Virgin of Montserrat is classified among the Black Madonnas.

The image is located in an alcove high in the wall behind the main altar. The alcove can be reached by climbing artistically decorated stairs to the side of the church. The stairs lead to a large room which is directly behind the alcove where the statue is enthroned. This large room is called the *Camarin de la Virgen,* the Chamber of the Virgin. A large group of people can be accommodated in this chamber and from here can pray beside the throne of the Blessed Mother. The pilgrim cannot touch the image, however, since it is protected by a glass covering.

Although not located on the peak of the mountain as are the sanctuaries of Monte Cassino and Le Puy, the monastery is situated high enough from the surrounding area to make one think it safe from attack. Yet the monastery did suffer considerable damage during the Napoleonic invasion. Additional damage was inflicted during civil wars and revolutionary disturbances. The treasured image of the Madonna and Child was hidden during these harsh times, but was soon restored to its place of honor when the church and buildings were repaired in a remarkably short time. These buildings were spared during the Spanish Civil War of 1936-1939 by the Autonomous Government of Catalonia.

Benedictines settled in the monastery centuries ago and still maintain the sanctuary and provide hospitality to the steady stream of pilgrims who visit there.

The number of historical figures who were connected to the sanctuary or who have visited it is considerable. One of its hermits, Bernat Boil, accompanied Christopher Columbus to the New World, thus becoming the first missionary to America. One of Montserrat's first abbots was Giuliano ella Rovere, who became Julius II, the Renaissance Pope for whom Michelangelo worked. Emperor Charles V and Philip II of Spain both died with blessed candles from the sanctuary in their hands. King Louis XIV of France had intercessory prayers said at Montserrat for the Queen Mother, and Emperor Ferdinand III of Austria made generous endowments to the monastery. All the kings of Spain prayed at the shrine, as did Cardinal Roncalli, who later became Pope John XXIII.

Among the Saints who visited there can be counted St. Peter Nolasco, St. Raymond of Penafort, St. Vincent Ferrer, St. Francis Borgia, St. Aloysius Gonzaga, St. Joseph Calasanctius, St. Anthony Mary Claret and St. Ignatius, who as a knight was confessed by one of the monks. After spending a night praying before the image of Our Lady of Montserrat, St. Ignatius embarked upon his new life and the founding of a new religious order. A few miles away is Manresa, a pilgrim shrine of the Society of Jesus. Located in this shrine is the cave wherein St. Ignatius Loyola retired from the world and wrote his *Spiritual Exercises.*

The Virgin of Montserrat was declared the Patron Saint of the Diocese of Catalonia by Leo XIII. The statue has always been considered one of the most celebrated images in Spain, as confirmed by the countless people who have visited there through the centuries. In modern times conservative estimates place the number of visitors each year at over a million.

One historian has written: "In all ages the sinful, the suffering, the sorrowful, have laid their woes at the feet of Our Lady of Montserrat, and none have ever gone away unheard or unaided."

DARKENED BY CANDLES and lamps that burned day and night before it, the statue of Our Lady of Montserrat pictured here dates back to the twelfth or thirteenth century. The statue is esteemed for its artistic value, as well as for its religious merit.

A MILLION PEOPLE each year visit Our Lady of Montserrat in Spain, as did St. Ignatius Loyola.

— 97 —

OUR LADY OF THE FORSAKEN

(Nuestra Señora de los Desamparados)
Valencia, Spain
1416

In the late fourteenth century, Padre Juan Gilabert Jofre, a friend of St. Vincent Ferrer, assisted in founding an order of brothers who devoted their lives and fortunes to the noble plan of rescuing children who had been abandoned by their parents. Later, after seeing some youths in the marketplace ridiculing a poor, mentally retarded man, the charity of the brothers was extended to include the elderly and the sick. After prayer and reflection, they named their community "The Brotherhood of Innocent Children and of the Mother of the Forsaken."

The statue venerated as Our Lady of the Forsaken has an origin clouded in mystery since there are no certain facts regarding the sculptor or the date of its completion. One source claims that Padre Juan Gilabert was consulted concerning a statue that would bear the title and represent the charity of the new community. The good priest supposedly arranged to have a statue sculptured by a respected artist of great talent. Heaven, it is said, intervened.

About the year 1416, three young men approached the monastery claiming to be sculptors. They offered to carve the statue for the honor and glory of the Mother of God if the community would provide them with wood or marble and the necessary tools. At their request they were locked in a room for three days, and although no sounds of activity were heard, a beautiful statue was discovered in their room on the fourth day. When no trace of the men could be found, it was surmised they had been sculptors sent from Heaven.

When this claim was made known, the citizens of Valencia flocked to the feet of the Madonna, and there numerous favors were promptly dispensed.

The statue is indeed a beautiful repesentation of our holy Mother. While leaning forward, Our Lady of the Forsaken stands about four feet tall. The Infant Jesus is held on her left arm, while the right hand holds a bouquet of lilies. Two small children, representing the first charity of the brothers, are on either side of the Blessed Mother. With hands folded in prayer they gaze upward while kneeling under the protection of the Madonna's mantle.

The statue is usually clothed in fabric of elegant design. On certain feast days Our Lady's many jewels are attached to her garments. These jewels and ornaments represent gifts given by her devotees who have received solutions to difficult problems or cures of physical afflictions. Because of the large collection of jewels and ornaments, Our Lady of the Forsaken is considered to be one of the most richly endowed images in Spain. Some of the costly tokens were donated by Queen Isabella II in 1859. Some years ago, the donations made by the queen were valued at $50,000. Christina of Bourbon, grandmother of King Alfonso, also gave costly presents to the sanctuary.

In Valencia's great cathedral, the miraculous statue of Our Lady is found in her own spacious chapel which was built especially for her in 1667. Standing high atop the altar, Our Lady is flanked by two large marble columns. At a lower level are located a statue of St. Vincent the Martyr and on the other side of the altar, St. Vincent Ferrer, a son and patron of Valencia.

The statue of Our Lady of the Forsaken was honored with a papal coronation on May 12, 1923. Many honors have been conferred upon Our Lady, and one of the more recent awards was given on May 13, 1961. A historic procession with the miraculous statue took place on that day, when Our Lady of the Forsaken was proclaimed Patroness of the region. Also carried in the procession was the framed papal document.

Of the many miracles and unusual events that took place as a result of prayer to Our Lady, we will relate one of the most extraordinary and most carefully witnessed. This involved a criminal condemned to death for murder. While being taken to the place of execution, he was permitted to stop at the cathedral to offer a prayer before the miraculous statue. While he was kneeling in prayer, the hand of the statue which held the lilies was seen to move several times, to the shouts and exclamations of the people. It was decided that such a miracle must indicate the man's innocence, and for this reason he was set free. The liberated man returned to this shrine of Our Lady numerous times to offer his gratitude.

A CONDEMNED CRIMINAL on the way to his execution was allowed to stop and offer a prayer before the miraculous statue, Our Lady of the Forsaken. While the man knelt there, everyone present was astounded to see one hand of the statue move several times. The miracle was interpreted as a sign of the man's innocence, and he was set free.

— 98 —

OUR LADY OF THE DEW

(Nuestra Señora del Rocio)
Almonte (Huelva) Spain
Fifteenth Century

The history of Our Lady of the Dew begins in the fifteenth century, when a hunter approached the great woods near the village of Almonte. His interest and curiosity were stirred when he heard something like the bark of a dog and saw a mysterious movement among a tangle of thornbushes. With great difficulty he guided his horse through the high grass, while small animals scurried away and birds fluttered overhead. His interest was no longer in hunting, but in following an inner prompting to travel deeper into the forest. Presently he saw a large bush and atop it a lily nestled among a cluster of thorns. Then, looking aside, he saw a vision of the Queen of Heaven.

Standing close beside a tree was a Woman of heavenly beauty and elegant bearing. Dressed in a linen tunic of pale green, she said nothing. She mysteriously disappeared, leaving behing a statue of remarkable beauty. Whether the statue itself had become animated or whether the vision was separate from the statue is unclear. What is known is that the hunter dismounted and stood in awe before the apparition. Filled with unbounded happiness at seeing the vision and then discovering the statue, the hunter wanted to share his happy experience and decided to carry the statue on his shoulders to the open road.

After walking three leagues to the town, he was extremely tired. The excitement of the apparition likewise added to his fatigue so that when he arrived home, he decided to rest before telling about his experience. In a few moments he fell fast asleep. Upon awakening he found the statue missing. Greatly troubled, he reported the happening to the clerk of the Cabildo, who journeyed with him to the woods accompanied by some others who had overheard the story. There in the forest beside the tree of the apparition, covered with dew, was the statue exactly as the hunter had found it. The beauty of the statue was immediately appreciated by all. Despite the dampness of the weather, the people were amazed that it had remained in excellent condition.

With all devotion and respect the statue was carried to the local church, and a temporary shrine was erected. In the woods, at the place of the apparition, a small chapel was soon built with the trunk of the tree serving as a pedestal for the miraculous statue. On the trunk was placed a sign on which was inscribed, *La Virgen de las Rocinas*.

Devotion to Our Lady of the Dew has been vigorous from the time of her discovery. Wearing a superb crown, she is constantly venerated in her famous sanctuary, where processions often take place—particularly on every Monday of Pentecost.

Every seven years she is dressed in a native costume depicting a shepherdess which includes a sombrero. Situated on a platform, she is carried by the men of Almonte during the round trip between Rocio, a pueblo of Almonte, and the city of Almonte.

With the passage of time the original chapel in the woods fell into disrepair, but was later rebuilt in a splendid fashion, with the trunk of the tree being carefully retained.

A HUNTER in fifteenth century Spain was graced with a vision of the Queen of Heaven just before he discovered the beautiful statue known as Our Lady of the Dew.

DEVOTION to Our Lady of the Dew continues to be vigorous today.

— 99 —

OUR LADY OF EINSIEDELN

Einsiedeln, Switzerland
853

The history of this miraculous statue begins with St. Meinrad, who was about 25 years old when he received the Benedictine habit at the monastery of Reichenau. The monks there enjoyed a great reputation for sanctity and learning, but after five or six years Meinrad felt called to a life of more complete seclusion. With the permission of his superiors, he left the monastery during the year 840 and took with him only a few pious books. He eventually settled in an isolated place on Mt. Etzel. There he built a cell and lived a hermit's life—until his retreat was discovered by the curious. He then left to establish a hermitage in the depths of a pine forest a short distance from Lake Lucerne. Here in the Dark Forest, he spent his days in prayer and penance. Northcote reports in his history of the shrine that a monk from Reichenau discovered Meinrad's retreat and was occasionally permitted to visit him. One night, he saw a brilliant light proceeding from the hermit's little chapel. Looking in he saw Meinrad reciting the night office while a young child, surrounded by brilliant rays, supported the book and recited with him the alternate verses. The monk did not enter, but returned to his monastery and made known to his fellow monks that Meinrad's retreat was visited by angels.

It is reported that Meinrad tamed and adopted two crows. It is also said that he was discovered by a woodcutter. Once his location was known, many people journeyed to him for spiritual instruction. Because of the great number of people who were visiting the hermitage, it was considered necessary that a chapel be provided for the celebration of Holy Mass and the administration of the Sacraments. During the year 853 a chapel was built adjoining the Saint's cell.

There are two accounts regarding Meinrad's acquisition of the miraculous statue. One tells that when he left Reichenau, he took not only his books, but the monastery's statue as well; another account reveals that he was given the statue after the chapel was built. Historians do agree, however, that the statue was the gift of Abbess Hildegarde of Zurich, who might also have arranged for the building of the chapel since she was able to provide the necessary funds from her father, the Emperor Louis.

The statue of Our Lady holding on her left arm the Divine Child is carved in wood and is three feet, four inches in height. The features are described as being regular, gracious and serene. Its color is now perfectly black; but whether this is the original color of the wood or the result of great age and long exposure to the smoke of burning tapers, it is impossible to determine.

This precious statue was placed by St. Meinrad over the simple altar of his little chapel. People flocked to pray there, and soon extraordinary graces were manifested. Because of these marvels pilgrimages soon wended their way to the hermitage to do honor to Our Lady of Einsiedeln.

Two thieves named Richard and Peter eventually heard that crowds of people were visiting the isolated chapel. Thinking that the people were donating jewels and valuables in return for the benefits they derived from praying there, the thieves visited the hermitage one winter's day in the year 863. We are told that the Saint was informed by supernatural means of their coming and their intent; nevertheless, St. Meinrad welcomed them kindly and offered them the hospitality of his humble dwelling. It is uncertain whether the thieves attacked the Saint before they searched for treasure, or whether they killed him from disappointment at finding nothing of value. It is told, however, that after the scoundrels placed St. Meinrad's body on his bed of leaves, two candles standing nearby were mysteriously lighted. Frightened at this marvel, they hastily left, but the two crows belonging to the Saint followed them to Zurich. Their sharp cries and flapping wings attracted the attention of many, including the woodcutter, who identified the birds as those which lived near the Saint. Suspecting that some danger had befallen his friend, the woodcutter hurried to the chapel and discovered the body. Burial of the Saint took place at the Abbey of Reichenau.

It is said that the two crows hovered over the scaffold the day the two thieves were brought to justice. Northcote tells us that there exists no reason for doubting the truth of this account about the crows, "which need not necessarily be regarded as in any way miraculous." In addition to many reproductions of the crows in sculpture and illuminations found in Swiss churches, the abbey of Einsiedeln bears the likeness of two crows on its armorial shield, and for many years an inn in Zurich was known as the Inn of the Two Faithful Crows.

After St. Meinrad's death the chapel was seldom visited, but in 903 Benno, a canon of Strasburg, made a pilgrimage there. Touched by devotion, he resolved not only to bid farewell to the world, but also to restore the hermitage. He eventually assembled a community of hermits. Later a community of Benedictine monks was established on the spot and a handsome church was erected around the holy chapel. This was so arranged that the chapel remained as a separate little building within the church. When the church was completed in 948 and its consecration was planned for September 14, a most astounding miracle occurred.

The evening before the planned ceremony, Conrad, the Bishop of Constance, who was to perform the consecration, decided to spend part of the night in prayer before the miraculous image. With him were some of the clergy. Shortly after midnight a bright light illuminated the sanctuary, while heavenly voices began to sing. Looking up, the prelate saw two choirs of angels chanting the hymns appointed by the Church for the solemn consecration of a church. He then beheld Our Lord Himself standing at the high altar, arrayed in pontifical vestments and preparing to celebrate the rite of dedication. Bishop Conrad identified St. Stephen, the protomartyr, who served as deacon, and St. Lawrence, who assisted as subdeacon. St. Peter, St. Gregory and St. Augustine stood around the altar. Seated nearby on a throne of light was the Queen of Heaven, attended by angelic spirits.

Amazed by what he was witnessing, the Bishop was not too awe-struck to notice that the angels made a slight alteration in the prayers. Instead of the words: "Blessed is He that cometh in the name of the Lord," the angels substituted: "Blessed be the Son of Mary, who has come down to this place; who reigns world without end."

At the completion of the ceremony, when the heavenly visitors departed, the Bishop remained in an ecstasy. According to one report, the Bishop remained in the church until the sun streamed through the eastern window. While early morning preparations were being made in the church and clerical dignitaries were gathering for the scheduled ceremony, the Bishop informed them of the vision he had seen during the night and advised them that the church was already consecrated. Nevertheless, he was persuaded to vest and take his place in the procession. When the first words of the consecration were about to be uttered, a voice was distinctly heard by all present: "Cease, for the church has been divinely consecrated." Thus the reality of the vision was proved beyond a doubt.

Bishop Conrad related the vision in his book entitled, *De Secretis Secretorum,* and 16 years later, on the deposition of the Bishop and other witnesses, the miraculous event was confirmed by a bull of Pope Leo VIII. The Pope likewise granted a plenary indulgence to all who would pilgrimage to Our Lady of Einsiedeln. The deposition of Bishop Conrad regarding the vision, dated 948, is still intact and preserved at the abbey.

Unfortunately, the building which was graced by heavenly consecration was destroyed by fire in 1028. The flames spared nothing except the chapel of St. Meinrad, which contained the holy image. When the church was rebuilt, a triple ceremony took place: the solemn consecration, the canonization of Meinrad by Pope Benedict IX, and the solemn translation of St. Meinrad's remains from Reichenau to Einsiedeln, the place of his martyrdom.

It is remarkable that in each of the five fires which reduced the church to ashes, only the holy chapel escaped injury. These fires occurred in 1028, 1214, 1465, 1509 and 1577.

The chapel was carefully preserved in its original form until the year 1467, two years after its miraculous escape from the third fire. In that year the outside of the chapel was protected with stone columns and pilasters. Following its escape from the fifth fire it was entirely encased in marble, which was later adorned with statues and bas-reliefs. Precious marbles also cover the inside walls.

The church containing the chapel of St. Meinrad and the miraculous statue of the Virgin always remained a place of popular pilgrimage, but during the French Revolution, when the French Republicans invaded the country, they seized the treasures of the church and conveyed them to Paris. The sacred image of the Blessed Virgin Mary was saved from sacrilege by being carried to safety by one of the monks. History reports that the monk placed the sacred image at the bottom of a peddlar's pouch and covered it with cloths and miscellaneous articles. When enemy soldiers asked to examine the pouch, the monk craftily opened it and offered for sale the various articles he was carrying, pretending as he did so that his only interest was to strike a profitable bargain. In this way both he and his precious cargo passed safely through enemy lines. The holy image was joyfully brought back to its shrine in the year 1803, when tranquility was again restored.

One historian relates that: "To enumerate a hundredth part of the royal and other illustrious personages who have made the pilgrimage of Einsiedeln would be a lengthy task." We should mention, however, that costly gifts were given to the shrine by the King of Prussia, the King of Sardinia, Emperor Napoleon III and Queen Hortense Eugenie. Three eminent Saints also visited Our Lady of Einsiedeln: St. Nicholas of Flue, the patron of Switzerland; St. Charles Borromeo; and St. Benedict Joseph Labre, whose visits were recorded on several occasions.

Throughout the centuries, miracles of every nature have been performed through the intercession of Our Lady of Einsiedeln; but the shrine claims as the most striking those graces which have invigorated faith and devotion.

In 1854 a group of religious from Einsiedeln were sent as missionaries to the United States. The first settlement established by them is well known as St. Meinrad's Abbey in southern Indiana.

The miraculous statue of Our Lady remains today in the little chapel and continues to attract pilgrims, as it has since its origin over a thousand years ago.

ST. MEINRAD placed the precious statue, Our Lady of Einsiedeln, in Switzerland, over the simple altar of his little chapel. People flocked to pray there, but two visitors had different plans. They murdered St. Meinrad, but were brought to justice for their crime due to the actions of two crows that St. Meinrad had trained as pets.

HEAVENLY VOICES began to sing in the year 948 as St. Conrad, Bishop of Constance, prayed before the sanctuary in preparation for the consecration of the church containing the statue known as Our Lady of Ensiedeln. The Bishop then saw two choirs of angels chanting hymns, Our Lord standing at the high altar, as well as St. Stephen, St. Laurence, St. Peter, St. Gregory, St. Augustine and the Queen of Heaven herself. Our Lady of Einsiedeln is pictured above on the golden altar, "dressed" in special garments.

— 100 —

OUR LADY OF PROMPT SUCCOR

New Orleans, Louisiana, United States of America
1809

The history of the miraculous statue that is enshrined above the altar in the chapel of the Ursuline convent in New Orleans began in France, when that country was just issuing from its great Revolution.

Mother St. Michel is mentioned in this history as a woman of rare ability and a teacher crowned with success. She was asked by the Ursulines in New Orleans to join them in educating Indians and Negroes and to help in administering their establishments, which included a boarding school and an orphanage. Despite the circumstances requiring her continued labors in France, she nevertheless saw the will of God in the American invitation.

Her bishop in France, however, rejected any thought of dispensing with her services and refused to give his permission for her to leave by declaring that such permission could be given only by the Pope. This was equivalent to an emphatic refusal, since Pope Pius VII was then a captive of Napoleon and lived under a strict injunction that prevented all communications, even those made by letter. Knowing that a reply from the Pontiff was impossible, the Bishop felt secure in the condition he expressed. Nevertheless, Mother St. Michel wrote to the Pope, setting forth her motives for wishing to leave. Before sending the letter she knelt before a statue of the Blessed Mother and prayed: "O most holy Virgin Mary, if you obtain a prompt and favorable answer to my letter, I promise to have you honored in New Orleans under the title of Our Lady of Prompt Succor." The letter left Montpellier on March 19, 1809. The favorable reply was received from the Pope one month later, on April 28. Although knowing the state of affairs in France and the need for such apostles of the Faith, the Pope nonetheless gave his permission and his blessing for Mother St. Michel to leave France for America with her group of religious aspirants.

Bishop Fournier acknowledged the swift response from the Pontiff as miraculous and blessed the statue of Our Lady that Mother St. Michel had ordered to be carved in accordance with her promise to Our Lady. On their arrival in New Orleans on December 30, 1810, the statue was solemnly installed in the convent chapel. Homage and veneration to Mary under the title of Our Lady of Prompt Succor has been constant since that time. The chronicles of the Ursuline monastery summarize the graces worked through this devotion with the statement: "Under this title the Most Blessed Virgin has so often manifested her power and goodness that the religious have unbounded confidence in her."

Two years after the installation of the statue, the Blessed Mother honored this confidence by demonstrating the promptness of her help to the urgent needs of her children. This occurred in 1812, when a great fire was engulfing the neighborhood near the convent. With the flames steadily advancing toward the Ursulines, city officials gave orders for the sisters to evacuate the building. Despite strong winds that whipped the flames toward them, and with the danger imminent, the statue of Our Lady of Prompt Succor was placed on a windowsill facing the fire. Mother St. Michel prayed aloud, "Our Lady of Prompt Succor, we are lost unless you hasten to our help." Immediately the wind changed the direction of the flames, the convent and the properties around it were relieved of danger and the fire died out. Witnesses promptly attributed the miracle to Our Lady and spread the news throughout the city.

Another miracle attributed to Our Lady features none other than General Andrew Jackson, who later became the seventh President of the United States. This miracle occurred on the outskirts of New Orleans in the confrontation with British forces which is known in history as the Battle of New Orleans.

Encouraged by their victory over Napoleon's forces, the British aimed their ambitions at the United States. After raiding Washington and setting fire to the White House, and after attacking Fort McHenry at Baltimore, they planned to conquer the central portion of America by capturing Louisiana. The expedition was described as being ". . . perfectly appointed in every way, commanded by officers some of whom had grown gray in victory. The elite of England's army and navy were afloat." Transferring to small boats, the troops arrived nine miles below the city of New Orleans on December 9, 1814. During the month, the British attempted several times to attack the city by tangent routes.

The troops that opposed each other consisted of approximately 20,000 well-trained and superbly equipped British militiamen, against a scraggly group of about 6,000. In this group were fishermen, farmers, flatboatmen, Tennessee frontiersmen and hurriedly trained city men who were led by General Andrew Jackson.

The night before the decisive battle, the wives, mothers and sisters of Jackson's band assembled in the Ursuline chapel before the statue of Our Lady of Prompt Succor. Thoroughly terrified that their menfolk would be killed and the city invaded, they prayed to the Blessed Mother throughout the night. At dawn, with the sound of cannonfire reaching the city from Chalmette plantation, the women prayed the more fervently. Later, during Holy Mass, a courier rushed into the chapel announcing the defeat of the enemy. A *Te Deum* was immediately entoned amid the most enthusiastic display of gratitude.

The British suffered enormous casualties, with one British writer stating: "They fell like blades of grass beneath the scythe." The American forces suffered few casualties. The British withdrew and made no further attempt to capture the city.

General Jackson did not hesitate to admit of a divine intervention on his behalf and went in person, together with his staff, to thank the Ursulines for their prayers and to express his appreciation to Our Lady of Prompt Succor.

During the night of prayer, the superior of the Ursulines made a vow to have a Mass of Thanksgiving sung annually, should the Americans be victorious. The vow has been honored every year since 1815 on the anniversary of the battle, January 8. The celebrant of the yearly commemoration is the Archbishop of New Orleans.

Ironically, this final battle of the war of 1812-1815 was fought after a treaty of peace had been signed, a fact unknown by the participants.

In accordance with a decree of Pope Leo XIII, issued in November of 1895, the statue of Our Lady of Prompt Succor was solemnly crowned. Another honor was rendered Our Lady when the Sacred Congregation of Rites, acting on the request of the Archbishop of New Orleans and two Bishops of surrounding regions, approved and confirmed on June 13, 1928, the choice of Our Lady of Prompt Succor as the principal patroness of the City of New Orleans and of the State of Louisiana.

THE MIRACULOUS statue, Our Lady of Prompt Succor is enshrined above the altar in the Ursuline convent in New Orleans.

OUR LADY OF PROMPT SUCCOR was offered prayers of gratitude by Andrew Jackson following the battle of New Orleans.

— SELECTED BIBLIOGRAPHY —

Adam, R., Cure d'Houdelaincourt. *Notre Dame Des Vertus, La Bonne Notre-Dame de Ligny.* Vagner. Nancy, France. 1940.

Aimond, Monseigneur. *Notre-Dame des Vertus.* Ligny en Barrois, France.

Aparicio, Emilio Maria. *Madre de Desamparados. Real Basilica de Santa Maria de los Desamparados.* Valencia, Spain. 1964.

Aradi, Zsolt. *Shrines to Our Lady Around the World.* Farrar, Straus & Young. New York. 1954.

Ball, Ann. *A Litany of Mary.* Our Sunday Visitor, Inc. Huntington, Indiana. 1988.

Boix, Maur M. *What is Montserrat.* Publicacions de l'Abadia de Montserrat. Montserrat. 1976.

Boymann, Dr. Guido Grobe and Olga Llop de Grobe Boymann. *The Basilica in Kevelaer.* 1979.

Bruguera, Dom Justino. *Montserrat.* Editorial Planeta. Barcelona, Spain. 1964.

Brusher, S.J., Joseph. *Popes Through the Ages.* D. Van Nostrand Company, Inc. Princeton, New Jersey. 1959.

Cartwright, John K. *The Catholic Shrines of Europe.* McGraw-Hill Book Company, Inc. New York. 1954.

Cassidy, Joseph L. *Mexico, Land of Mary's Wonders.* St. Anthony Guild Press. Paterson, New Jersey. 1958.

The Catholic Encyclopedia. The Encyclopedia Press, Inc. New York. 1912.

Chretiens A Boulogne S/Mer. Paroisse Notre-Dame. Boulogne-sur-Mer.

Cruz, Joan Carroll. *Relics.* Our Sunday Visitor, Inc. Huntington, Indiana. 1984.

de Liguori, St. Alphonsus. *The Glories of Mary.* Redemptorist Fathers. Brooklyn, New York. 1931.

De Montfort, St. Louis-Marie Grignion. *True Devotion to Mary.* TAN Books and Publishers, Inc. Rockford, Illinois.

De Montfort. *True Devotion to the Blessed Virgin.* Society of St. Paul. Staten Island, New York. 1962.

Devesa, Juan. *Real Monasterio Del Puig De Santa Maria.* (Paper.)

Dorcy, O.P., Sr. Mary Jean. *Shrines of Our Lady.* Sheed and Ward. New York. 1956.

Elenco Delle Sacre Relique Nella Patriarcale Basilica Liberiana. (Paper.)

Elias, Fr. Julio Maria. *Copacauana-Copacabana.* Santuario de Copacabana. Bolivia, South America. 1981.

Emiliano De La Huerga. *Covadonga.* Editorial Everest. Leon, Spain. 1989.

Farrell O.P., Walter. *A Companion to the Summa.* Sheed & Ward. New York. 1942.

Finucane, Ronald C. *Miracles and Pilgrims.* Rowman and Littlefield. Totowa, New Jersey. 1977.

Fremantle, Anne. *Age of Faith.* Time Incorporated. New York. 1965.

Gillett, H. M. *Famous Shrines of Our Lady.* Volumes I and II. The Newman Press. Westminster, Maryland. 1952.

Glories of Czestochowa and Jasna Gora. Our Lady of Czestochowa Foundation. Diocese of Worcester, Massachusetts. 1955.

Guida del Santuario Di Montenero. Livorno.

Haffert, John M. *The Meaning of Akita.* 101 Foundation, Inc. Asbury, New Jersey. 1990.

Heath, Sidney. *Pilgrim Life in the Middle Ages.* Kennikat Press. Port Washington, New York. 1911.

Huysmans, J. K. *Saint Lydwine of Schiedam.* TAN Books and Publishers, Inc. Rockford, Illinois. 1979.

Il Santuario Dell'addolorata di Rho. Edizioni F.IIi. Milano.

Jameson, Mrs. *Legends of the Madonna.* Houghton, Mifflin and Company. Boston. 1881.

Kavanaugh, O.C.D., Kieran and Otilio Rodriguez, O.C.D., Translators. *The Collected Works of St. John of the Cross.* Institute of Carmelite Studies. Washington, D.C. 1973.

Kendall, Alan. *Medieval Pilgrims.* G. P. Putnam's Sons. New York. 1970.

Kerkhoff, O.S.B., P. Dr. Radbert. *Kevelaer.* Pilgrimage Directorate. Kevelaer. 1986.

La Chiesa Monumentale Della Madonna Delle Lagrime. Desclee & Co. Rome. 1928.

La Fresque de Mater Admirabilis. Trinite des Monts. Rome. (Paper.)

La Madonna di Capocroce. Pia Unione di Maria SS. di Capocroce.

La Vergine Bruna e il Carmine Maggiore di Napoli. Napoli, Italy. 1988.

Manual of Devotions, National Shrine of Our Lady of Prompt Succor. Ursuline Convent. New Orleans, Louisiana. 1963.

Marengo, Aldo with Giuseppe Tuninetti, Jr. and Giuseppe Pollano. *La Madonna Consolata Patrona Della Diocesi di Torino, Venerata Nel Suo Santuario.* Santuario Della Consolata. Torino, Italy.

Maria Absam. Absam, Austria.

Miller, C.SS.R., Father D. F. and Aubin, C.SS.R., Father L. X. *Saint Alphonsus Liguori.* TAN Books and Publishers, Inc. Rockford, Illinois. 1987.

Mowatt, Archpriest John H. *The Holy and Miraculous Icon of Our Lady of Kazan.* Byzantine Center Domus Pacis. Fatima, Portugal.

Musumeci, Dr. Ottavio. *The Madonna Wept in Syracuse.* Santuario Madonna Delle Lacrime. Siracusa. 1954.

The New Catholic Dictionary. The Editors of the *Catholic Encyclopedia.* The Universal Knowledge Foundation. New York. 1929.

New Catholic Encyclopedia. Catholic University of America. McGraw-Hill Co. New York. 1967.

Northcote, D.D., Rev. J. Spencer. *Celebrated Sanctuaries of the Madonna.* Peter F. Cunningham & Son. Philadelphia, Pennsylvania. 1868.

Notre-Dame de Boulogne-Sur-Mer. Saep Edition. Pas-de-Calais, France.

Notre-Dame de Toutes Graces, de Chatillon-Sur-Seine. Chatillon-Sur-Seine, France.

Notre-Dame Du Cap. Juillet-Aout. 1987. (Magazine.)

Notre-Dame Du Cap Shrine. Quebec, Canada.

Nuestra Senora de los Remedios. Santuario Parroquia de Ntra. Senora de los Remedios. Naucalpan, Mexico. (Paper.)

Nuestra Senora Del Rocio. Almonte (Huelva) Spain.

Our Lady of Good Counsel, A History of the Ancient Sanctuary in Genazzano and of the Wonderful Apparition and Miraculous Translation of the Sacred Picture. Anthonian Press. Dublin, Ireland.

Our Lady Patroness of the Americas. Franciscan Marytown Press. Kenosha, Wisconsin. 1974.

Piat, O.F.M. Rev. Stephane Joseph. *Our Lady of the Smile.* Franciscan Herald Press. Chicago, Illinois. 1953.

Pietra, D. Pierluigi. *Shrine Madonna Del Divino Amore.* Rome. 1982.

Plank, O.S.B., Mag. Peter Benedikt. *Mariazell.* 1985.

Rahm, S.J., Harold. *Am I Not Here?* AMI Press. Washington, New Jersey. 1963.

Romanelli, Emanuele, *Santa Maria in Aracoeli*. Rome.

Salo, Juan Gasca. *Preve Noticia Del Pilar.* La Parroquia de Nuestra Senora del Pilar. Zaragoza. 1977.

Salus Populi Romani. Basilica of St. Mary Major. Rome. (Paper.)

Sanctuary of Our Mother of Good Counsel. Sanctuario Madonna del Buon Consiglio. Genazzano, Italy.

Sanctuary of Our Lady of the Guard. Marseille, France. (Paper.)

Santuario Madonna Della Quercia. 1981.

Santos, Javier Gonzalez. *El Santuario de Nuestra Senora de Covadonga.* 1989.

Sharp, Mary. *A Guide to The Churches of Rome.* Chilton Books. Philadelphia. 1966.

Schroeder, O.P., Rev. H. J. *Canons and Decrees of the Council of Trent.* TAN Books and Publishers, Inc. Rockford, Illinois. 1978.

Senhora do Fetal. Fetal, Portugal.

Valenti, Tommaso. *Curiosita Storiche Trevant.* Foligno, Italy. 1922.

Ventas, Pedro Gerrero. *De Santa Maria De Toledo, a ntra. Senora Del Sagrario.* Toledo, Spain. 1983.

The *Virgin of Peace and Good Voyage, a Historical Sketch.* (Paper.)

The Weeping Madonna. Sanctuary of Our Lady of Tears of Syracuse, 20th anniversary issue 1953-1973, and the silver jubilee issue 1953-1978.

Yasuda, O.S.V., Teiji. *Akita, The Tears and Message of Mary.* 101 Foundation, Inc. Asbury, New Jersey. 1989.

Yeo, Margaret. *Reformer: St. Charles Borromeo.* Bruce Publishing Company. Milwaukee, Wisconsin. 1938.

If you have enjoyed this book, consider making your next selection from among the following . . .

Visits to the Blessed Sacrament. *St. Alphonsus* 5.00
Moments Divine—Before the Blessed Sacrament. *Reuter* 10.00
Miraculous Images of Our Lady. *Cruz* 21.50
Miraculous Images of Our Lord. *Cruz* 16.50
Saints Who Raised the Dead. *Fr. Hebert*. 18.50
Love and Service of God, Infinite Love. *Mother Louise Margaret* 15.00
Life and Work of Mother Louise Margaret. *Fr. O'Connell* 15.00
Autobiography of St. Margaret Mary. 7.50
Thoughts and Sayings of St. Margaret Mary 6.00
The Voice of the Saints. *Comp. by Francis Johnston*. 8.00
The 12 Steps to Holiness and Salvation. *St. Alphonsus* 9.00
The Rosary and the Crisis of Faith. *Cirrincione & Nelson* 2.00
Sin and Its Consequences. *Cardinal Manning* 9.00
St. Francis of Paola. *Simi & Segreti* 9.00
Dialogue of St. Catherine of Siena. *Transl. Algar Thorold* 12.50
Catholic Answer to Jehovah's Witnesses. *D'Angelo* 13.50
Twelve Promises of the Sacred Heart. (100 cards). 5.00
Life of St. Aloysius Gonzaga. *Fr. Meschler* 13.00
The Love of Mary. *D. Roberto* 9.00
Begone Satan. *Fr. Vogl* 4.00
The Prophets and Our Times. *Fr. R. G. Culleton*. 15.00
St. Therese, The Little Flower. *John Beevers* 7.50
St. Joseph of Copertino. *Fr. Angelo Pastrovicchi*. 8.00
Mary, The Second Eve. *Cardinal Newman* 4.00
Devotion to Infant Jesus of Prague. *Booklet* 1.50
Reign of Christ the King in Public & Private Life. *Davies* 2.00
The Wonder of Guadalupe. *Francis Johnston* 9.00
Apologetics. *Msgr. Paul Glenn*. 12.50
Baltimore Catechism No. 1 . . . . 5.00
Baltimore Catechism No. 2. . . . . 7.00
Baltimore Catechism No. 3 . . . . 11.00
An Explanation of the Baltimore Catechism. *Fr. Kinkead*. 18.00
Bethlehem. *Fr. Faber* 20.00
Bible History. *Schuster*. 16.50
Blessed Eucharist. *Fr. Mueller* 10.00
Catholic Catechism. *Fr. Faerber*. 9.00
The Devil. *Fr. Delaporte* 8.50
Dogmatic Theology for the Laity. *Fr. Premm* 21.50
Evidence of Satan in the Modern World. *Cristiani* 14.00
Fifteen Promises of Mary. (100 cards). 5.00
Life of Anne Catherine Emmerich. 2 vols. *Schmoeger.* (Reg. 48.00). 40.00
Life of the Blessed Virgin Mary. *Emmerich* 18.00
Manual of Practical Devotion to St. Joseph. *Patrignani* 17.50
Prayer to St. Michael. (100 leaflets) 5.00
Prayerbook of Favorite Litanies. *Fr. Hebert* 12.50
Preparation for Death. (Abridged). *St. Alphonsus* 12.00
Purgatory. (From *All for Jesus*). *Fr. Faber*. 6.00
Bible History. *Johnson, Hannan, Dominica* 24.00
Fundamentals of Catholic Dogma. *Ludwig Ott*. 27.50
Spiritual Conferences. *Faber* 18.00
Trustful Surrender to Divine Providence. *Bl. Claude* 7.00
Wife, Mother and Mystic. *Bessieres*. 10.00
The Agony of Jesus. *Padre Pio*. 3.00

Prices subject to change.

Seven Capital Sins. *Benedictine Sisters* 3.00
Confession—Its Fruitful Practice. *Ben. Srs.* 3.00
Sermons of the Curé of Ars. *Vianney* 15.00
St. Antony of the Desert. *St. Athanasius* 7.00
Is It a Saint's Name? *Fr. William Dunne* 3.00
St. Pius V—His Life, Times, Miracles. *Anderson* 7.00
Who Is Therese Neumann? *Fr. Charles Carty.* 3.50
Martyrs of the Coliseum. *Fr. O'Reilly.* 21.00
Way of the Cross. *St. Alphonsus Liguori* 1.50
Way of the Cross. *Franciscan version* 1.50
How Christ Said the First Mass. *Fr. Meagher* 21.00
Too Busy for God? Think Again! *D'Angelo* 7.00
St. Bernadette Soubirous. *Trochu* 21.00
Pope Pius VII. *Anderson* 16.50
Treatise on the Love of God. 1 Vol. *de Sales. Mackey, Trans.* 27.50
Confession Quizzes. *Radio Replies Press* 2.50
St. Philip Neri. *Fr. V. J. Matthews.* 7.50
St. Louise de Marillac. *Sr. Vincent Regnault* 7.50
The Old World and America. *Rev. Philip Furlong* 21.00
Prophecy for Today. *Edward Connor* 7.50
The Book of Infinite Love. *Mother de la Touche* 7.50
Chats with Converts. *Fr. M. D. Forrest.* 13.50
The Church Teaches. *Church Documents* 18.00
Conversation with Christ. *Peter T. Rohrbach* 12.50
Purgatory and Heaven. *J. P. Arendzen* 6.00
Liberalism Is a Sin. *Sarda y Salvany* 9.00
Spiritual Legacy of Sr. Mary of the Trinity. *van den Broek* 13.00
The Creator and the Creature. *Fr. Frederick Faber* 17.50
Radio Replies. 3 Vols. *Frs. Rumble and Carty* 48.00
Convert's Catechism of Catholic Doctrine. *Fr. Geiermann* 5.00
Incarnation, Birth, Infancy of Jesus Christ. *St. Alphonsus* 13.50
Light and Peace. *Fr. R. P. Quadrupani* 8.00
Dogmatic Canons & Decrees of Trent, Vat. I. *Documents* 11.00
The Evolution Hoax Exposed. *A. N. Field* 9.00
The Primitive Church. *Fr. D. I. Lanslots.* 12.50
The Priest, the Man of God. *St. Joseph Cafasso* 16.00
Blessed Sacrament. *Fr. Frederick Faber* 20.00
Christ Denied. *Fr. Paul Wickens* 3.50
New Regulations on Indulgences. *Fr. Winfrid Herbst* 3.00
A Tour of the Summa. *Msgr. Paul Glenn* 22.50
Latin Grammar. *Scanlon and Scanlon* 18.00
A Brief Life of Christ. *Fr. Rumble* 3.50
Marriage Quizzes. *Radio Replies Press* 2.50
True Church Quizzes. *Radio Replies Press* 2.50
The Secret of the Rosary. *St. Louis De Montfort* 5.00
Mary, Mother of the Church. *Church Documents* 5.00
The Sacred Heart and the Priesthood. *de la Touche* 10.00
Revelations of St. Bridget. *St. Bridget of Sweden* 4.50
Magnificent Prayers. *St. Bridget of Sweden* 2.00
The Happiness of Heaven. *Fr. J. Boudreau* 10.00
St. Catherine Labouré of the Miraculous Medal. *Dirvin* 16.50
The Glories of Mary. *St. Alphonsus Liguori* 21.00
Three Conversions/Spiritual Life. *Garrigou-Lagrange, O.P.* 7.00

Prices subject to change.

ABOUT THE AUTHOR

Joan Carroll Cruz is a native of New Orleans and was educated by the School Sisters of Notre Dame. She attended grade school, high school and college under their tutelage. About her teachers Mrs. Cruz says, "I am especially indebted to the sisters who taught me for five years at the boarding school at St. Mary of the Pines in Chatawa, Mississippi. I cannot thank them enough for their dedication, their fine example and their religious fervor, which made such an impression on me." Mrs. Cruz has been a tertiary in the Discalced Carmelite Secular Order (Third Order) for the past 25 years; for eight years she served as Mistress of Formation (Novice Mistress). She is married to Louis Cruz, who owns a swimming pool repair and maintenance business.

Other books by Mrs. Cruz include *Prayers and Heavenly Promises, Secular Saints, The Incorruptibles* and *Eucharistic Miracles,* all published by TAN Books and Publishers, Inc.; *The Desires of Thy Heart,* a novel with a strong Catholic theme published in hardcover by Tandem Press in 1977 and in paperback by Signet with an initial printing of 600,000 copies; and *Relics,* published by Our Sunday Visitor, Inc. For her non-fiction books Mrs. Cruz depends heavily on information received from foreign shrines, churches, convents and monasteries. The material she receives requires the services of several translators. Mrs. Cruz is currently working on another book which also involves a great deal of research.